Palgrave Studies of Sustainable Business in Africa

Series Editor

Allam Ahmed
University of Sussex
Brighton, United Kingdom

In partnership with the World Association for Sustainable Developmnet (WASD), The Palgrave Studies of Sustainable Business in Africa series aims to provide a global perspective and understanding of international business as a context for sustainable business practices in Africa. Providing new methodologies through which goods and services are produced and managed using sustainable business practices in Africa, books in this series offer a sound grounding in the terminology of sustainable business. In doing so, the series develops a number of tools of analysis in order to conceptualize various business and management theories that can be used to address the challenges posed to the development of African businesses. Adopting and adapting western business and management theories, it will provide a practical application of various theoretical and practical frameworks in order to develop new ways of doing business in Africa.

Including case studies, ground-breaking research and new conceptual approaches, the Palgrave Studies of Sustainable Business in Africa series includes contributions from a range of African scholars and leaders of major African academic and research institutions, as well as scholars from around the world. The merging of these perspectives examines how the future of African business and management should be shaped in order to better address the needs of African business development both now, and for future generations.

More information about this series at
http://www.springer.com/series/15060

Allam Ahmed
Editor

Managing Knowledge and Innovation for Business Sustainability in Africa

palgrave
macmillan

Editor
Allam Ahmed
University of Sussex
Brighton, United Kingdom

Palgrave Studies of Sustainable Business in Africa
ISBN 978-3-319-41089-0   ISBN 978-3-319-41090-6   (eBook)
DOI 10.1007/978-3-319-41090-6

Library of Congress Control Number: 2016957375

Cover illustration: © Sergio Azenha / Alamy Stock Photo
Cover design by Paileen Currie

Printed on acid-free paper

This Palgrave Macmillan imprint is published by Springer Nature
The registered company is Springer International Publishing AG
The registered company address is: Gewerbestrasse 11, 6330 Cham, Switzerland

Series Preface

We are pleased to present the first volume of a series of books devoted to Sustainable Business in Africa. The Palgrave Studies of Sustainable Business in Africa series is published in partnership with the World Association for Sustainable Development (WASD). The series aims to highlight the difficulty in attaining successful business management in Africa, a continent with a weak technological and knowledge base.[1] The most profound and encouraging change in African economies over the past decade has been the rapid advancement towards integration into the global economy.

Since the Rio summit in 1992 sustainable development (SD) is increasingly becoming a major concern for both developed and developing countries (DCs). Yet translating SD principles into effective economic and environmental policies seems to be a major challenge for all countries.

Many of the countries in Africa have undertaken significant economic reforms: improving macroeconomic management, encouraging a conducive private investment climate, liberalising markets and widening the

---

[1] WASD is a unique global forum that brings together people from across the world to promote the exchange of knowledge, experience, information and ideas among academicians, scholars, professionals, policy- and decision-makers, industry, executives and students. to improve the mutual understanding of the roles of science, technology, business and management in achieving sustainable development across the world. See more at: www.wasd.org.uk.

space for business and entrepreneurship to drive strong and inclusive growth. However, understanding the nature of problems, challenges and opportunities in Africa is a very difficult task for many people outside its territories.

The book series therefore calls for the development of new methods and approaches to suit the challenges and opportunities of globalisation. Africa represents one of the world's most intractable development challenges, with its peculiar and seemingly insurmountable environmental inhibitors, including very high transportation costs, small markets, low agricultural productivity, very high disease incidences, environmental despoliation, adverse geopolitics and very slow diffusion of strategic technology from abroad.

A sustainable management approach is seen by many scholars and policymakers as a way to enhance organisational performance in the current era. The book series argues that it is essential that research and policy development fully takes account of the differing perspectives of sustainability and makes explicit their particular perspective(s).

The book series aims to outline the methodologies by which goods and services are produced and managed using sustainable business practices. It is also important to note that all significant *sustainability initiatives* are necessarily dependent on the engagement of the people working in the organisation. Without engagement, change will falter and ultimately fail. This book series goes behind the scenes of business management to help managers, consultants and practitioners implement sustainable business development approaches for their organisations.

Underpinned by academic models and theories of sustainability, the series explores the ideas behind the tools to provide the reader with the link between theory and practice. It gives educators and business managers the confidence and knowledge to assess the factors affecting an organisation's 'readiness' and to effectively manage these throughout the sustainability life cycle. It addresses current challenges, such as how to understand the environmental context driving the need for sustainable business practices; how to initiate and sustain momentum throughout the sustainability programme; how to institutionalise structural and behavioural change; and how to create a compelling vision. With case studies from various academic and business sources, the book series provides practice-based insights into the realities of leading sustainable change in business practices.

The series presents many African academic and practical business case studies. In practical terms, this series will demonstrate that SD is a multidisciplinary process that involves many areas including science, innovation, technology, research and development, information technology, human capital development, business and management, trade and so on for knowledge-based economies and sustainable inclusive growth. Ideas and techniques explored in the book series are therefore illustrated and supported throughout with various case studies contributed by senior academics, scholars and business managers from a wide range of private- and public-sector organisations, for example universities, education, industry, central government, engineering, banking and so on.

All books in the series are of a consistent academic quality. All chapters are structured logically around a coherent central theme, and there is also a balance between theoretical/methodological and empirical chapters in the books.

The series publishes original manuscripts, conceptual studies (proposing approaches and solutions), literature reviews, reviews (sectors, industries, systems, methodologies, etc.), case studies (empirical work, industry cases, country-specific studies, etc.), research (original data), viewpoints and opinions, technical works (technical systems, processes, etc.), conference reports, management reports, book reviews, notes, commentaries and news. It expects to publish three to four books annually.

The series will present many illustrative African examples, rather than exhaustive research-oriented case material.

Finally, we would like to congratulate the authors for their valuable contributions, and we hope that the ensemble of chapters presented in this series will help to stimulate debate amongst scholars, researchers and policymakers within and outside Africa with a view to defining common, effective responses to tomorrow's challenges that will ultimately lead to a more integrated and multidisciplinary approach to policy design.

We are also grateful to all reviewers for graciously offering their invaluable comments, which have enriched the quality of the volumes in this series, and also for making available to us their valuable time and efforts. The suggestions and criticisms of these leading world experts greatly enhanced the quality of the book series, and much credit goes to them for the quality of this series. We also would like to thank Palgrave Macmillan and most sincerely Liz Barlow (Senior Commissioning Editor, Scholarly Business) and Maddie Holder (Assistant Editor, Business and Management) for giving us the opportunity to publish this book series.

London June 2016   Allam Ahmed

Acknowledgements

It has taken me a long time to complete this book. A series of this nature and scope can only be completed through the hard work and dedication of many people. It is difficult to mention all of them but we would like to congratulate the authors for their valuable contributions and we are grateful to all the reviewers for graciously making available to us their valuable time and efforts. Their suggestions and criticisms have greatly enhanced the quality of this volume. Finally, I would like to thank my wife, Samar, and daughters, Waad, Shahd, Lena and Salwa, for their patience and all the happiness they have brought to my life while editing this book.

London June 2016   Allam Ahmed

Contents

Notes on Contributors

Marwan A.A. Adam Sudanese Knowledge Society, Sudan

Marwan A. A. Adam received his BSc in Electrical Engineering, University of Khartoum in 2002. In 2004 he joined Mobitel (now ZAIN-SD) as a Maintenance Engineer. He was part of the BSS Technical Support team from 2008–2012, participating in an innovative team that examined the modernisation of Network Energy and developing a strategy to introduce alternative energy and other solutions after the success broad-spectrum trials. He then took the position of Power Manager, where he guided the network towards efficiency and optimisation in operational, environmental and quality dimensions by putting green solutions to work with optimum economic structure and lower CO_2 emissions. He guided the work by blending TQM, System Modelling and research approaches. In 2015, he moved from ZAIN-SD to become a freelance engineer and an active member of the Sudanese Knowledge Society (SKS), which he currently chairs.

Allam Ahmed President World Association for Sustainable Development

Allam Ahmed is a senior lecturer at the University of Sussex, UK, Founding President of the World Association for Sustainable Development, and Founding Director of the Middle Eastern Knowledge Economy Institute. He is also a Fellow and Chartered Marketer of the Chartered Institute of Marketing, UK, has advised the African Capacity Building Foundation and the EC, and held the position of International Coordinator for UNESCO Chair on Transfer of Technology.

Constantia Anastasiadou Edinburgh Napier University, UK

Constantia Anastasiadou is Reader in Tourism at Edinburgh Napier University Business School, Edinburgh, UK. She has a PhD and MSc in Tourism from Strathclyde University, UK and a BA (Hons) in Economics from the University of Macedonia in Greece. She has published extensively on the impact of regional trading organisations on international tourism in Europe and beyond, and her research interests focus in particular on policy and planning and inter-organisational dynamics in tourist destinations. She has undertaken research projects on cross-border collaboration in tourism in Southern Africa, tourism marketing technologies and community engagement in events. Previously she worked as a qualitative social researcher on tourism-related and employability projects and was involved in knowledge transfer activities on an EU Tempus project involving four Russian regions.

Adil A. Dafa'Alla Airbus UK, UK

Adil A. Dafa'Alla graduated in Mechanical Engineering from the University of Khartoum, Sudan in 1981 and received his PhD from the University of Manchester Institute of Science and Technology (UMIST), UK, in 1988. He is currently a Specialist Member of the Aero Data for Loads Group at Airbus UK Ltd. As part of his quest for continuous development, he became a Chartered Engineer (C.Eng.), a designation granted by the British Engineering Council and recognised worldwide as proof of a high standard of professional experience and conduct. He followed that up to become EurIng, the European sister of the C.Eng., granted by the European Federation of the National Engineering Associations (FEANI). His current research interests include aircraft safety and airport capacity planning. He has published his research in a number of journals and conference papers in addition to many technical reports. Coming from a Sudanese background, he also has a special interest in topics related to industry, education and sustainable development in Africa. He is an active member of the World Association for Sustainable Development (WASD) and has been Associate Editor of the *Journal of World Review of Science, Technology and Sustainable Development* (*WRSTSD*) since its inception in 2003.

Abdelkader Djeflat University of Lille, France and Oran University, Algeria

Abdelkader Djeflat currently teaches industrial economics and the economics of technical change and innovation at the University of Lille, France. He was previously Full Professor of Economics at the University of Oran in Algeria, where he held the position of Dean of the Faculty of Economics. He is the founder and current Chairman of the MAGHTECH (Maghreb Technology) Network (http://www.Maghtech.org/) and Senior Researcher at the CLERSE (CNRS). He is also Vice President of the Scientific Committee of the Globelics Network (http://www.Globelics.org). He has published several articles in international journals on the issues of technology transfer, innovation and the knowledge economy. He has also written and edited several books and done extensive consulting for several international organisations.

Hany El Shamy Tanta University and British University in Egypt, Egypt

Hany El Shamy is Associate Professor of Economics at Tanta University, Egypt. He received his PhD in Economics from the University of Surrey, UK, and his MPhil in Economics, MSc in Economics (First class) and BSc in Commerce (First class) from the University of Tanta, Egypt. His principal research interests are in productivity. In particular, his PhD investigated the impact of technological change on UK manufacturing. This included producing econometric results to show the importance of research and development (R&D) expenditure as a technological indicator. His future research plans are to build on the foundations of his PhD to further develop models to study the impact of technological change, as measured by such things as technical standards, on productivity in UK manufacturing.

Eman Elish British University in Egypt

Eman Elish is a lecturer in the Economics Department, Faculty of Business Administration, Economics and Political Science at the British University in Egypt. Prior to joining the university she was a lecturer at the University of Modern Sciences and Arts from 2004–2007. She was also employed as an assistant research expert at the Institute of National Planning (INP) in Egypt from 1998, assigned to write and publish economic research focusing on the Egyptian economy and other developing economies, as well as contributing to the preparation of the 'Human Development Report' and the 'Annual Economic Report' published by the institute. At the INP she taught post-graduate students in the Economic Planning master's degree programme. She has published research papers in international and regional conferences and in well-established academic journals. Her research interests are in economic development, foreign direct investment and public debt.

Mavis Gutu Edinburgh Napier University, UK

Mavis Gutu, is a 2nd year PhD candidate at Edinburgh Napier University, UK. Her PhD research area is in Foreign Direct Investment and Determinants, with a focus on Zimbabwe. She holds a Masters' Degree in International

Business Management and a BA (Hons) Degree in Business Studies, both from Edinburgh Napier University, UK. She is an Associate Member of the Institute of Chartered Secretaries and Administrators. Mavis has attended and presented papers at International Conferences in Foreign Direct Investment. Her research interests are in international business, global marketing, emerging markets, and branding. Prior to commencing her studies at Edinburgh Napier University, she held senior finance and research positions with the University of Exeter in England, and has worked in senior finance and management roles in the private sector in Zimbabwe

Elmouiz S. Hussein Airbus UK, UK

Elmouiz Siddeg Hussein is a Mechanical Engineering graduate of the University of Khartoum, Sudan (1999). After graduating he gained work experience as a mechanical engineer at a private workshop in North Khartoum, Sudan. During this period, he also worked part time as a teaching assistant at the Faculty of Engineering, University of Khartoum. He subsequently moved to the University of Portsmouth, UK, to do his MSc in Advanced Manufacturing Technology (2003–2004). In 2006, he joined Airbus UK as a Manufacturing Engineer. Currently he develops and integrates the industrial system for the A350XWB Wing, develops and optimises business processes and manages industrial risk.

Sherif Kamel American University in Cairo, Egypt

Sherif Kamel is Vice President for Information Management and Professor of Management at the American University in Cairo. He was Founding Dean of the School of Business (2009–2014). He led a major repositioning of the School by focusing on entrepreneurship, innovation, leadership and responsible business. During his tenure as Dean, he initiated and achieved the EQUIS, AMBA and ACCET accreditations and got the school reaccredited by AACSB, joining 70 business schools worldwide that are known as triple-crown accredited. He established the Center for Entrepreneurship and Innovation and the university's Venture Lab, which has become Egypt's primary university-based incubator. He has served as Associate Dean for Executive Education (2008–2009), Director of the Management Center (2002–2008) and Director of the Institute of Management Development (2002–2006). Before joining the university, he was Director of the Regional IT Institute (1992–2001), and helped establish and manage the training department of the Cabinet of Egypt Information and Decision Support Center (1989–1992). He is an Eisenhower Fellow (2005), a board member of the Egyptian American Enterprise Fund (2012–present), a member of the Egypt–US Business Council (2013–present) and a member of the AACSB International Middle East Advisory Council (2015–present). He was previously a member of the World Bank Knowledge Advisory Commission (2012–2014). He is a founding member of the Internet Society of Egypt and chairs the Education Committee at AmCham Egypt.

Nahlaa A. Khalifa King Abdulaziz University, Saudi Arabia

Nahlaa A. Khalifa is an assistant professor at the Clinical Nutrition Department, Faculty of Applied Medical Sciences, King Abdulaziz University in Jeddah, Saudi Arabia. She holds a PhD in Food Science and Nutrition from Khartoum University in cooperation with Hanover University in Germany. She is Coordinator of the evaluation and quality assurance programme, Chairperson of the academic advising committee, Member of the strategic planning committee, Coordinator of the undergraduate curriculum development, revision and accreditation programme, Thinkbuzan Licensed Instructor (TLI) and Train of Trainer (TOT). She has been awarded certificates for her contributions to health, community and educational missions. Having published articles on food science and nutrition, her main interests are in alternative medicine, nutigenomics and medical nutrition therapy. She is also interested in the application of modern information technology in educational systems and accreditation.

Jerry Kolo American University of Sharjah, UAE

Jerry Kolo is a professor in the Master of Urban Planning Program at the American University of Sharjah (AUS) in the United Arab Emirates. Prior to joining AUS in 2006 he was a professor of Urban Planning at Florida Atlantic University in Fort Lauderdale, Florida, USA, and the founder and director of the Center for Urban Redevelopment and Empowerment (CURE), an applied research and community outreach programme. His teaching and research areas are sustainable community planning processes, land use planning and tourism development. He also has extensive consultancy experience in public-sector planning and community capacity building.

Lynette Louw Rhodes University, South Africa

Lynette Louw is Raymond Ackerman Chair of Management, Department of Management and Deputy Dean, Faculty of Commerce at Rhodes University in Grahamstown, South Africa. She obtained her Doctor Commercii in Business Management at the University of Port Elizabeth in South Africa. She is the recipient of research awards, serves on journal editorial boards, and has co-authored and edited textbooks on management and strategic management. She is the leader of an international project in Africa, 'Chinese Organisations in Sub-Saharan Africa: New Dynamics, New Synergies'. Her areas of speciality include strategic management, international organisational behaviour, and intercultural and cross-cultural management. She has international teaching experience in Germany, the Netherlands and China.

Kelly Mua Kingsly Harvard University, USA

Dr Kelly Mua Kingsly holds a Ph.D. in Public Finance from Charisma University, and several Masters Degrees, including a Master in Public Administration and Management from Harvard University at the John F. Kennedy School of Government.

Dr Mua is currently the deputy director for Finance Operations at the Cameroonian Ministry of Finance. Before this recent appointment, Dr Mua has more than 10 years experience within the Cameroonian ministry of finance. He has occupied among others, the position of technical Adviser in the Cameroonian Ministry of Finance, programme portfolio manager at the African Development Bank (AfDB), and assistant resident representative-operations within the United Nations Development Programme. He is alternatively adjunct lecturer at the AGENLA Academy on Forensic Accounting and project Management. Author of four books, Dr Mua areas of specialisation are operations Management, supply chain management, forensic Accounting and forensic investigation.

Samuel Muiruri Muriithi Daystar University, Kenya

Samuel Muiruri Muriithi is a senior lecturer in the School of Business and Economics at Daystar University, Kenya where he teaches graduate courses in management, strategic management and cross-cultural management. He also coordinates the MBA research and thesis programme at the school. He holds a PhD in Management from Rhodes University (South Africa), an MA in Communications from Wheaton Graduate School (USA) and an MBA from Seattle Pacific University (USA). He has extensive experience as a consultant in strategic management and cross-cultural management, besides having a keen interest in the banking industry in Africa. He is a member of several committees involved in research, examination and curriculum development besides lecturing in different universities. He has authored articles on leadership and management and several books, including *African Crisis: Is There Hope?* and *African Development Dilemma: The Big Debate.*

Alain Ndedi Saint Monica University, Cameroon

Dr Alain A. Ndedi is a Professor of Entrepreneurship, Organisation, and strategy. Advisory board member of the Bioinfo Publications, the Journal of Business and Management Economics, the Journal of Business and Management of the Centre of Excellence for Scientific and Research Journalism, the African Journal of Business Management, Dr Ndedi is Director of the Think Tank Comerci, and Past President of Young Entrepreneurs for the New Partnership for Africa's Development (YENEPAD). He has consulted for the UNDP, the World Bank, and the United Nations. He has been involved on monitoring and evaluation research and training since 2002. He is member of many networks including, AfrEA, SAMEA, 3ie and NONIE.

Professor Ndedi holds a doctorate in Business Management with the focus on corporate entrepreneurship. Author of more than 20 books, Dr Ndedi has lectured entrepreneurship in many tertiary institutions for the past 15 years. His areas of expertise are entrepreneurship, corporate innovation and creativity, monitoring and evaluation.

Maktoba Omar Coventry University, UK

Maktoba Omar (Reader in Marketing Strategy) completed her PhD at the University of Leeds entitled "Contextual Determinants of Standardisation and Entry Strategies in Internationalisation". Since then she has published and acted as editor and referee for a number of academic journals and performed as track chair, presenter and member of the Vetting Panel for a number of national and international conferences. She has won the Emerald LiteratiNetwork outstanding paper Award 2008. She also acted as consultant and leading academic in a number of projects and Knowledge Transfer Partnership (KTP) and has generated a substantial amount of funds in the UK and overseas. Currently her main research focus is a study of the impact of branding, emerging markets and foreign direct investment in relation to UK companies.

Collins Osei Edinburgh Napier University, UK

Collins Osei is Marketing Lecturer at Edinburgh Napier University. He has been involved in delivering a number of undergraduate and postgraduate modules. He also supervises doctoral students. He completed his PhD at Edinburgh Napier University in August 2014. His thesis, entitled 'UK Foreign Direct Investment in Ghana: Determinants and Implications', empirically investigated the relative significance of the determinants of UK foreign direct investment in Ghana. He also holds an MBA in Marketing from the University of Leicester and a BA (Hons) from the University of Cape Coast in Ghana. His key research interests are emerging markets, global marketing, branding, international marketing, international business and research methods. He has presented papers at conferences and seminars and published in refereed journals and books.

Stephen Bolaji Peluola Yaba College of Technology, Nigeria

Stephen Bolaji Peluola is a senior lecturer at the Centre for Entrepreneurship Development, Yaba College of Technology, Lagos, Nigeria. He is a member of the Institute of Management Consultants of Nigeria and the African Association of Entrepreneurs Nigeria. He is a member of the Examination Committee at the Centre for Entrepreneurship Development. He is a patron of a number of students' associations at the Yaba College of Technology. He has led a team of staff and students to award-winning national entrepreneurship exhibitions and inventions. His research interests focus on developmental issues and entrepreneurship.

Luqman Raimi Yaba College of Technology, Nigeria

Lukman Raimi is Senior Lecturer and Coordinator of Training and Part-Time Programme at the Centre for Entrepreneurship Development, Yaba College of Technology, Lagos, Nigeria. He holds a PhD in Entrepreneurship and CSR from the Leicester Business School, De Montfort University, Leicester (UK). He is a Fellow of Cumberland Lodge, Windsor (UK). He is a member of the British Academy of Management, the Nigerian Institute of Management, the American Economic Association and the African Association of Entrepreneurs Nigeria. His research interests focus on developmental issues and entrepreneurship. He has over 26 public academic papers to his credit, including 'Corporate Social Responsibility, Waqf System and Zakat System as Faith-Based Model for Poverty Reduction', which was awarded the Highly Commendable Academic Paper for 2015 by the *World Journal of Entrepreneurship, Management and Sustainable Development.*

Morufu Oladimeji Shokunbi Yaba College of Technology, Nigeria

Morufu Oladimeji Shokunbi is Lecturer II at the Centre for Entrepreneurship Development, Yaba College of Technology, Lagos, Nigeria. He is a member of the National Entrepreneur Educators of Nigeria and the African Association of Entrepreneurs Nigeria. His research interests focus on human resources development issues and entrepreneurship. He is a member of the Examination Committee at the Centre for Entrepreneurship Development, a public affairs analyst, and a coach for the Young Children's Association in Nigeria.

List of Figures

List of Tables

Part I

Introduction

1

Managing Knowledge and Innovation for Business Sustainability in Africa

Allam Ahmed

Today, more than ever before, the African continent is confronted with many challenges on its path to sustained growth and development. There is no denying the fact that Africa needs to substantially improve growth performance if it is to achieve the Millennium Development Goals (MDGs).

It is evident from various recent international reports that nearly all African countries' attempts to transform their economies during the past three decades have not delivered the desired outcomes when measured against the principal indices for sustainable development (Ahmed and Nwankwo 2013). Overall progress towards the attainment of the MDGs has been patchy and less than robust given Africa's peculiar and seemingly insurmountable environmental inhibitors, including very high transport costs, small markets, low agricultural productivity, very high disease incidences, environmental despoliation, adverse geopolitics and very slow diffusion of strategic technology from abroad.

A. Ahmed(✉)
Science Policy Research Unit (SPRU), University of Sussex, Brighton, BN1 9SL UK

© The Author(s) 2017
A. Ahmed (ed.), *Managing Knowledge and Innovation for Business Sustainability in Africa*, DOI 10.1007/978-3-319-41090-6_1

At the same time, there is no suggestion that Africa has cocooned itself away from the rest of the world. In fact, many countries have opened up their economies, implemented political and market reforms, and undertaken variants of structural reforms to foster and sustain market responsiveness with the concomitant goal of improving the overall well-being of their people.

Poverty remains amongst the most important challenges facing all African countries today due to the failure of macroeconomic policies, market imperfections and inequalities as well as the inability of African governments to enhance productivity. Knowledge, innovation and technological learning in building a knowledge-based economy in Africa are therefore of paramount importance for the continent's efforts to achieve sustainable development.

Due to inadequate knowledge absorption and innovation, technological development in Africa lags behind that in other regions. The majority of African countries are mired in the very early stages of their development. The African region is neither digitally nor politically well positioned to leverage factor endowments in financial and natural resources in a productive way that fosters the development of knowledge economies.

As a result, there is an urgent need for a public sector that is knowledgeable, efficient, empowered and committed; a private sector that is not only innovative and growth oriented, but also driven and competitive; civil society that is constructively responsive and capable of collaborating with both the public and private sectors with a view to achieving the MDGs; a political system that is responsive to its citizens and premised on good governance; and a socio-economic and geopolitical environment that is enabling and inclusive of all.

Moreover, a substantial amount of literature has been written about the role that science, technology and innovation (STI) plays in building an enabling environment to foster economic growth and promote the knowledge economy (see Ahmed 2005, 2012; Danofsky 2005; Hamel 2005; Mansell and When 1998).

A 'pure' knowledge economy generates creativity to produce new ideas instead of making use of existing knowledge. This creativity is innovation. Innovations contribute to knowledge creation and technological learning, which represent the core fundamentals of the knowledge economy.

The focus in national strategies should be on investment in research and development (R&D) and training to strengthen capacity for knowledge absorption and information dissemination.

Based on a synthesis of policy prescriptions for a renascent Africa, it has become clear that solutions to extreme poverty in Africa will have to come from Africans themselves. Africa is not in want of policy prescriptions; problems often arise from implementation failures. The point needs to be made, however, that Africa is not poor because the people are poor.

Over the years, contemporary works by thinkers such as P. T. Bauer and William Easterly (e.g., *From Subsistence to Exchange* and *The White Man's Burden*) have demonstrated that indigenous entrepreneurship provides a strong foundation for development. The logic is simple: Africans, through progressive indigenous efforts at social change, could bring about enterprise-led institutional change which, in turn, could foster the evolution of rules of social cooperation and thus realise the immense gains of trade through entrepreneurial activities (Boettke 2007).

The most profound and encouraging change in African economies over the past decade has been the rapid advancement towards integration into the global economy. Many of the countries have undertaken significant economic reforms: improving macroeconomic management, instigating a conducive private investment climate, liberalising markets and widening the space for entrepreneurship to drive strong and inclusive growth. Concurrent with institutional reforms are policies to improve the conditions for enterprise to thrive and provide a dynamic source of growth. By and large, African economies are opening up and beginning to respond to genuine market signals.

The purpose of this first book in the series is to address issues that will be central to Africa's various attempts to manage effectively knowledge and innovation for sustainable business management.

The book is also very timely with the recently launched *Science, Technology and Innovation Strategy for Africa 2024 (STISA-2024)* by the African Union (AU), emphasising the critical role of science, technology and innovation in Africa's socio-economic development and growth. Among the key pillars for the AU strategy are the promotion of entrepreneurship and innovation as well as providing an enabling environment for STI development in the African continent.

The theme—knowledge and innovation management for business sustainability in Africa—has been very carefully chosen. However, building on this discussion, a number of policy implications can be derived to improve the management of knowledge and innovation within Africa countries and consequently achieve sustainable development (SD).

This book also provides an opportunity to discuss and clarify how universities can contribute to the generation of wealth in Africa through the transfer of finalised knowledge and the creation of new firms, new industries and business opportunities. Moreover, the book presents a number of case studies relating to the expansion of networking and collaboration between education and research institutions, and between private and public entities, as well as the commercialisation of research and innovation outputs.

This book takes a holistic multidisciplinary and multisectoral approach to provide in-depth analysis and a state-of-the-art overview of the efforts made by different African countries to tackle various issues relating to knowledge and innovation management in Africa.

The results of many comprehensive research programmes undertaken in different countries in Africa and other parts of the world over the last few years are presented here. More than 27 chapters, covering a wide range of topics, were considered for possible inclusion in this volume of the series. The 12 chapters that appear here were chosen following a blind peer review process. The chapters cover a wide geographical area and were written by more than 20 renowned international experts from Africa and the rest of the world.

This volume comprises five sections:

Introduction (2 chapters)
Innovation and Entrepreneurship (3 chapters)
Education (2 chapters)
Capacity Building and Human Capital (2 chapters)
Investment (1 chapter)
Banking and Finance (2 chapters)

In Chap. 2, Kolo proposes some strategic initiatives for African governments, corporations, non-profits and citizens to take, in an effort to deploy innovation and knowledge to build the capacity of entrepreneurs, thereby enabling them to produce goods and services that are profitable in the marketplace. Kolo argues that Africa's role and presence in the global creative economy are weak. Africa is in a race against time as the population explodes, driving rapid urbanisation and the growth of slums, and the need for schools and health centres places enormous pressure on the meagre resources of states. These issues are exacerbated by extraneous factors such as climate change, terrorism and global economic volatilities. Kolo's fascinating research should equip and enable entrepreneurs to produce goods and services for local and international markets. His proposed initiatives are simple, pragmatic, feasible, innovative and knowledge-based, and their adaptation could trigger the change needed to catapult African entrepreneurs into the global theatre of the creative economy.

Innovation and Entrepreneurship

Following on Kolo's research, Kamel's chapter (Chap. 3) describes the role of an innovative information and communication technology (ICT)-based entrepreneurial evolution in Africa's development, helping to realise business and socio-economic development based on different channels of information acquisition and knowledge creation and dissemination. This will in turn allow for the creation of a global information society with innovative means of communication that can help increase competitiveness for individuals, organisations and societies. Using the case of university-based incubators, Kamel addresses the developments taking place in Africa in the space of ICT with an emphasis on the evolution of the entrepreneurial ecosystem and its implications for business and socio-economic development. The chapter demonstrates how ICT, coupled with skilled human capital and timely infostructure, are vital to improving the balance in economic and social progress between nations, leveraging economic growth, boosting capacity to face societal challenges, enhancing the progress of democratic values, and augmenting cultural creativity, traditions and identities. Moreover, Kamel demonstrates the growing role of innovation and entrepreneurship and the emergence of start-ups that capitalise on ICT to help transform society, boost the private sector and improve standards of living across the continent.

Continuing on the theme of entrepreneurship in Africa, Raimi, Peluola and Shokunbi explore the prospects and challenges of managing clusters as entrepreneurship interventions for SD in Nigeria. According to Raimi et al., clusters development has the prospect of strengthening Nigeria's food industry, by making it strong enough to produce semi-finished and finished products. The food clusters afford interaction and collaboration among farmers, food processing companies and other stakeholders. However, the findings of Raimi et al. need to be strengthened with further quantitative and empirical research in Nigeria.

In most cases, failure is perceived as a disappointment and drags down the person experiencing this misfortune, but it is also possible for failure to be a blessing in disguise. Using the case of the founders of WhatsApp, Ndedi and Kingsley demonstrate how any failure may lead to innovation and success. In doing so, Ndedi and Kingsley undertake a thorough literature review focusing on the linkages between failure, success and innovation. According to Ndedi and Kingsley, success and innovation result from rapidly fixing mistakes rather than getting things right the first time.

Education

The next part of the book focuses on the important role of education in African sustainable business practices. Dafa'Alla, Hussein and Adam investigate the role of education in achieving SD and whether it can reasonably be expected to improve on Africa's state of underdevelopment. Using Sudan as a case study and building on their previous research, Dafa'Alla et al. assess the Sudanese education system's ability to meet the objectives of the national development plan of the country. Lessons learned are then generalised to the case of Africa, and recommendations for an 'Action Plan for Education in Africa' are made. They find that good-quality education and SD are synonymous. Education drives innovation, which in turn drives economic growth and SD, as has been clearly demonstrated in many emerging economies worldwide. Dafa'Alla et al. argue that weak education is the root cause of the underdevelopment of Africa, and that Africa must build an innovation-based economy.

Following on the same theme of education, Khalifa studies the use of mind mapping (MM) as an unconventional but valuable technique in knowledge retrieval and critical thinking in medical education and clinical problems. According to Khalifa, mind mapping is a visual technique that accelerates the learning process, inspires problem-solving and critical thinking, and supports effective teaching. However, there is a lack of significant previous research on using MM in medical institutions in Africa, and she argues that MM methodologies could be more widely implemented in most African medical institutes.

Capacity Building and Human Capital

The first chapter in this section investigates the difficulties faced by many African countries in building innovation systems in their countries. Djeflat argues that amongst the components of innovation dynamics, the issue of design and engineering (D&E) is drawing more and more attention from international organisations and a growing corpus of researchers, both in the North and in the South. Yet, D&E raises various questions related to the concepts, the tools and the instruments it uses, but more profoundly and in particular, its links with R&D and innovation. It also raises questions regarding the policies needed to build D&E capabilities. Finally, it raises questions with regards to the practices of D&E and interactive learning at the enterprise level. To assess the real situation, Djeflat examined a small sample of 20 Algerian firms (small and big enterprises), both in the public and the private sector, from 11 different industries. According to Djeflat, D&E is a neglected function throughout the North African region, and this explains why local industry is still highly dependent on external sources for technical change and innovation. This is due to a host of factors, namely the low level of policy awareness, weak linkages with the training system, out-of-date syllabuses, and little practice of reverse engineering.

The next chapter, by Elish and El Shamy, investigates the relationship between labour productivity, human capital and international R&D spillover during the period 1982–2011 in Egypt. Elish and El Shamy estimate a single equation model which employs long-run cointegration analysis and short-run analysis (ECM) using annual data collected from the World Bank and the Ministry of Planning in Egypt and the OECD database. The results show a conventional result for international R&D and human capital. Elish and El Shamy's study stresses that human capital's absorptive capacity, enhanced by high-quality education, intensifies the positive effect of R&D spillover on labour productivity.

Investment

In sub-Saharan Africa (SSA), the performance of foreign direct investment (FDI) differs considerably between Zimbabwe and its neighbouring countries. Gutu, Anastasiadou, Omar and Osei examine FDI determinants for SSA with particular emphasis on the comparison between Zimbabwe and Botswana. Using secondary data analysis, their study examines why Botswana was attracting more FDI than Zimbabwe in the period 2002–2012. According to the study, Botswana is attractive due to the stability of the political and legal environments, high human capital and governance that promotes technological adoption. In contrast, Zimbabwe's political instability and the government's unwillingness to address the challenges the country is facing impedes FDI attraction and retention. Gutu et al.'s research is very useful for policymakers as they plan and implement policies, and for foreign investors for understanding how different determinants impact on location attractiveness.

Banking and Finance

In the final part of the book we examine the financial and banking sector in Africa and its impact on sustainable business practices in Africa. The banking industry is a major driver of economic development for world economies. By offering different types of services, such as facilitating money transfers between countries and ensuring that savers and borrowers are brought together in well-organised structures, the industry determines countries' economic development and long-term sustainability. According to Muriithi and Louw, the Kenyan banking industry is considered to be the most mature, fastest-growing and largest in East Africa, thereby making it the regional financial leader. The industry has, however, been a victim of both global and domestic financial challenges. Between 1980 and 2000, the country's financial industry was characterised by major financial upheavals that led to the collapse of many banks, while others were in and out of receivership. Muriithi and Louw explore the importance of enhancing and strengthening the Kenyan banking internal control mechanisms and developing sustainability strategies, focusing on business practices and product development geared towards healthy economic, social and environmental activities.

In the final chapter of the book, Ndedi assesses the importance of the Douala Stock Exchange (DSX) in Cameroon. Ndedi argues that without financial markets, borrowers would have difficulty finding lenders, and that these structures are seen as platforms for the economic prosperity of nations, especially in Africa. Accordingly, the future development of the DSX will occur when market players are able to reach mutually acceptable compromises regarding the terms of financial transactions. Ndedi develops an appropriate strategy for sequencing the development of the DSX by arguing that instruments that require simpler and more easily verifiable compromises must be launched in the first place at the DSX. The chapter also shows that the path of development will depend on economic, legal, political, institutional and cultural factors—the framework that prompts policymakers to ask the right questions in diagnosing the deficiencies and hurdles. Finally, Ndedi provides guidance for designing suitable policies for the development and functioning of the DSX that will contribute to the emergence of Cameroon by 2035.

Finally, this book is intended as a first step in paving the way towards further reflection on the future position and role of Africa in the world, and we hope it will be utilised as a guide by policymakers and senior managers to enhance their ability to think strategically towards achieving SD.

References

Ahmed, A. (2005). Digital publishing and the new era of digital divide. *International Journal of Learning and Intellectual Capital, 2*(4), 321–338.

Ahmed, A., & Nwankwo, S. (2013). Entrepreneurship development in Africa: An overview. *World Journal of Entrepreneurship, Management and Sustainable Development, 9*(2/3), 82–86. Emerald Group Publishing Limited, UK.

Boettke, P. (2007). Editorial: Entrepreneurial response to poverty and social conflict: The enterprise Africa project. *Journal of the Institute of Economic Affairs, 27*(2), 2–5.

Danofsky, S. (2005). *Open access for Africa: Challenges, recommendations and examples, United Nations ICT Task Force working group on the enabling environment.* New York: The United Nations Information and Communication Technologies Task Force.

Hamel, J. L. (2005). Knowledge for SD in Africa towards new policy initiatives. *World Review of Science Technology and SD, 2*(3), 217–229.

Mansell, R., & When, U. (1998). *Knowledge societies: Information technology for SD. UN commission on science and technology for development.* New York: Oxford University Press.

2

From Innovation to Sustainability: Life-Cycle Polylemmas and Strategic Initiatives for Entrepreneurship in Africa

Jerry Kolo

Introduction and Purpose

The context and aim of this chapter are based on the contention, and simple but profound and irrefutable evidence, that Africa is experiencing economic growth but without commensurate development, or at least not enough for the teeming and desperately poor population of the continent, despite the continent's vast natural, mineral and human resources, and the goodwill and support of the international community. The lag of development behind growth, two concepts that development scholars categorically distinguish (Fik 2000), is significant in understanding and explaining what this chapter terms Africa's 'schizophrenic' development experience, as exemplified by the Africa Rising and African growth tragedy debate (Easterly and Levine 1997; Rowden 2013, 2015; Gibney 2015; Spooner 2015). While the growth/development mismatch places

J. Kolo (✉)
College of Architecture, Art & Design, Master of Urban Planning Program, American University of Sharjah, Sharjah, UAE

© The Author(s) 2017
A. Ahmed (ed.), *Managing Knowledge and Innovation for Business Sustainability in Africa*, DOI 10.1007/978-3-319-41090-6_2

13

the primary burden on political leaders and policymakers to develop feasible mitigation measures, it also places responsibility on other stakeholders, including scholars and academics, to engage in diagnosing and prescribing reasonable initiatives for Africa to work its way out of poverty and despair, thereby achieving sustainable development. This chapter posits that entrepreneurship, fostered and enabled by innovation and knowledge management, holds enormous potential for Africa to achieve sustainable development. In the life cycle of entrepreneurship in Africa, there are perennial polylemmas that must be addressed or mitigated in order for entrepreneurs to be successful in terms of profitability and sustainability. The idea of polylemmas suggests that Africa's entrepreneurial challenges and obstacles are deeply rooted, long-standing and formidable. Therefore, none of the mitigation measures and options are optimal, yet choices must be made between the options. The analysis and insights that may be useful for informed tactical and strategic policy, programme and project choices is part of the purpose, implication and value of this chapter for policymakers, technocrats, entrepreneurs and entrepreneurial advocates in Africa.

Methodology

This chapter resulted from two basic research methods that allow for a fair and robust exploration and analysis of an issue that is as subjective yet complex and multifaceted as sustainable entrepreneurship in a continent as vast and diverse as Africa. One was the desktop method, where conceptual and empirical materials from various scholarly, professional and governmental sources were reviewed on the subject of discourse. The second was a series of unstructured conversational interviews with entrepreneurs from five African countries: Kenya, Morocco, Nigeria, South Africa and South Sudan. Information from the desktop method provided very rich insights into extant conceptual discussions on innovation, knowledge management and entrepreneurship, as well as insights on country-specific practices and applications of innovation, knowledge and entrepreneurship. The interviews were aimed at understanding the diverse terrain of entrepreneurship across Africa based on the knowledge, experiences, observations and perspectives of the interviewees. The information and insights from both methods were used to develop Table 2.1.

Overview and Relevance of Concepts

Some of the critical concepts used in this chapter hardly need to be defined from the standpoint of the literature and professional practice, as they have already been robustly, almost ubiquitously, discussed and researched. The relevant concepts are innovation, knowledge economy or creative economy, knowledge management and entrepreneurship. What this chapter finds common to all the concepts are, firstly, they are multidisciplinary in origin, study and application. Secondly, they are widely used in most fields today for problem-solving, change or improved action. Thirdly, there is no universal consensus on their interpretation and, particularly, their measurement or assessment (El Houssamy 2016; Weheba 2015). Fourthly, they combine, depend on or require knowledge and skills that are cognitive, experiential and intuitive. Finally, the end result for all of them is the same: cost-effective problem-solving or improvement in the condition or performance of a phenomenon (situation or thing). In light of these commonalities, the terms are used and defined 'operationally' and annotated 'apropos' in this chapter. The use of these terms in this chapter notwithstanding, quite noteworthy is the rationale and relevance for their use in anchoring the discourse in the chapter, one which is discussed next.

The discourse in this chapter is predicated or premised on the contention, indeed conviction, that the world economy today is powered by innovation and knowledge (Kolo 2009). This economy is known popularly as the knowledge economy (KE) or the creative economy (CE). According to Piotrowski (2015), 'the term "knowledge economy" was coined in the 1960s to describe a shift from traditional economies to ones where the production and use of knowledge are paramount'. He referenced the four pillars of KE identified by the World Bank as 'institutional structures that provide incentives for entrepreneurship and the use of knowledge, skilled labor availability and good education systems, ICT infrastructure and access, and, finally, a vibrant innovation landscape that

Table 2.1 Business life cycle polylemmas and strategic initiatives for African entrepreneurship

Goal clusters	Initiation	Planning	Financing	Operations	Sales	Stabilisation	Modernisation
	Concept Idea Vision	Research Design Protocol Strategy Consults	Registration Permitting Budgeting Equipment Lead team	Staffing Contracting Take off Testing Production Refining	Promotion Marketing Distribution Placements	Streamlining Consolidation Branding	Expansion Diversification Acquisition Merger Restructuring Transfer
Political Polylemmas	N/A	No T/A No seed funds No grants	No T/A No seed funds No grants Bureaucracy Regulations Charges/Fees	N/A	Bureaucracy Regulations Charges/Fees	N/A	Bureaucracy Regulations Charges/Fees
Initiatives	Create Business Enterprise Development Office to provide T/A and conduct business research Establish One Stop Shop and streamlined permitting programme Establish business finance grants and low-interest loans Provide fee waiver and reduction incentives Contract universities to provide business seminars and training and T/A for local businesses Offer or promote entrepreneurial education curriculum in schools and universities Establish a credit bureau Invest in infrastructure and technology development, repairs and upgrades Invest in smart technologies to serve citizens and businesses Provide business references in local library (translate as feasible)						
Economic Polylemmas	N/A	No bank loans High interests No credit	No bank loans High interests No credit	No bank loans High interests No credit High leases No insurance	No bank loans High interests No credit	No bank loans High interests No credit	No bank loans High interests No credit

Initiatives	Provide low-interest and flexible business loans	Provide credit counselling and repair programmes with or through non-profits providing business T/A	Partner with universities to provide business capacity training and business planning T/A	Establish business mentoring programme for prospective lenders	Provide smart banking business programmes
Psychosocial					
Polylemmas	Poverty No business literacy	Poverty No business literacy	Poverty No business literacy	Poverty No business literacy	Poverty No business literacy
Initiatives	Entrepreneurs should establish business savings account with local banks	Establish and/or repair credit	Attend business training programmes, seminars and training workshops	Provide healthy workplace	
Built Environment	N/A				
Polylemmas	Poor infrastructure Energy cost No technology	Poor infrastructure Energy cost No technology	Poor infrastructure Energy cost No technology	Poor infrastructure Energy cost No technology	Poor infrastructure Energy cost No technology
Initiatives	N/A	N/A	N/A	N/A	N/A
Natural Environment	N/A				
Polylemmas					
Initiatives					

Source: Compiled by the author

Notes: T/A is Technical Assistance. Bureaucracy implies personnel-related hurdles, including corruption includes academia, the private sector and civil society'. A parallel term, CE, was first used by Howkins (2001) to describe the current global economy, although the term has been popularised more widely by scholars such as Florida (2002). Creativity lies at the heart of the CE, and, as Howkins (ibid.) noted, 'creativity is the ability to generate something new. It means the production by one or more people of ideas and inventions that are personal, original and meaningful. It is a talent, and aptitude.' He noted further that 'the creative economy has been midwifed by the technologies of information and communications', adding that 'perhaps the greatest impact of the creative economy is not only within the traditional creative industries but in the way their skills and business models are being used to create value in other areas of life'. In the CE, he said, 'people with ideas – people who own ideas – have become more powerful than people who work machines and, in many cases, more powerful than people who own machines'.

The contextual relevance of the foregoing brief overview of the concept of the KE to this chapter is that Africa cannot afford to be left behind, marginalised or ostracised, by default or because of some handicaps, from the creative global economy. At the World Summit on Sustainable Development in Johannesburg, South Africa in 2002, Ngubane (2002) posited that poor nations must embrace the KE or be left behind in the global economic race, stating that 'it is the knowledge and technological capacity to apply the inputs of labor, capital and resources that make modern economies work'.

Akin to the concept of KE is that of knowledge management (KM). As earlier stated, there is a plethora of scholarly and professional literature on KM from a multidisciplinary standpoint (Barclay and Murray 1997), although there is no consensus on its definition (Dalkir 2005). In his own view, Dalkir (ibid.) defined KM as 'the deliberate and systematic coordination of an organization's people, technology, processes, and organizational structure in order to add value through reuse and innovation. This coordination is achieved through creating, sharing, and applying knowledge as well as through feeding the valuable lessons learned and best practices into corporate memory in order to foster continued organizational learning.' He noted that 'the ability to manage knowledge is becoming increasingly more crucial in today's knowledge economy. The creation and diffusion of knowledge have become ever more important factors in competitiveness.' Again, the contextual relevance of this definition in this chapter is that African countries must understand and adopt or apply the basic tenets of KM, even if for the purposes of managing, and protecting through patents, trademark and intellectual property rights, indigenous or primordial knowledge that has been used to produce goods and services in local communities for centuries. It is not unlikely that this type of knowledge, if unprotected and poorly managed, can lose its value, can 'migrate' legally or illegally, or can be lost totally to future generations.

Next is the concept of innovation, which this chapter deems to be the 'zeitgeist' of business, management, technology and social enterprise discourse and practice today (Elahi et al. 2013). Satell (2013) posited that innovation 'has become management's new imperative', adding that the 'innovate or die' maxim is often heard at conferences and meetings. It is, he noted, 'a messy business which creates novel solutions to important problems'. He went further to delineate what he deems to be 'the three pillars of innovation' as competency, strategy and management. Foster (2016) cautioned that 'innovation does not mean simply inventing ideas; innovation is being flexible, adapting your business model and making changes in order to deliver better products or services to respond to the needs of your customers'. He added that 'if you establish the right culture and are brave enough to challenge thinking, then anyone's bright idea can be turned into value adding innovation'. According to Schirtzinger (2016), 'true innovation begins with an exciting new idea, but extends to its execution. So, in its fullest expression, innovation is also about spurring—and successfully managing—organizational change.' He was pragmatic in adding that 'real innovation is really, really hard'. Interestingly, unlike other innovation analysts such as Shaughnessy (2013), and quite pertinent to the aim of this chapter, he opted to address what he called '10 innovation killers—and how to neutralize them'. Of the ten, the seven that this chapter finds apropos for the African context are famine (resource scarcity, mainly budget, people, time and technology); trying to go it alone; institutional knowledge (dismissing an idea which someone said they had tried before and was futile); no short-term vision (thinking of end result and overlooking the 'now' hurdles); the 'right' way (stuck to one way and ignoring options); the sunk-cost fallacy (not cutting losses, but throwing good money at bad); and uncertainty (one's insecurities). The other less relevant three are feast (vast resources to work with, leading to wastage); too much data (data deluge, leading to analysis paralysis); and all work, no play (the 'live to work' type).

While innovation discourse generally tends to focus on the positive aspects of innovation, Hanekom (2013) observed that 'innovation can have a downside', and in the context of social equity he posed a rather ethical question: 'Through innovation we may remain globally competitive, but at what cost to the poorer members of our society?'

The final concept reviewed for its relevance in this chapter is entrepreneurship. Judging by the scope and time frame of scholarly, professional and policy discourses of entrepreneurship, this chapter surmises that entrepreneurship lies at the heart of market capitalism, industrialisation and the creative economy. In the light of the scope of the literature on entrepreneurship, suffice it to say that one of the earliest and most insightful scholarly analyses of entrepreneurship was by the economic doyen Schumpeter (1934), who married the concepts of entrepreneurship and innovation by depicting entrepreneurs as innovators who implement entrepreneurial change within markets. He identified five dimensions of entrepreneurship as the introduction of a new or improved item; the unveiling of a new method of production; discovery or opening of a new market; tapping into a new source of supply; and restructuring or re-engineering of business management processes. Another management guru, Drucker (1985), described an entrepreneur as someone who actually searches for change, responds to it and exploits it as an opportunity. In perhaps the most lay terms, the US Department of State (2007) defined an entrepreneur simply as 'a person who organizes, operates, and assumes the risk for a business venture'.

Rationalising Entrepreneurship

What is relevant for this chapter from the referenced definitions of entrepreneurship is the need to grasp, for policy and planning purposes, what it entails to nurture or groom Africans who are able, or have the capacity and wherewithal, to capitalise on opportunities to produce and market valuable and profitable goods and services for consumption both locally and beyond. Essentially, African governments and entrepreneurs must understand what it takes to engage profitably in the creative economy. While there is historic evidence that entrepreneurship is an age-old practice and tradition across Africa (Kolo 2006), the view in this chapter is that such practice has existed and served only at the subsistence level. The issue today is the ability of African entrepreneurs to produce and market goods and services that can command patronage and value in the global marketplace. This is the critical issue that this chapter addresses in the light of the extant creative global economy. At the heart of this issue are the vibrancy, resilience, profitability and sustainability of African enterprises for the short and long hauls, that is, throughout their life cycle.

In further pondering the reference issue as an African development scholar, several difficult, troubling and interrelated questions arise that lead to the contention that African entrepreneurs face several polylemmas in the life cycle trajectory from business innovation to business sustainability. Firstly, given the dismal level of international trade by the aggregate of African countries relative to other regions of the world, what are the prospects that entrepreneurship would now make a difference in Africa's engagement in the creative global economy? Secondly, with the relative failure of 'special' trade programmes designed to incentivise African trade with the world, such as America's 2000–2025 African Growth and Opportunity Act (AGOA), how and why would entrepreneurship make a difference? Thirdly, with the cascade of domestic political, security, economic, environmental, health and infrastructure problems that beset Africa and constantly threaten political stability, governance and the investment climate, what are the chances for sustainable entrepreneurship in such environments? Yet, many more similar questions can be posed, while many other obstacles can be identified, such as climate change, food insecurity, terrorism and xenophobia. Paradoxically—and this is the crux of the rationale for advocating sustainable entrepreneurship through innovation and knowledge management in this chapter—these very obstacles, problems and challenges harbour enormous opportunities for entrepreneurs, as defined in the literature as strategic risk managers, to be innovative, productive and profitable within and beyond the shores of Africa. Mugabe (2009) mounted a strong and evidence-based case for the deployment of knowledge and innovation for development in Africa, on the grounds that there are significant positive changes occurring across all spectrums of African countries, all pointing to a ripe and conducive time to create an enabling environment for sustainable entrepreneurship in the continent. The view in this chapter is that a Marshallian effort across the continent, especially through interregional and international collaboration, would help develop the entrepreneurial capacity that would answer some of the questions posed above, and mitigate some of the development and quality of life problems currently threatening public interest across the continent.

Business Life Cycle Polylemmas and Strategic Initiatives

Information from the desktop research (Murray et al. 2010) and personal interviews conducted for this chapter were used to construct Table 2.1 below. First, an analytical framework consisting of society's main goal clusters was developed in order to cluster the information from both sources. Goal clusters are categories of all people's needs and desires, based on the primary societal resources that would be needed or appropriate to address the needs. This is critical to understand the real causes of the problems and challenges of entrepreneurs, and for strategic development of initiatives and deployment of resources. Second, ideal phases were delineated for the life cycle of an enterprise, from cradle (initiation) to Grave (modernisation). Sustainable entrepreneurship is about a perpetual life for an enterprise, which is a rarity for African enterprises. Third, for each phase, the polylemmas identified from the literature and interviews for each goal cluster were summarised. Four, for each polylemma, strategic or actionable initiatives were proposed.

Conclusion

The argument and position in this chapter revolve around Africa's weak role and presence in the in the global economy, and the need to strengthen and expand this role by stimulating, developing and nurturing a robust entrepreneurial capacity in the continent through innovation and knowledge, along with other requisite political, economic and institutional reforms. Entrepreneurship has been the key to the economic success and, to some extent, political and strategic supremacy of countries around the world. From Norway's preponderance in communications technology to Japan's excellence in automobile manufacturing and America's and China's ubiquitous presence in all economic and industrial sectors, entrepreneurship has proven to be the *sine qua non* for success. Not to be left out is the ability of nations to feed, house and employ their citizens, resulting in political stability, self-reliance and patriotism. Finally, entrepreneurship has accounted for wealth creation and generation all over the world, while the sustainability of enterprises has accounted for the successful intergenerational transfer of wealth. All or most of these dividends of entrepreneurship remain a dream for most Africans. Yet, the demand for the dividends continues to grow as population and urbanisation rates rise above world averages.

Having examined the key factors of production, namely land, labour, capital, technology, infrastructure and entrepreneurial skills (Fiks 2000), this chapter contends that post-colonial African governments embraced, willingly, blindly and/or in compliance with the dictates of international development agencies such as the World Bank and International Monetary Fund, classical or modern economic models which have inadvertently or by design shifted the control, ownership and access of and to these factors from the vast majority of Africans to a privileged few. In sum, across Africa today, most people are landless; labour is cheap but crude and skill-less; access to affordable credit is limited to a few privileged people; technology is obsolete, non-existent or overly costly; and knowledge is handicapped by inadequate educational infrastructure. Add to these population, urbanisation and slum explosions, unaffordable health care, crumbling institutions, and unemployed and very restless youths (Anderson and Galatsidas 2014; Tinsley 2015). The consequence of all these is a stagnant or declining standard of living and overall quality of life for the majority. In this context, innovation and entrepreneurship become extremely difficult or nearly impossible for the majority of citizens who have the ambition and talent, but lack the production factors needed to move through the trajectory of innovation or entrepreneurship.

To address Africa's challenges, there have been advocates, such as Wadongo (2014) (Afro-realism), Elemelu (2015) (Africapitalism) and Sarfo (2013), for new development paradigms in Africa. It is in this context that this chapter advocates unlabelled entrepreneurship, which deploys innovation and knowledge to provide African entrepreneurs with the capacity to engage profitably in the creative global economy. The conclusion of this chapter is that innovation is pragmatically the time- and resource-intensive process of converting ideas into products and/or services that, firstly, are of value to others and command a price; secondly, yield dividends to the proprietor or owner of the product or service; thirdly, bring a sense of accomplishment and satisfaction to the owner; and finally, encourage or motivate the owner to share dividends with those who cannot afford to pay for the product/service. At the individual/ corporate ownership level, these four would translate, respectively, into productivity, profit, self-fulfilment/corporate success and giving back to society (service)/corporate social responsibility.

The phases and initiatives proposed in this chapter for the trajectory or life cycle of African enterprises will require radical changes in the thought processes, attitudes and viewpoints of those interested in entrepreneurship. These shifts will trigger some of the risks of innovation and entrepreneurship in the creative economy. As Hanekom (2013) opined, for example, 'policy-makers have to be more thoughtful about where and how innovation takes place. Otherwise they risk promoting economic growth that leaves people even further behind than before.' What this implies is that innovation is not risk-free. However, the conviction in this chapter is that there is hardly any viable or sensible alternative for Africa to become an active and profitable player in the creative economy. Among the strategic imperatives for dealing with any risk that innovation may portend are mutual collaboration among all societal stakeholders, leveraging of roles and resources, and vertical and lateral integration of institutions locally, regionally and internationally.

References

Anderson, M., & Galatsidas, A. (2014). *Urban population boom poses massive challenges for Africa and Asia.* Available at: http://www.theguardian.com/ global-development/2014/jul/10/urban-population-growth-africa-asia-united-nations

Barclay, R., & Murray, P. (1997). What is knowledge management? *Knowledge Praxis*. Available at: http://www.media-access.com/whatis.html

Dalkir, K. (2005). *Knowledge management in theory and practice*. Burlington: Elsevier Butterworth–Heinemann.

Drucker, P. F. (1985). *Innovation and entrepreneurship*. New York: Harper Business.

Easterly, W., & Levine, R. (1997). Africa's growth tragedy: Policies and ethnic divisions. *The Quarterly Journal of Economics, 112*(4), 1203–1250 Available at: http://www.hks.harvard.edu/fs/pnorris/Acrobat/stm103%20articles/ Easterley_Levine_Ethnic_Divisions.pdf.

El Houssamy, N. (2016). *Exploring knowledge and innovation in Africa*. Available at: https://knowledgemaze.wordpress.com/2015/01/05/exploring-knowledge-and-innovation-in-africa/

Elahi, S., de Beer, J., Kawooya, D., Oguamanam, C., & Rizk, N. (2013). *Knowledge and innovation in Africa: Scenarios for the future*. Cape Town: Open A.I.R. Network.

Elemelu, T. (2015). *Africapitalism: A philosophy for the era of sustainable development*. Available at: http://www.vanguardngr.com/2015/10/africapitalism-a-philosophy-for-the-era-of-sustainable-development/

Fik, T. J. (2000). *The geography of economic development: Regional changes, global challenges* (2nd ed.). New York: McGraw-Hill.

Florida, R. (2002). *The rise of the creative class: And how it's transforming work, leisure, community and everyday life*. New York: Basic Books.

Foster, T. (2016). *What is innovation?* Available at: http://www.packagingnews. co.uk/features/comment/soapbox/tony-foster-what-is-innovation-27-04-2016

Gibney, J. (2015). *Debate continues: Why Africa isn't rising, resource curse and how everyone – Including the west, World Bank – Is all in on it*. Available at: http://mgafrica.com/article/2015-12-29-the-debate-continues-why-africa-isnt-risingresource-curses-and-how-everyone-is-all-in-on-it-including-the-west-and-the-world-bank

Hanekom, D. (2013). *Knowledge economies risk leaving the poor behind*. Available at: http://www.scidev.net/global/knowledge-economy/opinion/knowledge-economies-risk-leaving-the-poor-behind.html#sthash.kdnGq5O1.dpuf

Howkins, J. (2001). *The creative economy: How people make money from ideas*. New York: Penguin Books.

Kolo, J. (2006). An analysis of strategic issues in institutionalizing a financial systems approach for microenterprise development in Africa. *Managerial Finance, 32*(7), 594–605.

Kolo, J. (2009). The knowledge economy: Concept, global trends and strategic challenges for Africa in the quest for sustainable development. *International Journal of Technology Management, 45*(1/2), 27–49.

Mugabe, J. (2009). *Knowledge and innovation for Africa's development: Priorities, policies and program.* Prepared for the World Bank Institute. http://info. worldbank.org/etools/docs/library/250707/Knowledge%20and%20 Innovation%20for%20Africas%20Dev.pdf

Murray, R., Caulier-Grice, J., & Mulgan, G.(2010). *The open book of social innovation. The young foundation.* http://www.nesta.org.uk/publications/open-book-social-innovation.#sthash.2jWd8Zft.dpuf

Ngubane, B. (2002). *Poor nations must embrace knowledge economy.* Available at: http://www.scidev.net/global/knowledge-economy/opinion/poor-nations-must-embrace-knowledge-economy.html#sthash.K39KzJzS.dpuf

Piotrowski, J. (2015). *What is a knowledge economy?* Available at: http://www. scidev.net/global/knowledge-economy/feature/knowledge-economy-ict-developing-nations.html

Rowden, R. (2013). *The myth of Africa's rise.* Available at: http://foreignpolicy. com/2013/01/04/the-myth-of-africas-rise/

Rowden, R. (2015). *Africa's boom is over.* Available at: http://foreignpolicy. com/2015/12/31/africas-boom-is-over/

Sarfo, A. (2013). *The uncomfortable truth: The myth of Africa's rise.* Available at: http://globalfusionproductions.com/featured/the-uncomfortable-truth-the-myth-of-africas-rise/#sthash.q5K650aW.dpuf

Satell, G. (2013). *How to manage innovation.* Available at: http://www.forbes. com/sites/gregsatell/2013/03/07/how-to-manage-innovation-2/#2328284e33d9

Schirtzinger, A. (2016). *10 Innovation-killers – And how to neutralize them.* Available at: http://www.forbes.com/sites/salesforce/2016/04/26/10-innovation-killers-and-how-to-neutralize-them/#148ae7b240f4

Schumpeter, J. A. (1934). *The theory of economic development: An inquiry into profits, capital, credit, interest, and the business cycle.* Cambridge, MA: Harvard University Press.

Shaughnessy, H. (2013). *Six ideas driving the future of innovation.* Available at: http://www.forbes.com/sites/haydnshaughnessy/2013/08/30/six-core-ideas-for-the-future-of-innovation/#7378148423aa

Spooner, S. (2015). *Africa rising narrative takes a hit as index shows business environment declining since 2011.* Available at: http://mgafrica.com/

article/2015-10-05-africa-rising-narrative-dealt-a-blow-as-business-environment-showing-a-decline-in-latest-governance-index

Tinsley, R. (2015). *Africa's angry young men.* Available at: http://foreignpolicy.com/2015/07/02/africas-angry-young-men/

U.S. Department of State (Bureau of International Information Program). (2007). *Principles of entrepreneurship: What is entrepreneurship?* Available at: http://www.ait.org.tw/infousa/zhtw/DOCS/enterp.pdf

Wadongo, E. (2014). *Africa rising? Let's be Afro-realistic.* Available at: http://www.theguardian.com/global-development-professionals-network/2014/nov/07/africa-rising-lets-be-afro-realistic

Weheba, N. (2015). *Why we need to reconsider how knowledge and innovation are measured.* https://knowledgemaze.wordpress.com/2015/10/01/why-we-need-to-reconsider-how-knowledge-and-innovation-are-measured/

Part II

Innovation and Entrepreneurship

3

The Role of an Innovative ICT-Based Entrepreneurial Evolution on Africa's Development: The Case of University-Based Incubators

Sherif H. Kamel

Overview

Technology has not only changed the world, it has also increased its potential (Figueres 2003). Innovative ICT, coupled with globalisation and the role of societal norms, values and cultures, is constantly affecting societies around the world and helping to transform many aspects of life, whether at the personal or professional level. It is forcing organisations and corporations to rethink and re-engineer the way they manage their operations and resources and face competition both locally and globally. Moreover, it is having a major impact on the way development and competition are taking place. It is fair to claim that the processes of globalisation are increasingly dependent on ICT (Musa 2006). This situation has generated new forms and structures of economic, business and social organisations that are no longer affected by geographic or time

S.H. Kamel (✉)
The American University in Cairo, Cairo, Egypt

© The Author(s) 2017
A. Ahmed (ed.), *Managing Knowledge and Innovation for Business Sustainability in Africa*, DOI 10.1007/978-3-319-41090-6_3

constraints but depend mainly on teleworking, which is emerging as the platform for business and socio-economic development in the twenty-first century. Examples of such organisations include the growing platform of incubators and accelerators that are spreading round the world, Africa included, in order to support, nurture, mentor and help develop tech start-up companies offering a variety of products and services that are innovation-based and that cater for today's mobile marketplace. Today, there are a number of innovative ways to do business in Africa that cannot be found in other countries, all of which are enabled through cutting-edge ICTs. African tech-savvy entrepreneurs are coming up with original, innovative ways to do business, and consequently a lot of intellectual property is being developed in Africa (Arlove 2016).

Africa, a continent with many resources and a variety of economies in transition, has been investing in building its ICT infrastructure for many decades in order to overcome its status as the most unconnected continent when it comes to ICT, although it faces a broad spectrum of developmental challenges (Figueres 2003). The deployment of emerging ICT infrastructure in the African continent can also benefit from a unique opportunity by capitalising on the experiences and learning from the lessons of the past witnessed by other nations in the developed world. In that respect, ICT can lead to an industrial and societal evolution based on information acquisition as well as knowledge creation and dissemination, allowing the creation of an emerging information-based society with innovative means of communication that could help increase competitiveness for individuals, organisations and societies (Branscomb 1994).

In 2015, the African population reached 1.1 billion people and is expected to reach 2 billion by 2050. It is by far the youngest continent in the world, with over 50 % of the population under the age of 19, and is known for its huge and young labour force, multiple languages and dialects and diversified cultures. Algeria is the largest country in terms of land, and Nigeria has the largest population. In terms of trading, as an example of the changes that are taking place, Chinese exports to the continent increased from US$11 billion to US$166 billion during the period 2006–2016. Economically, Africa has been the second-fastest-growing continent (Leke 2016). In other words, the transformation process is taking place but is not yet complete. There is still a lot that is taking place in terms of building and completing the infrastructure, improving government laws and regulations, as well as investing in human capital whether in training, vocational development, education or lifelong learning at large.

During the 1990s, there was an unprecedented link between the technological innovation process and economic and social organisations. Moreover, as the links between economic development, productivity and the availability of information resources became invaluable, governments round the world started to invest heavily in building their National Information Infrastructure (NII) (Petrazzini and Harindranath 1997). This led to major changes and transformations in the activities and relationships of individuals and organisations within the society, leading to the evolution of the information society, where the services provided by ICT represent a set of challenges and opportunities for the global society. However, it is important to note that although access to ICT is a prerequisite to its use, individual differences in time and space as well as capabilities and choice may play a role in the use, value and application of ICT (Alampay et al. 2003). Many African countries are facing massive challenges, including poverty and unemployment, yet again the continent is becoming, since the 1990s, home to many of the fastest-growing economies in the world, in many ways due to the growing number of entrepreneurs that are capitalising on tech start-ups that address the needs of the continent. The full impact has not yet been realised, but with sustainability, and scalability, the real impact will be felt across the continent in the years to come.

In general, the ICT infrastructure makes information more accessible, with more benefits for society (Shapiro and Varian 1999), which puts more pressure on firms round the world to exploit all possible opportunities to leverage productivity and efficiency. Businesses are becoming increasingly aware of the indispensability of ICT to stay competitive, with other global implications for productivity, employment and profits to the extent that organisational operations are becoming unthinkable without the effective and efficient use of ICT, especially in a global society, where information travels across national boundaries (Branscomb 1994). Therefore, many nations in Africa have taken concrete measures in that direction, such as Egypt, South Africa, Tunisia, Morocco and Kenya, which have restructured initiatives in telecommunications and informatics as part of an overall strategy that targets socio-economic development in the continent and where small and medium-sized (SMEs) enterprises play a vital role. This includes deregulation, encouraging private investment and foreign direct investments (FDI), and the use of tools such as public–private partnerships (Kamel 2009a). In the information age, ICT is an opportunity for the development of Africa because it is a powerful tool for economic growth, social inclusion and poverty eradication, which can facilitate the integration of African nations into the emerging, digital global marketplace (Annan 2003). Africa stands to gain a great deal from participating in the globally connected economy. However, it must first establish the necessary ICT infrastructure, and government and economic conditions to attract and maintain an effective position in the global economy (Ajayi 2004). Moreover, the legal and regulatory environment for those companies should be put in place to enable the proliferation of innovative and impact-driven start-ups as well as their scalability and sustainability. The African continent, with 54 countries and massive diversity across different countries, stands on the brink of a massive rise-up that can turn its fortunes around. According to the World Bank, six of the 12 fastest-growing economies in the world from 2014 to 2017 will be in Africa. They include Ethiopia, Democratic Republic of Congo, Mozambique, Tanzania, Côte D'Ivoire and Rwanda. It is important to note that, since 2015, Africa has been attracting some of the biggest names in international finance, whether state-owned funds such as China Investment Corporation, or private equity groups such as Blackstone and the Carlyle Group, or institutional investors such as Goldman Sachs.

More than one decade into the twenty-first century, the world is becoming smaller and the public is rapidly gaining access to new and dramatically faster ICT (Shapiro and Varian 1999). Moreover, the gradual move towards establishing the information society is irreversible and will have implications for all aspects of society. The formulation of information-based companies and societies at large will positively contribute to the creation of the global information society and will lead to the creation of a powerful platform for knowledge dissemination and sharing that is mobile, dynamic and iterative (Kamel 2009b). Moreover, the above-mentioned high-tech directions will result in further investments in telecommunications and infrastructure, as well as digital platforms such as eGovernment, eCommerce and many more digital initiatives that began to appear in the mid-1990s (Sorensen and Sayegh 2007). In 2016, in sub-Saharan Africa alone there were more than 42 top digital platforms. The advantage of Africa is the diversification of its economies across different countries. The misconception is that Africa is one country and is homogeneous, which is not the case. Africa is big and has similarities across its nations, but also many differences. It is worth noting that the world's financial crisis in 2008 turned the attention of many investors away from the traditional markets and destinations of investments and toward the African continent (Arlove 2016). This represents a unique opportunity for Africa, and home-grown talents and initiatives should take the necessary measures to capitalise on that. Some of those companies are gradually making the news, such as Africa's first tech unicorn, the Africa Internet Group (AIG), which is a privately held technology company valued at US$1 billion or more. AIG is the parent to a network of more than ten consumer-driven Internet businesses, including but not limited to Jumia and eCommerce platform; Zando, focused on shoes and clothing; Hellofood, a food delivery platform; Laymu, an online resale marketspace; Lamudi, a real estate platform; EasyTaxi, a cab service; and more (Knowledge@Wharton 2016).

The information society is becoming a global force and a fundamental element of change in the global society (Garito 1996). The information infrastructure (infostructure) is a factor for socio-economic improvement and represents a major support mechanism that can assist African nations in leapfrogging stages of development towards achieving a better standard of living and quality of life. In the current competitive context, access to and mobilisation of information are becoming the central aspects of productivity and competitiveness, and the investment required to set up ICT infrastructures directly supports growth and contributes to structural improvements in various services and industries (Kamel 2009a). The move towards an information society, and the opportunities it provides, will eventually be as important as the first industrial revolution (Kamel 1995a). It is difficult to predict the pace at which this change will take place, but the economies that will be the first to succeed in completing this change satisfactorily will have major competitive advantages. There are examples to demonstrate such development, such as Kenya, where the business environment is much further advanced as a result of having improved the legal and regulatory framework that can enable such development (Arlove 2016).

ICT and Socio-Economic Change

Change, transformation, competition, innovation, collaborative work and partnerships could be institutionalised through customised strategies targeting the diffusion of best practices and the development of ICT applications, which are the fundamental objectives in view of the contribution they can make to leveraging development and growth as well as strengthening competitiveness. Such a process should include the liberalisation of the telecommunications sector, the provision of a regulatory framework, the provision of a broad range of attractive tariff options for users, and the organisation of specialised training and human resources development programmes focusing on the needs of ICT industries and rendering information to be timely, shared and publicly available (Branscomb 1994). This is because the lack of a basic telecommunications infrastructure is a severe hindrance to the growth of the Internet in many countries (Mbarika 2002), especially where most of the development is taking place in the capitals and major cities (Kamel 2005). For example, the developments taking place in Africa in the space of mobile payments are all interesting to follow in order to analyse their impact on the economy and the society at large (Arlove 2016). There are multiple ways to look at such new spaces, with various recent additions including FinTech.

During the 1990s, ICT became a vital platform for business and socio-economic development with the growing role of the Internet (Kamel 1995b). This led to the development of the global information society, with new global trends and challenges such as competing in time, time to market, customer-oriented services, the online society, smart communities, social inclusion, eReadiness, the market economy, intellectual capital, investing in human resources and the sharing of information and knowledge. Therefore, the Internet and open data networks at large became major driving forces of change in the global marketplace (Kamel 1999). Changes are taking place globally, and the move towards an information age, coupled with emerging ICT innovations since the 1980s, has led to rapidly falling costs for ICT and major managerial, economic and organisational transformations, as well as the creation of a window of opportunity for massive developments and a chance to accelerate business and socio-economic growth in Africa. With the increasing high-level commitment from African leaders to bring about change in the way ICT is perceived, more ICT-enabled entrepreneurial initiatives could transform the way business is done in Africa and consequently positively affect societies across the continent. It is perceived that such a trend represents a unique opportunity for Africa's younger and growing generations to adapt and adopt new tools and techniques using state-of-the-art ICT. Africa, more than ever, is prepared to capitalise on the capacities enabled by emerging ICT to help leverage its development process and engage actively in the global information society, by transforming its societies into being more socially inclusive, digitally connected and electronically ready. Today Africa is a cash-based economy, but it is gradually becoming a digital economy (Sinare 2016).

ICT Evolution in Africa

Few doubt the significance of ICT for African economic and social development (Odedra-Straub 1993). Three major development goals have been articulated by African leaders who represent the driving force behind the embarkation on ICT evolution across the continent. The primary target is improving the quality of life for every African, working on the integration of the economies of the different African nations and leveraging trade linkages with other regions outside Africa based on mutual development purposes and growth targets. Consequently, building the African Information Infrastructure (AII) has become essential for the future of Africa, since it is perceived to form the backbone of the comprehensive socio-economic development plans for the continent in the twenty-first century and beyond. ICT is perceived to have the ability to improve the lives of people with low incomes who have limited access to services such as health care and education (Qureshi 2007). ICT is an invaluable platform for the creation of opportunities for underprivileged communities and societies, especially in a global community transformed through mobility. Moreover, ICT holds the promise of development by connecting people to more accurate and up-to-date sources of information and knowledge (Ahmed 2007).

Moreover, a number of civil society initiatives are under way, with the informal sector playing a major role through non-governmental organisations (NGOs) in contributing to ICT development in Africa. NGOs are very active in contributing to the eradication of poverty, to the social, educational and political empowerment of the underprivileged with a focus on women and children, and to universal access to ICT services through innovative and affordable technologies (Okpaku 2003a). Many are also involved in mentoring entrepreneurs across the continent, including in Egypt, such as Injaz (Junior Achievement). There are also industry-based initiatives such as the digital factory, which aims to create capacity in Africa for the development of software applications at global standards to support the global ICT industry as well as, and more importantly, to meet the indigenous continental demand (Okpaku 2003b). Some ICT introduction and diffusion initiatives have been nation-based, such as those in Egypt, Rwanda, Cameroon and Kenya. For example, the Free-Internet model was formulated in Egypt and migrated to a number of developing nations in both Africa and beyond. In the case of Rwanda, with its ambitious Vision 2020 programme approved in 2000, ICT has been anchored into broader economic, social and development policies and strategies in the form of the National Information and Communication Infrastructure (NICI) plan. The essence of the programme is to help build the Rwandan information society and to start integrating it into the global information society.

In the case of Cameroon, an integrated national ICT strategy was developed, initiated by the United Nations Economic Commission for Africa (UNECA) and supported by the United Nations Development Programme (UNDP). The strategy benefited from the input of all stakeholders in the marketplace including the government, the private sector and civil society. It is always important to engage and empower all stake-holders. In the case of Kenya, the approach was different because, while the private sector took the lead, the government was reluctant at first to embrace ICT for socio-economic development. However, momentum built up in a later stage and was embedded in the nation's poverty reduction strategy, which positioned ICT at the core of the national development plan. Currently, an integrated ICT-driven socio-economic development plan for Kenya has gone from being supported and driven only by the private sector to becoming the cornerstone for the development of the Kenyan information society (UNECA 2003). Recently, Kenya produced M-Pesa, which is setting the pace when it comes to mobile payments in Kenya and beyond. It is a mobile phone-based money transfer and micro finance service that was launched in 2007. It then expanded to Tanzania, South Africa, India and Eastern Europe. In general, the diffusion of ICT across Africa aims at supporting and accelerating business and socio-economic development across the continent.

The impact of emerging ICT is no longer confined to the technology domain. It is predicted that by 2020 over 12 billion, if not more, computing facilities will be connected to the global information infrastructure. However, as per the reports of UNECA, there are a number of priority challenges which hinder development in Africa and the opportunities that ICT offers African nations. They mainly relate to job creation, health, education and research, culture, trade and commerce, tourism and food security, among others. It is important to note that the main challenge facing African nations is to formulate effective strategies to bridge the gap between the penetration, use and effective implications of ICT within the African continent when compared to other regions in the world. In that respect, the New Partnership for Africa's Development (NEPAD) has set a number of ICT development objectives that address this challenge. They include doubling teledensity to two lines per 100 people, reaching an adequate level of access per household, lowering cost and improving reliability of service, achieving electronic readiness for all African nations, developing a pool of ICT-proficient youth from which Africa can draw trainees, software developers and engineers, and developing local content based on local culture (Okpaku 2003a). It is important to note that since the 1990s, many of these elements were realised and more are expected to do so moving forward. Universal access to ICT and the Internet is really coming into place across the African continent. In 2014, the number of Internet users in Africa reached 205 million, representing 18 % of the population, and the number of mobile phone users reached 750 million, representing 67 % of the total population, according to the International Telecommunications Union.

Universal access is an important element in introducing and diffusing ICT within the community and minimising the inter- and intra-digital divide, with an emphasis on rural and underprivileged areas and communities, where around 70 % of the population in developing nations lives (World Bank 2007). Improving public access is an important step in the development of the information society for Africa. This could be realised by setting up universal access funds to encourage infrastructure development in rural communities, and establishing community access centres and telecentres, as is the case in Egypt, where IT access centres have had major implications for remote locations, reaching thousands of access locations. Clearly, this could also be replicated in other African nations. Moreover, public–private partnerships (PPP) could prove to be effective in the ICT space. In Ethiopia, for example, low-cost personal computers (PCs) are being supplied to the community to help increase the penetration rate and usage levels (World Bank 2007). Additionally, in Egypt, multiple PPP programmes and initiatives have been introduced, such as Egypt PC 2010, IT clubs, mobile IT units and free Internet, with effective outcomes. This also applies to mobile telephony, which is constantly on the rise across the continent.

Role of Human Capital in Development

The transformational change could be realised through the proper investment in human capital. In today's economic, business and social space, communities around the world face a set of challenges related to growing unemployment, changing market dynamics and tough business conditions, among others. However, they are also regularly presented with a variety of opportunities given the development of new markets, the growing role of ICT, the rapid population growth especially in African economies, and their associated prospects and implications for global markets. While the pressures of those challenges will affect investments in different socio-economic directions, it should not affect the continuous investments in both human capital and in developing the proper infrastructure needed to help promote and create SMEs and start-ups, given the size and the demographics of the population in many of the emerging markets around the world. For example, one of the largest African nations, Egypt, with 58 % of its population under the age of 25, presents entrepreneurship with a unique opportunity to thrive. Thus, policy- and decision-makers, including the primary stakeholders—the government, the private sector and civil society—should collaborate and synchronise their strategies and plans and focus on how to optimise the use of the various limited resources to cater for the growing lifelong learning needs that could help establish an enabling environment for an agile and competitive entrepreneurial culture. In a nutshell, investing in people is investing in the future of Africa.

Consequently, the formulation of innovative strategies, clear objectives and nationwide training and professional development policies that can support the overall build-up of business culture becomes extremely invaluable in addressing market and industry needs in terms of providing human capital with the much-needed skills and capacities that can positively influence business and economic development and growth. Do more entrepreneurs mean more jobs and consequently a better economy? How can that happen? What is the infrastructure required? What is needed to entice youth and job seekers in general to engage with the private sector? How can we change the culture from looking for employment to looking to be self-employed? Is the environment ready to help create a start-up culture? Are the skills and capacities that could turn the society entrepreneurial available? What can be the role of ICT-based start-ups? Is entrepreneurial education and lifelong learning embedded in the curricula? The answer to all these questions and more relate directly to the way education and knowledge is being disseminated and shared, and the manner in which the culture in the community perceives business as a profession and entrepreneurship as the way to go. This too relates to the future of Africa and Africans. Investing in human capital through awareness and lifelong learning paves the way to the development of skills and capacities that are becoming increasingly important to prepare future generations to grow into agents of change and transform their society.

Investing in people is investing in the future and making the individual, the organisation and the community at large more agile, more competitive and ready to compete in a changing and dynamic global marketplace. It is important to note that while access to capital, among other factors, is key for entrepreneurs, human capital is the primary building block in creating an entrepreneurial culture and hence a strong private sector that can turn around the economy. Therefore, lifelong learning, with its different forms and means, should be considered as the engine of socio-economic development and the base for a start-up culture and a start-up continent. In every region of the world, Africa included, investing in youth specifically and in human capital at large helps unlock the society's potential for socio-economic development and growth. They want to learn, unlearn and relearn in a world that is constantly changing to be able to make a difference. Human capital remains the game changer and is gradually becoming the deciding factor in both emerging and developed societies. In many ways, in my view, human capital is the oil of the twenty-first century and represents the most invaluable resource in countries round the world.

In 2013, the emerging markets' total gross domestic product was US$44.4 trillion compared to the US$42.8 trillion generated by developed markets. Having said that, there is never one size that fits all; the process of adoption, diffusion and adaptation varies across different countries. Therefore, the content, the approach, the set-up and the tools to educate a community vary based on culture, norms, values, work patterns and the way business is conducted. Clearly, it is not only academic degrees, or even extended experiences and diversified exposure, for that matter, that will enable entrepreneurship to flourish. Rather, the community will become more entrepreneurial if the environment provides opportunities for everyone to think differently and have the space and time to act creatively and attempt to follow their passion, take risks and accept failures, all as part of the continuous learning process. It is important to understand that in entrepreneurship, mistakes represent opportunities for learning and improvement.

The required education–knowledge–experience infrastructure, in other words lifelong learning, goes beyond the boundaries of the classroom, school or university. It is the market knowledge and experience that counts, and the way the community prepares its current and future generations to be ready to unleash their potential. It is more related to openness, innovation, forward-looking and moving from the traditional and the predictive mindset into the unconventional and the uncertain. The knowledge shared should embed creative and timely content using cutting-edge methodologies and critical thinking and should be driven and focused on catering for the global job market requirements. Universities and professional institutions round the world offer entrepreneurship programmes to nurture an entrepreneurial spirit and provide potential entrepreneurs with the right tools and methodologies to launch their start-ups. This should be well diffused in the 100+ business schools across the African continent. In addition, this should be coupled with multiple informal settings such as advisory sessions, mentorship and awareness campaigns, seminars and networking events. Since 2008, throughout the Middle East and North Africa (MENA), more than 140 programmes, initiatives and organisations have been established to promote the culture of entrepreneurship. These include university-based incubators and accelerators, non-governmental organisations, private set-ups and funds, and chapters of international students and youth associations.

The entrepreneurial culture needs to be nurtured throughout the education system and beyond. It is time to establish additional university-based incubators. There also needs to be more focus on and encouragement toward the private sector in schools, teaching youth about entrepreneurship throughout the curricula as well as developing the appropriate policies and directions to ensure an impact-oriented entrepreneurial education. This should include exposure to business successes and failures and role models in the society as well as extracurricular activities that promote innovation and creativity. There is a need for a transformational change in the societal mindset by appreciating more the role of the private sector and demonstrating the role it plays that complements the role of the public sector and the civil society. They all contribute in different ways to the welfare of the community and that notion needs to be disseminated through degree and non-degree programmes as well as orientation and awareness seminars and the media. The community needs expertise in idea generation, leadership, governance, responsible business, business ethics, problem identification and solving, project management and more.

Given the demographics in emerging economies such as most of Africa, as well as the need to enlarge the private sector through the proliferation of SMEs, economies in many ways will be shaped by how effective entrepreneurial education is developed and integrated universally across the different communities. Some would argue that entrepreneurship cannot be taught and that it is a gift or talent; I would argue otherwise. While some definitely are born with more talent than others in some respects, everything can be improved and fine-tuned through proper education, mentorship, exposure and the opportunity to showcase one's own capacities and skills. The key strategic objectives of entrepreneurial lifelong learning include, but are not limited to, fostering innovation, leveraging responsible business, introducing business and management skills and techniques, helping develop high-growth SMEs, commercialisation of ideas, empowering and engaging youth, and more. Identifying talent should be universally based across different communities, unlike the conventional wisdom in emerging economies that everything happens in the capital and the big cities. Talent is everywhere, and more often than not it is found in remote locations and small villages and towns, where the need for change and a better life encourages youth to think differently and creatively to develop solutions and ideas that could transform their communities—further proof that it is not just academic degrees, but the overall educational experience and knowledge dissemination in both its explicit and tacit ways, that can make a difference.

For example, among Egypt's 85 million citizens, 7.1 million work as civil servants. That leaves a huge population ready for a more robust private sector. It would be a big mistake for Egypt not to utilise its most precious resource, human capital, to establish a strong private sector. The preparation of future leaders and entrepreneurs in Egypt should be aiming at realising sustainability, societal impact and scalability to accommodate the fast-growing population. The ICT platform will be driven by an incredibly passionate youth contingent that is technology-savvy, reaching 100 million (117%) mobile users and more than 40 million (47%) in 2015. This youth contingent possesses the creative minds and innovative solutions needed to help transform the society while focusing on the incredible number of untapped opportunities across a variety of sectors. The notions of productivity, velocity, accuracy and consistency should be at the core of the learning process, since they will be among the deciding factors in preparing the entrepreneurs who will have the ability and stamina to handle the pressure and market dynamics while continuing to make a difference. The future of Egypt, and consequently Africa, depends on the next generation of business leaders and entrepreneurs being able to transform the economy through the creation of a robust and competitive start-up Egypt. It is invaluable to understand that what really counts is human capital, and that they are ready and engaged to influence the economy. The process of building a start-up culture would eventually lead to creating a start-up society and consequently a start-up nation, which would in many ways help create an ecosystem in which more entrepreneurs lead to more jobs and a better economy.

The Impact of University-Based Incubators/ Accelerators

The development of an entrepreneurial culture should follow a bottom-up approach that spreads across the community and becomes embedded in the way people think, plan, work, study and go about doing different things in business and society. The stakeholders in the entrepreneurial ecosystem are many and diverse; each plays an important role in developing, institutionalising and promoting entrepreneurship and innovation. One of the growing and invaluable key stakeholders in the ecosystem that provides the rich and much-needed body of knowledge associated with the academic set-up that supports entrepreneurs is the university-based incubator (UBI). The concept of campus incubators is spreading, and they are growing in number, impact and role when it comes to the entrepreneurial ecosystem in the society. Generally, campus incubators are widely perceived as platforms providing a nurturing environment for new business ventures and business start-ups that stem from ideas generated and developed by university undergraduate and graduate students (Kamel 2013a). To support such a growing community, some universities, in addition to developing an incubator, either open offices to support entrepreneurship or establish technology tracking offices that are focused on promoting innovation and helping start-ups, especially those that are technology-based. Some define the university incubators as the equivalent of a career office, where the ultimate outcome for entrepreneurs is a gateway to the marketplace with all the support, opportunities, mentorship and funding possible (Kamel 2014). Incubators could be the gateway to the marketplace with the right idea and a value proposition to the society.

Entrepreneurial universities in general are increasingly becoming essential agents in generating knowledge and innovation while capitalising on emerging ICTs. Such a mandate serves their purpose as academic institutions focused on research and education, but also supports their quest to fortify their invaluable role in knowledge creation, dissemination and transfer as well as the commercialisation of innovative ideas, especially through technology-based ventures and the creation of start-ups (Kitagawa and Robertson 2012). Universities could be teaching and researching entrepreneurship, rather than being entrepreneurial themselves in everything they do. The latter are those who really have an impact on creating the entrepreneurial culture in the society (Kamel 2014). It is not just about teaching entrepreneurship in the classroom; it is all about the case studies, extracurricular activities, the teaching method, the interaction with industry and business, and the blending of course content and the amalgamation between theory and practice. It is the mindset and the culture that need to be created and embedded in campus life (Kamel 2012).

The importance of having UBIs is invaluable for the formulation of a vision and a strategy for the promotion of innovative research in technology-based start-ups, which is becoming increasingly important in today's global competitive economies, and more important for emerging economies such as most of the African economies that are looking for a platform to make a difference and realise socio-economic development (Scaramuzzi 2002). Unlike stand-alone business incubators that mainly provide the incubation, funding and mentorship required by new business start-ups in a classical environment, the ones located on university campuses play an important role in developing solid and effective relationships between the academic establishment and different businesses and industries across the society (Kamel 2013b). UBIs are intended to link ICTs, resources and human capital to entrepreneurial talent for the objectives of accelerating the development of start-ups and consequently accelerating the commercialisation of technology. Respectively, multiple universities around the world started establishing their incubators, providing policymakers and aspiring entrepreneurs insights into the various facility design, management policy, and value-added aspects of this emerging tool employed by some entrepreneurial universities as a strategy for supporting the development of new start-ups and helping economies at large (Kamel 2014). Such evolution needs to occur in Africa too; the potential is huge and the resources, ideas, passion and need are there.

UBIs offer many advantages, including access to university facilities, faculty, staff, mentors, library resources and student support; entrepreneurial clinics provide free advice and counselling on campus 24/7 and are often buzzing with students and mentors (Robertson and Kitagawa 2011). The growing interest in and passion for UBIs stem from the significant potential of the interdisciplinary nature of the environment that could be created from among the academic disciplines offered on campus, including business, engineering, chemistry, biotechnology, art and more, and the diverse groups of stakeholders off campus involved and engaged in the ecosystem (Kamel 2013a). In addition, the research outcome that could result from assessing the incubated start-ups becomes increasingly important for businesses, industries and entrepreneurs across different sectors in today's competitive and changing global marketplace (Manimala and Vijay 2012). The learning environment on campus provides the proper context for the creation of the entrepreneurial culture among the youth—the future leaders and entrepreneurs, the ultimate agents of change.

As early as the 1980s, more than 50 universities in the United States had established business and technology UBIs. Since then the concept has spread worldwide across different regions, with a growing number of universities funding UBIs as an integral element of the educational experience to leverage their research, teaching and service outcomes. Moreover, the partnership between universities, industries and businesses represents another effective platform that can contribute to socio-economic development, productivity and growth (Kamel 2013b). Campus incubators are a great fit for the learning process: they relate theory and practice and can effectively guide the interested students not only to become knowledgeable about entrepreneurship but also to become entrepreneurial themselves (Mian and Oswego 1996). UBIs encourage innovative new businesses, help disseminate knowledge (which schools specialise in), and complement the teaching of entrepreneurship in the classroom by closing the gap between academia and the business world. With SMEs growing in number and impact in driving both developed and emerging economies, universities can stimulate the economy by supporting the proliferation of start-ups (Scaramuzzi 2002). This is the way to create an entrepreneurial mindset that can help create the required culture for a start-up nation, one that can have a positive impact with respect to job and wealth creation (Kamel 2012).

In general, UBIs are perceived as an important venue for research through theoretical inquiry and access to faculty and different facilities as well as for helping foster university–industry and business entrepreneurial linkages and partnerships to support the development and growth of the incubated start-ups (Mian and Oswego 1996). The model differs across different universities. Experience clearly indicates that no one size fits all. Some have accelerators that are profit-oriented, others develop their own incubators or labs that are purpose-oriented, and some establish their own centres or institutes (Robertson and Kitagawa 2011). However, the one thing all universities are focused on is leveraging their entrepreneurial education with hands-on experience that can provide their students and different stakeholders with a platform to apply theory to practice. The ultimate strategic objective is to create a societal impact on the economy and contribute to the betterment of society (Manimala and Vijay 2012).

The Entrepreneurial Ecosystem

In this pivotal time for Egypt, the notion of start-ups, a strong entrepreneurial culture and an innovative mindset is needed more than ever to become the driver and catalyst to rebuild Egypt on strong, solid and sustainable foundations. Entrepreneurship is not new to Egypt. Egyptians throughout history have been known as successful entrepreneurs across different sectors, including trading, agro-business and the textile industry, moving between provinces in Egypt and across nations in Africa, actively involved in establishing and growing businesses in different sectors. This mindset shifted some time ago, however, so that the aspiration of many

Egyptians more recently has been to work for the government or in the public sector, to secure a job with minimal risk and challenge. A culture developed in which the primary focus was on securing a safe job regardless of the opportunities that presented themselves elsewhere in the marketplace (Rizk and Kamel 2013). However, that mindset gradually started to change in the late 1990s with a growing young population that is technologically savvy, better educated, more exposed and willing to venture into the business world at a younger age. In 2008, such change started to take a more definite shape with the proliferation of business associations, organisations and business plan competitions supported by investors, mentors, local companies and multinationals (Kamel 2014).

Consequently, since 2010, more than 140 organisations in Egypt and the region were established and/or started to provide different types of support, whether financial or non-financial, to the entrepreneurial ecosystem. Several factors contributed to the change, including, but not limited to, an average population growth rate of 2.1 % per annum in Egypt, in a population of 85 million that is overwhelmingly young, with 58 % under the age of 25, coupled with a growing belief that the nation's future can only be improved with a more agile and competitive private sector (Kamel 2011). Moreover, the change was also assisted by the growing diffusion of ICT usage and increasing investment in entrepreneurial awareness campaigns and educational and training programmes. Accordingly, over the last decade many cases have emerged in Africa of promising entrepreneurs who have great ideas for start-ups that can have positive implications for the societies of the region. Given the demographics of Africa, and with a growing and young population increasingly exposed through various technology and social media platforms, there is no shortage of ideas that can spawn start-ups in different sectors and industries such as health, environment, tourism, education, agriculture, energy, recycling, music, entertainment and more.

In Egypt, the government has developed several strategies to encourage entrepreneurship. They include training programmes, financing opportunities and technical support (Hattab 2010). Rules and regulations have also seen some shifts. Regarding the ease of doing business, Egypt was considered one of the top global reformers when it came to simplification of administrative work in 2007 (OECD 2009). For example, the creation of 'one-stop shops' to consolidate government services in one location have helped streamline and facilitate the process of starting a new business (IBRD 2012). However, most of these reforms have targeted large investors and corporations, rather than small start-up companies. The government has also supported entrepreneurship (albeit mostly SMEs, rather than high-growth innovative entrepreneurship) through financial opportunities. For example, public banks such as the National Bank of Egypt, Banque du Caire, Banque Misr and the Bank of Alexandria have created departments to address the particular needs of SMEs (AFDB 2009). Moreover, the Social Fund for Development and the Industrial Modernization Center, both quasi-governmental entities, have created SME support programmes (AFDB 2009). Looking at the entrepreneurial ecosystem holistically, El Dahshan, Tolba and Badreldin (2010) identified some of the most active organisations in Egypt that support entrepreneurship. These organisations include the Information Technology Industry Development Agency (ITIDA), the Middle East Council for Small Business and Entrepreneurship, Nahdet El Mahrousa, Ashoka, Entrepreneurs Business Forum, Endeavor, Alashanek ya Baladi, the Egyptian Junior Business Association, the American University in Cairo and the Center for Entrepreneurship at Cairo University. There are also many others including Cairo Angels and the American Chamber of Commerce in Egypt. However, this is a dynamic space that needs to be monitored on a regular basis given its fluid nature and the continuous changes that take place as players come on board or leave the ecosystem. The American University in Cairo since 2009 has tried to help build the entrepreneurial ecosystem by engaging different players and becoming their educational partners, and by bringing everyone together to contribute what can really be a game changer for Egypt.

Building a University-Based Entrepreneurial Ecosystem: The Case of the AUC Venture Lab

Within the context of emerging economies, UBIs are gradually growing in numbers to cater for the needs of their societies, especially those with demographics that are predominantly young and that are interested in establishing a solid, diverse and competitive private sector. In the case of Egypt, entrepreneurship and investment in human capital for the creation of a competitive private sector is key. There is a youth population that is interested in creating a start-up culture that could transform the society (Kamel 2014).

Therefore, in 2013, the American University in Cairo (AUC) organised the soft launch of the first full-fledged UBI in Egypt—the Venture Lab (V-Lab), aiming to translate technologies and innovations developed by selected start-ups across the country into commercially viable ventures. The V-Lab is managed by the Entrepreneurship and Innovation Program (EIP) of the AUC School of Business, established in 2010 as part of the school's 2010–2015 strategy aimed at promoting and supporting a growing entrepreneurial culture in Egypt. The strategy was focused on helping to create an entrepreneurial culture supported by three distinct pillars: innovation, leadership and responsible business (Ismail and Kamel 2013). EIP was transformed in 2014 into the Center for Entrepreneurship and Innovation (CEI), which identifies and assists mentors, as well as incubates, connects and supports talented youth and facilitates their success beyond AUC, into Egypt, Africa and the Middle East. The V-Lab capitalises on the resources and reach of the university at large and its state-of-the-art campus facilities in terms of people, knowledge and technology infrastructure (Ismail and Kamel 2013).

At the early stages of building the EIP ecosystem, discussions and meetings were held with various stakeholders sharing a common entrepreneurial passion. These conversations involved faculty, students, alumni and business leaders with specific interest in the area. To formalise these discussions, the school established the Entrepreneurship and Innovation Council to act as an advisory body, which had among its members faculty and business leaders with an interest in entrepreneurship. Over time, they became judges and mentors in competitions, acted as angel investors and provided advice in designing the various EIP programmes and activities. EIP also established a network of practitioners, business executives and academics interested in mentoring and coaching entrepreneurs at various stages of their start-up journeys (Ismail and Kamel 2013). EIP takes a comprehensive ecosystem approach in designing its action framework, focusing its activities on six key areas: entrepreneurs, ideas, networks, mentors, funding and start-up ventures. The programme focuses especially on partnerships with other organisations associated with entrepreneurship to implement its activities. Table 3.1 demonstrates the primary focus areas of the framework. Working with young entrepreneurs highlighted the need for providing additional in-depth services to serious early-stage entrepreneurs/start-ups as they worked through their business modelling and planning, fundraising, and setting up their operations and partnerships. These services are best provided to a smaller number of start-ups through an acceleration/incubation programme. This provided the motivation to expand the scope of the entrepreneurship ecosystem at AUC by establishing the AUC V-Lab, as already indicated.

Since 2008, EIP activities have supported more than 5,000 entrepreneurs from several provinces in Egypt including Cairo, Giza, Mansoura, Alexandria and Aswan as well as from other countries in MENA such as Lebanon and the United Arab Emirates. Since its inception, EIP positioned itself in the entrepreneurship ecosystem as the educational partner, becoming the primary platform for knowledge sharing and dissemination in the space of entrepreneurship and innovation and collaborating with the different main stakeholders in the ecosystem, including Injaz Egypt, Flat6Labs, Endeavor Egypt, Enactus and others. As indicated previously, AUC V-Lab, as a university-based incubator, was established to provide in-depth support services for a small number of serious entrepreneurs and their start-ups. The findings from background research conducted on start-ups in Egypt demonstrated that there is a huge 'white space' in the market (Ismail and Abdallah 2013). Many start-ups were in need of services that could easily be offered by a university-based incubator, such as mentorship and coaching, networking and connections, and access to university facilities, faculty and students.

The business model of the V-lab was based on research on other university-based incubators in the world (Ismail and Abdallah 2013). This provided insights into the various business models of university-based incubators, which helped shape the V-Lab business model. Globally, for example, universities tended to select companies that matched their own internal competencies. Many indicated a significant interest in technology, and the time period between affiliation and incubation ranged from several months to several years. Many also offered

Table 3.1 EIP primary focus areas

Focus area	Description
Entrepreneurs	Raising awareness about entrepreneurship among different participants. They vary in terms of education, demographics, socio-economic background and age group. This stage acts as a catalyst for start-up team formation and exposes the entrepreneurs to the venture process and the entrepreneurial ecosystem
Ideas	Generating attractive ideas, conceptualising business opportunities and developing business plans; all responding to market needs in Egypt. Leadership panels, partnerships with incubators and summer camps represent the major activities of this area
Network creation	Collaborating with 28 universities, companies and international institutions and the involvement of business executives from a variety of sectors where participants are exposed to real-life examples of entrepreneurship. Meetings and discussions are carried out between like-minded entrepreneurs, industry experts and local leaders
Mentorship	Coaching and mentoring potential entrepreneurs through the development of their business plans and launch of their start-ups. Furthermore, mentors provide internships in start-ups. The mentoring process is done through the university mentors' network, and supported by faculty advice, workshops and training
Start-up ventures	Encouraging entrepreneurs to seek funds. They are connected to venture capitalists, angel investors and potential investment partners. EIP also offers financial awards through start-up competitions. Consequently, some entrepreneurs are admitted to business incubators and others are assisted in promoting their ideas to the market. This is done by connecting start-ups to incubators and accelerators, supporting incubated start-ups in partner organisations or providing visibility and access to start-ups

multiple incubator types and stages, allowing a diversity of entrepreneurs to enter their programmes. Compared to the United States, emerging market programmes tended to offer longer incubation periods (up to 18 months), and university faculty also tended to demonstrate a more intimate, one-on-one relationship with the incubated entrepreneurs. It was also found that short-term incubators were a double-edged sword: on the one hand, they might push entrepreneurs to get their products to market more quickly, but they might also rush products that need more time to develop (Ismail and Shabana 2013). AUC V-Lab was established to operate in addition to all the above-mentioned EIP activities and programmes, and offers a few serious entrepreneurs a variety of services aimed at assisting the start-up process, increasing business survival rates and providing avenues for access to funding from angel investors, venture capitalists or other sources. The V-Lab utilises the university's capabilities (knowledge, faculty, staff, facilities, space, brand name and services) to help companies with strong growth potential launch successfully. AUC V-Lab offers workspace, facilities including the library, as well as engineering, multimedia, and technical labs, funding, business skills training, seminars, business plan competitions, networking events, mentorship, coaching, and assistance through professional services such as human resources, recruitment, communication, marketing and legal assistance. In addition to access to faculty members, students and facilities of the university, but also unique to the V-Lab, is access to students for product testing, class projects and internships. Moreover, the V-Lab organises two regular events: a weekly event where the university community is invited to meet the start-ups and give feedback on the products or services, as well as a biweekly event where mentors are invited to share experiences, both successes and failures, with the entrepreneurs of the start-ups being incubated.

To date, multiple rounds have been completed, with over 23 start-ups incubated since the inception of the V-Lab. Initially, over 500 applications were presented, but only the short-listed start-ups were given around US$3,000 each, in return for zero equity. The incubation cycle is designed to last for eight months. The initial cycle included six start-ups from diverse sectors with products ranging from wearable gadgets to mobile applications. The V-Lab is funded through sponsorships and the school budget. UBIs are usually sponsored by different businesses and industries. In the case of the V-Lab, SODIC, one of the leading real estate development companies in Egypt, and the Arab African International Bank (AAIB) are the primary sponsors. It is important to have earmarked sponsors to provide sustainable financial support to the start-ups in their initial phase. The V-Lab enables the entrepreneurs of the incubated start-ups to capitalise on AUC's world-class facilities and knowledge base, connecting them to the university's alumni network and fostering a thriving ecosystem of innovation, education and business. The V-Lab provides a space for young, passionate and promising Egyptian entrepreneurs to develop innovative business ideas and solutions to some of the most pressing problems in the community. Participants are not supposed to be primarily AUC students, since the model was developed from the start to serve Egypt's young and promising entrepreneurs regardless of where they are from. In that context, AUC is determined to provide the mentorship and support network that will give these talented young people an opportunity to make their dreams a reality. UBIs are established to empower entrepreneurs and foster innovation in an attempt to contribute to socio-economic development through the creation of jobs, and if the proposed ideas can be translated into successful products and services, the economy will be in much better shape (Scaramuzzi 2002). Innovation and entrepreneurship can be a key driver for competitiveness of the economy and for accelerating inclusive economic growth. In that sense, this is exactly what the V-Lab was established to realise, with an additional mission to help fill the existing gaps in the emerging entrepreneurial ecosystem in Egypt. One of the primary strategic objectives is to capitalise on AUC's intellectual capital and world-class resources, select a few high-potential innovative start-ups and help transform these teams into scalable start-ups.

A number of promising start-ups were incubated during the early incubation cycles, including Mubser, a technology-based start-up providing cutting-edge technology for the visually impaired around the world through a wearable gadget that can be integrated into a smartphone or through the device's customised pocket computer. With the help of algorithms, it can detect the obstacles in front of the user and notify him/her through a vibration bracelet in the user's hand and/or through a Bluetooth headset in the user's ear. It is important to note that in 2013, Mubser won first place in the ICT track at the Idea to Product competition held in Brazil. Other start-ups incubated at the V-Lab covered ideas related to media and news, edutainment, transportation logistics and textiles. A number of the V-Lab incubated start-ups and their founders have been recognised by a variety of international awards, including candidates among the 30 most promising young entrepreneurs in Africa by Forbes. While UBIs are popping up everywhere,

AUC's programme seems to be the first incubator in the region to support entrepreneurs across the community. While some are limited to specific technologies, others only serve their own students. The V-lab prides itself on being open to entrepreneurs from across Egypt. With several different models on which to base the V-Lab operations, the key here is to find a strategy that is right for Egypt, one that can help bring the different stakeholders in the ecosystem together and help realise a scalable and sustainable impact.

The V-lab has adopted best practices from global university and private incubators alike, but the team is forging ahead with their own adapted and localised model, one that can help optimally realise the strategic objectives it was initially created for. The longer incubation option, welcoming applications from across the country and two start-up competitions a year are all elements that the AUC School of Business has chosen in order to maximise its ability to support job creation in Egypt. The model is gradually being adapted with continuous efforts to improve the management and governance structure. To assess the success of the V-Lab, the university has developed a number of key performance indicators (KPIs). The main indicators of success are the number of start-ups the V-Lab creates in addition to the number of entrepreneurs trained through the V-Lab learning programme, the number of start-ups incubated and supported by services offered, and the number of start-ups able to access funding (and the amount of funding) as a result of the V-Lab incubation.

In 2013, a new Swedish organisation was established to provide international ranking for university-based incubators and to help establish standards and best practices for their operations. UBI Index ubi-global. com provides benchmarking and best practice sharing services to university-based incubators, as well as advice to corporations and governments on how to best support these programmes. In 2014, AUC V-Lab was selected as one of the five most promising university incubators in Africa, based on the first round of incubation. As V-Lab develops its programmes, it is learning from the benchmarking exercise and also joining an international network of peers. It is important to note that UBIs are increasingly becoming the ultimate resource base and the most convenient environment conducive to the development of successful technology-based start-ups and hence promoting technology-based entrepreneurship. However, there are issues that remain of primary importance for continuous research, relating to different entrepreneurial elements in the equation: the individual, the process, the organisation and the environment.

The experience of the V-Lab resulted in a number of accumulated experiences that could be summarised in the following: (a) the importance of using partnership models when collaborating with different stakeholders in the ecosystem including the venture capital funds, the angel investor networks, and the providers of training and professional development including non-profit organisations is a critical success factor; (b) the importance of building on the resources and facilities on campus, including utilising available services across the university such as faculty, labs, research centres and students and focusing on areas where the start-ups could benefit from being incubated within a university, is invaluable. For example, the first two start-ups incubated at the V-Lab were created by AUC professors and alumni; both were based on innovations in science and engineering in the areas of biotechnology and solar energy. In each case, the start-up was working with AUC students to improve their business plan, implement marketing research, conduct additional technical research and connect with the AUC network of funders and mentors. Through this integration with the university, these start-ups benefited tremendously and contributed to both university and students. This relationship makes a university-based incubator distinctive from any off-campus incubator; (c) the use of an iterative experimental approach in growing the scope of activities, by creating awareness about entrepreneurship across the campus among faculty, students and alumni, followed by the creation of partnerships with key actors in the ecosystem and expansion of the number of activities, followed by the phase of building the UBI, then creating a vehicle to fund the incubated start-ups. Such an approach provides the ability to experiment and learn, to build a stronger network with key stakeholders and to invest the resources efficiently; (d) the creation of locally engaged stakeholders helps build a solid support base and lay a foundation for long-term sustainability. Individuals and institutions who are engaged in the process, whether they are from within or outside the university, tend to have greater interest (Ismail and Kamel 2013). These stakeholders become strong long-term supporters of the UBI, which is invaluable for a scalable and sustainable impact on the entrepreneurial ecosystem coupled with the invaluable role that entrepreneurs play in advancing a country's economy (AFDB 2009), which in many ways points to the important role of universities in fostering and promoting an ecosystem for innovation and entrepreneurship.

The V-Lab Business Model

The V-Lab targets start-ups after the idea stage and prior to entering the market. This phase fits well with the university-based incubator model, as at this point entrepreneurs have a general idea of what their product or service will look like and a prototype or pilot, but still require a significant amount of technical and business support. Start-ups entering the programme must have or be working on a prototype, pilot or proof of concept for their product or service. The V-Lab is sector-agnostic, but requires that entrepreneurs have an innovative approach to solving or filling existing demand with a unique value proposition. Through its partners, the V-Lab has reached out to students in all 17 public universities in Egypt to ensure a diverse and interesting pool of applicants. Start-ups go through a rigid two-month selection process that includes a detailed application, initial presentations and finally the pitching of ideas to a panel of seasoned entrepreneurs and investors. The selection criteria cover three main areas: firstly, the business opportunity or idea must be original, impact on a problem, fill a market gap, be innovative and fit with the V-Lab service offerings; secondly, the business must have passed the idea stage and have developed a prototype, and the viability of its revenue model and cash burning rate will be examined; thirdly, the entrepreneur must demonstrate commitment to the business, managerial capabilities and an acceptance of feedback. The selection process is designed to add value to the entrepreneurs, even if they are not selected for incubation. Before the final presentations on demo day, all companies are required to attend an interactive training programme that focuses on building business skills. This also enables the V-Lab to work closely with each entrepreneur and evaluate his or her talents, abilities and motivation. The programme is designed and led by AUC faculty, business practitioners and executives selected from our mentors' network.

Based on the selection process, start-ups are admitted into a four-month acceleration programme. During this period, the V-Lab educates start-ups on basic business skills, works with them to finalise business models and develop functioning prototypes of products or services, and connects them to business leaders and mentors. A 'start-up boot camp' training programme explores basics business principles, as coaching and mentorship is offered in tandem. Facilities including labs, theatres and mass communications are offered, as well as workspaces. Entrepreneurs are offered help in recruiting other students, especially interns, to join their projects. The acceleration phase provides training to students in five areas of business management. Firstly, they are taught the basics of planning a business, including the business model, market, product and value proposition. They are introduced to project planning tools and taught how to create a business plan. The second aspect involves developing a 'product that works'. Next, launching that product requires skills in marketing, advertising and sales. Financial management explores aspects such as equity management, financing, budget and cash flow management, as well as accounting and taxes. Finally, training on 'organising for growth' helps start-ups learn how to manage people, as well as organisational values/culture, in an early-stage organisation. Upon finishing the four-month cycle, start-ups are expected to have a finalised business plan, a working product or prototype and a financial plan.

The coaching programme supports the team in areas that do not require deep expertise but rather general management experience. Coaches are selected based on expressed interest, as well as matching during events (for example, speed mentoring). Each start-up is assigned one coach, who is asked to meet with them frequently. Coaches are generally individuals with relevant work experience and a deep interest in the company's idea/business model. They also should have the capability to pitch and/or defend the idea in front of investors. Speaking and networking events are also held on a regular basis. These are open to outside entrepreneurs, and include pitches, speed mentoring, sharing of success stories and relevant topic-based speeches. In addition, AUC V-Lab assists with fundraising by providing access to an angel network and support in negotiating deals. Promising start-ups may be offered an additional nine-month 'incubation' period. This primarily involves customised support for the start-up, such as workspace, use of facilities and guidance. Entrepreneurs may be advised on human resources and legal support and participate in three- to nine-month mentorship programmes. Table 3.2 lists a sample of the start-ups that have been incubated since the establishment of the V-Lab.

Table 3.2 Sample profile of AUC venture lab start-ups

D-Kimia is the first biotech spin-off from AUC Labs. Based on knowledge, research and technologies developed at AUC, D-Kimia develops novel and affordable diagnostic solutions to detect a broad range of diseases, initially focusing on the identification of the hepatitis C virus

KarmSolar is dedicated to providing innovative off-grid solar energy solutions that are commercially viable and easy to use in the agricultural, industrial and business sectors. Through developing unique approaches to each project, we develop systems that harness the power of the sun and replace diesel-powered processes, thereby producing energy that is affordable, stable, reliable and environmentally friendly

Mubser develops wearable tech to aid visually impaired people in their everyday lives. Mubser's pilot product, Sensify, coordinates the user's smartphone or Mubser pocket computer to detect obstacles and notify the user through vibrations on a bracelet and a Bluetooth headset

Bus Pooling is a subscription-based bus service that transports commuters between home and work. After receiving a request, Bus Pooling matches individuals living in the same area who share the same work location and hours, and supplies a bus and schedule customised to meet their needs

Kashef Labs is developing a ground-penetrating radar capable of detecting the many landmines left by the Axis forces in WWII on Egypt's borderlands. Using an unmanned aerial surveillance tool that is lightweight and utilises minimal power, the radar flies one meter above desert rock and sand to scan the ground

Jozour is working on producing wooden panels from date palm midribs using innovative and unique machines. We design and manufacture our own machines. We also develop different types of wooden boards to be supplied to furniture manufacturers and interior designers

Creative Bits applications provide snowball technology to help people create electronic applications and provides an E-robot kits to teach children programming, electronics and to make their own toys

Conclusion

Based on interviews with the EIP and V-Lab teams, programme beneficiaries and entrepreneurs, four key lessons learned were identified. Firstly, it is very important to use a partnership model to collaborate with other players in the ecosystem. This ensures that synergies are established with outsiders while strengthening the ecosystem. Secondly, it is critical to build on the assets and strengths of universities in designing the programme and establishing the incubator. For example, there is a need to focus on areas where there is interaction between the incubated start-ups, outside students and faculty. In addition, there is a need to link start-ups with the university facilities, labs and services. Thirdly, it is advisable to use an experimental/gradual approach, for example, starting with a small number of start-ups and focusing on their growth. Finally, the creation of local stakeholders within and outside the university is an important factor for the success of the programme.

Partnerships form a base of supporters and stakeholders who care about the programme and seek its success, which is critical in overcoming many of the challenges and risks associated with operating in emerging markets. The V-Lab has developed a number of KPIs to measure its performance and impact. The main KPI is the number of successful start-ups the V-Lab will create; however, additional indicators include the number of entrepreneurs trained, the number of start-up ventures incubated and supported by the V-Lab services, and the percentage of start-ups that access funding (and the amount of that funding) as a result of being incubated. Mentors' ability to link entrepreneurs with business executives and entrepreneurs, as well as the creation of partnerships between start-ups, business, government and educational institutions, are additional indicators of success. Despite the important role of UBIs in initiating new ventures and in part in sustaining start-ups, entrepreneurs must learn not only how to survive, but also how to sustain and scale up on their own.

ICT is transforming the global economy and creating new networks that cross cultures as well as great distances. The progress made by many African nations has been remarkable, but they are still a long way from reaching a competitive stage with the rest of the world on a more scalable level. The transformation from the formulation of policies and directions to the implementation and institutionalisation of such programmes and projects represents the greatest challenge to strategically deploying ICT in the African continent. Exciting times are coming Africa's way with the changing leadership in the continent. The new leadership is moving the continent forward by helping individuals and organisations achieve their potential by having business take the lead.

One of the most important roles to be played in the information age will be the collaboration among different stakeholders, including the government, the private sector and civil society. This role will be determined by how governance will be exercised in the information-based world. In that respect, while the framework has yet to be defined, information society services will probably be provided by the private sector, with governments providing a supporting regulatory framework based on greater public participation and consensus. Development of the information society in Africa cannot be left to market forces; it deserves and needs the attention of the highest political decision-makers. Thus, nations should prioritise information needs for business and socio-economic development in the same way they do for different sectors such as industry, agriculture and health. Consequently, governments have a responsibility to take a strategic view in facing the coming information-intensive world. These strategies should include creating a shared vision of the new communication era, intensifying the process of information acculturation, developing the required human capacities and accelerating the development of the communications infrastructure. The integration of information, communication and computing developments with other social and economic policy goals is one of the priority issues globally. Table 3.3 demonstrates the path to building a start-up Africa.

African nations will have different priorities in the transformation process and in the use of information for socio-economic and cultural development. These priorities will change over time. However, success in achieving pervasive development lies in the proper design and delivery of applications that would fit the needs and requirements of the sectors targeted. In any case, special attention would have to be directed to human and professional development, especially to the skills and knowledge needed to provide employment in an information society and the incentives needed to provide both the ability and the willingness for

Table 3.3 Start-up Africa matrix

	Sustainability	Social impact	Economic impact	Scalability	Nurturing agents of change
Aiming at					
Driven by	Youth/passion	Information/ communication technology	Untapped opportunities	Creative minds/ innovative solutions	Building a start-up culture
Focused on	Responsible business	Ethics	Education/ vocational training	Leadership/ governance	Building a start-up community
Targeting	Entrepreneurship	SMEs/start-ups	What really counts is 'human capital'	Innovation is key	**Building a start-up Africa**

citizens to participate in an information society. Unless these prerequisites are available and efficiently maintained, the information society will not yield its targeted objectives. Africa should focus on its youth, be driven by innovation and entrepreneurship, and invest in its future leaders—those who will make a difference and transform society. These are most likely to be those capitalising on the power of technology who are at the same time knowledgeable and have access to timely, relevant and accurate data.

References

African Development Bank. (2009). *Egypt private sector country profile.* African Development Bank.

Ahmed, A. (2007). Open access towards bridging the digital divide – Policies and strategies for developing countries. *Journal of Information Technology for Development, 13*(4), 337–361.

Ajayi, S. (2004). What's in it for us? How Africa can make good on globalization? *Convergence, 3*(3), 66–68.

Alampay, E., Soliva, P., Justimbaste, L., & Tenedero, C. (2003, June). *Evaluating the impact of universal access models, strategies and policies in ICTs on poor communities in the Philippines: Final report.* Manila: National College of Public Administration and Governance Forum.

Annan, K. A. (2003). Information and communications technologies: A priority for Africa's development. In J. O. Okpaku (Ed.), *Information and communications technologies for African development: An assessment of progress and the challenges ahead* (pp. xv–xvii). New York: United Nations ICT Taskforce.

Arlove, R. (2016). *Before investing in Africa, investors need to shed two major misconceptions.* Special Report on The entrepreneurs spurring Africa's rise, pp. 6–8.

Branscomb, A. (1994). *Who owns information?* New York: Basic Books.

El Dahshan, M., Tolba, A., & Badreldin, T. (2010). *Enabling entrepreneurship in Egypt: Towards a sustainable dynamic model.* Alexandria: Entrepreneurship Business Forum.

Figueres, J. M. (2003). Preface. In J. O. Okpaku (Ed.), *Information and communications technologies for African development: An assessment of progress and the challenges ahead.* New York: United Nations ICT Taskforce.

Garito, M. (1996). The creation of the Euro-Mediterranean information society. In *Proceedings of the European Union meeting on the creation of the information society,* Rome.

Hattab, H. (2010). *Global entrepreneurship monitor: Egypt entrepreneurship report*. Cairo: The Industrial Modernization Centre.

IBRD. (2012). *Doing business in a more transparent world*. Washington, DC: The International Bank for Reconstruction and Development.

Ismail, A., & Abdallah, R. (2013). *AUC venture lab business model*. Unpublished Report, The American University in Cairo, Cairo.

Ismail, A., & Kamel, S. (2013, March 4–5). EIP@AUC: A case study of a university-centered entrepreneurship ecosystem in Egypt. In *Proceedings of the international conference on innovation and entrepreneurship*, Amman, Jordan.

Ismail, A., & Shabana, S. (2013). *Benchmarking university-based Incubators*. Unpublished Report, The American University in Cairo, Cairo.

Kamel, S. (1995a, May 21–24). Information superhighways, a potential for socioeconomic and cultural development. In *Proceedings of the 6th Information Resource Management Association International Conference (IRMA) on managing information and communications in a changing global environment*, Atlanta, GA, USA.

Kamel, S. (1995b). IT diffusion and socioeconomic change in Egypt. *Journal of Global Information Management, 3*(2), 4–16.

Kamel, S. (1999). Building the African information infrastructure. *Journal of Scientific and Industrial Research*, Special issue on Management of information technology organizations and beyond, New Delhi: National Institute of Science Communication, March–April, pp. 118–144.

Kamel, S. (2005, 15–18 May). Assessing the impacts of establishing an internet cafe in the context of a developing nation. In *Proceedings of the 16th Information Resources Management Association International Conference (IRMA) on managing modern organizations with information technology*, San Diego, CA, pp. 176–181.

Kamel, S. (2009a). Building the African information society. *International Journal of Technology Management, 45*(1–2), 62–81.

Kamel, S. (2009b, January 4–6). The evolution of the ICT sector in Egypt – Partnership4Development. In *Proceedings of the 11th International Business Information Management Association (IBIMA) conference on innovation and knowledge management in twin track economies: Challenges and opportunities*, Cairo, Egypt, pp. 841–851.

Kamel, S. (2011). Managing after the Arab spring. *Global Focus, 5*(3), 56–59.

Kamel, S. (2012, November/December). Entrepreneurial uprising. *BizEd*, pp. 46–47.

Kamel, S. (2013a). Investing in human capital and creating and entrepreneurial culture: The Egyptian experience. *The Journal of Information Technology Management, Cutter IT Journal, 5*(26), 32–35.

Kamel, S. (2013b). Is entrepreneurial education the solution. *AUC Business Review (ABR), 1*(1), 10.

Kamel, S. (2014). Investing in entrepreneurial lifelong learning would lead to more entrepreneurs, more jobs and a better economy. *Entrepreneur* – Egypt Edition, No. 1, pp. 89–91.

Kitagawa, F., & Robertson, S. (2012). High-tech entrepreneurial firms in a university-based business incubator. *Entrepreneurship and Innovation, 13*(4), 227–237.

Knowledge@Wharton. (2016, April). Meet Africa's first tech unicorn – Are more to come?.

Leke, A. (2016). *Why inclusive growth is key to Africa's rise*. Special Report on The entrepreneurs spurring Africa's rise, pp. 20–21.

Manimala, M. J., & Vijay, D. (2012). *Technology business incubators: A perspective for the emerging economies*. Bangalore: Indian Institute of Management.

Mbarika, V. W. A. (2002). Re-thinking information and communications technology policy focus on internet versus teledensity diffusion for Africa's least developed countries. *Electronic Journal of Information Systems in Developing Countries, 9*(1), 1–13.

Mian, S. A., & Oswego, S. (1996). The university business incubator: A strategy for developing new research/technology-based firms. *The Journal of High Technology Management Research, 7*(2), 191–208.

Musa, P. F. (2006). Making a case for modifying the technology acceptance model to account for limited accessibility in developing countries. *Information Technology for Development, 12*(3), 213–224.

Odedra-Straub, M. (1993). Critical factors affecting success of CBIS: Cases from Africa. *Journal of Global Information Management, Summer*, 16–31.

OECD. (2009). *Overcoming barriers to administrative simplification strategies: Guidance for policy makers*. Paris: OECD Publishing.

Okpaku, J. (2003a). Background on information and communications technologies for development in Africa. In J. O. Okpaku (Ed.), *Information and communication technologies for African development – An assessment of progress and challenges ahead* (pp. 23–46). New York: United Nations ICT Task Force Publications.

Okpaku, J. (2003b). Information and communications technologies as a tool for African self-development: Towards a re-definition of development. In J. O. Okpaku (Ed.), *Information and communication technologies for African development – An assessment of progress and challenges ahead* (pp. 1–22). New York: United Nations ICT Task Force Publications.

Petrazzini, B., & Harindranath, G. (1997). Information infrastructure initiatives in emerging economies: The case of India. In B. Kahin & E. Wilson (Eds.), *The national information infrastructure initiatives*. Cambridge: Massachusetts Institute of Technology Press.

Qureshi, S. (2007). Information technology innovations for development. *Information Technology for Development, 13*(4), 311–313.

Rizk, N., & Kamel, S. (2013). ICT and building a knowledge society in Egypt. *International Journal of Knowledge Management, 9*(1), 1–20.

Robertson, S L., & Kitagawa, F. (2011). *University incubators and knowledge mediation strategies: Policy and practice in creating competitive city-regions*. Centre for Learning and Life Chances in Knowledge Economies and Societies, Research Paper 28.

Scaramuzzi, E. (2002). *Incubators in developing countries: Status and development perspectives*. Washington, DC: The World Bank.

Shapiro, C., & Varian, H. (1999). *Information rules*. Boston: Harvard Business School Press.

Sinare, S. (2016). *Thinking big about investments in Africa*. Special Report on The entrepreneurs spurring Africa's rise, pp. 37–38.

Sorensen, M., & Sayegh, F. (2007). The initiation, growth and sustainment of SDI in the Middle East – Notes from the Trenches. *Information Technology for Development, 13*(1), 95–100.

United Nations Economic Commission for Africa-UNECA. (2003, October). Policies and plans on the information society: Status and impact.

World Bank. (2007). *Building knowledge economies: Advanced strategies for development* (pp. 157–166). Washington, DC: World Bank Publications.

4

Prospects and Challenges of Managing Clusters as Entrepreneurship Development Interventions for Sustainable Development in Nigeria: A Discourse Analysis

Lukman Raimi, Morufu Oladimeji Shokunbi, and Stephen Bolaji Peluola

Introduction

Clusters have played a significant role in the technological progress, new innovations and economic prosperity in industrial districts such as Silicon Valley, California and Route 128, Boston, Massachusetts in the USA, Bangalore in India and Hsinchu Science Park in Taiwan (Cai et al. 2007). Learning from the industrial experiences of the world, Nigeria vigorously pursued the establishment of clusters as an industrial development strategy, but these clusters were later abandoned by the military government, to be reactivated again by successive governments in Nigeria. Policy reversal is a common feature not only in Nigeria but in the whole of Africa as a result of a defective political philosophy in this part of the globe Mazrui (1986:16) laments:

L. Raimi (✉) • M.O. Shokunbi • S.B. Peluola
Yaba College of Technology, Yaba, Lagos, Nigeria

© The Author(s) 2017
A. Ahmed (ed.), *Managing Knowledge and Innovation for Business Sustainability in Africa*, DOI 10.1007/978-3-319-41090-6_4

... in a technologically underdeveloped society in the twentieth century, ultimate power resides not in those who controlled the means of production (entrepreneurs and capitalists contrary to the mindsets of many), but in those who controlled the means of destruction (political class with powers, ammunitions and who have final say on matters of the states).

Refocusing on clusters as entrepreneurship development intervention (EDI) after years of neglect fits perfectly into Nigeria's extant agenda; this agenda seeks to revamp Nigeria's industrial development strategy with a view to making it one of the top economies by the year 2020. One of the industrial strategies that has fast-tracked the technological progress of America, Europe and emerging economies like Brazil, Russia, India and China is official development and promotion of industrial clusters by both the public and private sectors. At the Annual Continental Conference of the Pan African Competitiveness Forum in Abuja, Nigeria in 2013, the Ministry of Science and Technology (MS&T) stated that the Federal Government had approved the establishment of 9,555 industrial clusters in the country based on comparative advantage and natural resource endowment in the identified districts. The management of the 9,555 will be in collaboration with the various state and local governments, as well as the involvement of non-governmental organisations (NGOs), local development partners, financial institutions and multinational companies (Amaefule 2012).

The eagerness to promote clusters for strong industrial development has attracted the attention of academics, leading practitioners and international organisations because of the inherent opportunities of clusters (Kuah 2002; Iwuagwu 2011). The economic benefits of clusters include reduced operational costs; emergence of new businesses/spin-offs; emergence of new innovations; cheaper technologies; increased specialisation/ division of labour and collaboration among companies in the clusters; leveraging of social infrastructure; and consistent knowledge sharing for greater competitiveness (Porter 1998; Ellison and Glaeser 1999). These benefits will be further elaborated in the subsequent discussion.

Apart from the introduction above, the chapter is organised in five parts. The first part focuses on the conceptualisation of clusters. The second part discusses the rationale for clusters. The third part examines the rationale for clusters development. The fourth part examines the plausibility of developing clusters in the packaged food industry vis-à-vis the opportunities and challenges. The last part concludes with recommendations and policy prescriptions on sustainable clusters in Nigeria.

Conceptual Issues

The term 'cluster' emerged from the works of Alfred Marshall and Michael Porter. According to Kuah (2002), Alfred Marshall articulated the cluster theory in 1890 as a concentration of specialised industries operating in districts or localities for mutually beneficial economic interests, or agglomeration economies. Michael Porter popularised the clusters concept in both in theory and practice. Porter (1990, 1998) prescribed clusters as a desirable and worthwhile industrial strategy based on competitive advantages or agglomeration economies. These competitive advantages will be discussed in the relevant part of this chapter.

Furthermore, the Department of Trade and Industry (1998:22) defined clusters as the 'concentration of competing, collaborating and interdependent companies and institutions which are connected by a system of market and non-market links'. From another perspective, clusters are defined as geographic concentrations of interconnected businesses, specialised suppliers, service providers, firms in related industries and other organisations that peacefully cooperate and compete with one another in particular industries (Martin and Sunley 2003; Porter 1998). Similarly, Boja (2011) defined clusters as geographical areas with competitive advantage where companies simultaneously compete and collaborate to gain economic advantages which are not available in other regions.

Summing up the various definitions above, the term cluster could be operationalised as the geographical concentration of interrelated small and large companies in the same value chain, which together collaborate to promote technological development, wealth creation, regional competitiveness and export of goods and services for long-term relationships.

In all clusters across the globe, the outputs of some companies are the inputs of others, like a circular food chain. The large and multinational companies operating in industrial clusters get their raw material, components and value-added services cheaper and more quickly from the smaller companies in what could be described a symbiotic relationship.

Some classic examples of model clusters include the wine clusters in California (USA), the textiles industry in northern Italy, shipbuilding clusters in Glasgow (Scotland, UK), steel clusters in Pittsburgh (Pennsylvania, USA) and car manufacturing clusters in Detroit (Michigan, USA) (Kuah 2002; Mueller et al. 2006). In Nigeria, there are a number of clusters in industrial cities such as Nnewi, Aba, Enugu and Owerri. The Nnewi Automotive Parts Industrial Cluster in particular is known for exports of fabricated automotive parts to West African countries, while in Latin America, the Brazilian Shoe Cluster of Sinos Valley is the world's leading leather shoes cluster, where leather shoes are produced and exported to other parts of the world (Amobi 2006).

Beyond the above discourse, the meaning of clusters extends to knowledge-based institutions and financial institutions that cluster together in a particular location, providing training, research and consulting services in various disciplines to society.

Rationale for Clusters Development

The cluster is a model of industrialisation which has economic justification both in theory and in practice. Theorists and practitioners argue that when several companies in related fields or industries cluster together, their costs of production decline; they enjoy access to multiple suppliers of raw materials at reduced costs; and they enjoy increased specialisation and division of labour (Amobi 2006; Ellison and Glaeser 1999; Kuah 2002; Porter 1998). Furthermore, Glaeser (2010:1) restates that:

> *Agglomeration economies are the benefits that come when firms and people locate near one another together in cities and industrial clusters. These benefits all ultimately come from transport costs savings: the only real difference between a nearby firm and one across the continent is that it is easier to connect with a neighbour.*

Several years back, Michael Porter justified the importance of clusters in his treatise *The Competitive Advantage of Nations*. He argued that clusters serving different industries have the potential to stimulate competitiveness in three ways: firstly, they increase the productivity of companies operating in the clusters; secondly, clusters propel products and services innovation; and thirdly, clusters stimulate the emergence of new businesses or spin-offs within the industrial clusters (Porter 1990, 1998; Amobi 2006).

On the strength of the reviewed literature, there are seven justifications for the development of clusters in clear terms. The first is that clusters as industrial strategies reduce transaction costs and lower risk premiums on the capital of companies (i.e., cost of production is lower in clusters than elsewhere). Secondly, clusters foster productivity and specialisation among collaborating small and large companies operating in a particular industry. Thirdly, clusters afford companies opportunities to exploit their specialties, thereby fostering innovation, the emergence of new businesses or spin-offs, and technological improvements of process and products. Furthermore, companies that operate in well-established clusters are in a position to work out joint solutions to common operational challenges. The fifth justification is that clusters give companies the opportunity to build a labour pool, technology, infrastructure and knowledge sharing, and team competitiveness. The sixth justification rests on the argument that clusters located in areas where there is greater factor endowment provide opportunities for utilisation of abundant natural resources, access to markets and fostering increased upstream and downstream employment for the growing number of unemployed people. Finally, clusters offer lower barriers to entry and exit for companies (Porter 1990, 1998; Boja 2011; Kuah 2002; Amaefule 2012).

Having understood the rationale and justification for clusters development in both developed and developing countries, it is important to identify the types of clusters that exist across the globe.

Cluster Typologies Across the Globe

There are different cluster typologies across the globe, namely: (a) Sectoral clusters, (b) High-tech clusters, (c) Historic know-how-based clusters, (d) Factor endowment clusters, (e) Horizontal clusters, (f) Vertical clusters, (g) Low-cost manufacturing clusters and (h) Knowledge services clusters.

(a) **Sectoral clusters:** These are clusters formed on the basis of the sectors of the economy where the companies operate. For instance, media clusters accommodate newspaper houses, TV stations, the film industry and so on, while commercial clusters house supermarket chains, bookshops and so forth.

(b) **High-tech clusters:** The high-technology-oriented clusters are found in most developed countries where products like ships, aircraft, arms and armaments, cars and so on are produced. Such clusters are often supported by research institutions and specialised universities. Some examples of high-tech clusters are Silicon Valley, the East London Tech City, Paris-Saclay and several other locations in Germany and France.

(c) **Historic know-how-based clusters**: These are clusters where expertise, mastery of certain skills and historical advantage in the production of certain products and services have been centred for centuries. Notable examples are the London financial clusters, leather clusters in northern Nigeria, shoe and spare-part fabrication clusters in Aba and so on.

(d) **Factor endowment clusters:** These are specialised clusters created to gain competitive advantage as a result of their presence in certain geographical districts. For example, Burgundy and Champagne clusters in France have for years enjoyed comparative advantages in wine production over other places because they are located in mountainous districts, where quality grapes are found and grown.

(e) **Horizontal clusters:** These are clusters that accommodate many companies in the same industry, producing the same or similar products and competing for the same market, but deliberately cooperating and acting like a jointly owned business. Examples are many companies producing different brands of shoes in the shoe clusters, compute clusters and wrist watches clusters.

(f) **Vertical clusters:** These are clusters which accommodate many companies producing different but related products/services that could be integrated. In these clusters, the products of some companies are the inputs of others within the industry's value chain. An example is car clusters, where companies produce related products like car tyres, auto engines, upholstery products, iron doors and so on which are assembled as a complete car.

(g) **Low-cost manufacturing clusters:** These are clusters that emerged in certain regions of the world because of access to cheap labour, land/rent, low-cost consulting services and affordable energy/overhead costs. These types of clusters are often found in developing countries such as in rural China, Mexico, Argentina, Africa, Eastern Europe and Latin America, where factor inputs are extremely cheap.

(h) **Knowledge services clusters:** These clusters are established because of collaborative linkages with institutions that provide low-cost engineers, unhindered access to the low-cost services of other experts/professionals and low-cost consultancy fees from knowledge-based institutions.

Developing Clusters in the Packaged Food Industry: The Opportunities

The thrust of Nigeria's extant industrial policy is to accelerate economic growth and sustainable development through active involvement in agriculture, semi-processing, full-fledged manufacturing, construction and services, thereby making Nigeria one of the Top 20 economies with 'a minimum GDP of $900 billion and a per capita income of no less than $4000 per annum' (Vision 2020 Blueprint 2009:9). To achieve the industrial target above, the clusters offer a realistic and workable model for actualising Nigeria's industrial policy. Clusters have the capacity to boost the total factor productivity of collaborating companies through knowledge sharing, risk pooling, cost sharing and skill-intensive production. In the developed countries and emerging economies where clusters have formed the foundation of their industrial development strategy, forward and backward clusters that span different industries are encouraged (Amobi 2006). Nigeria, like the rest of Africa, suffers from food insecurity. Therefore, an attempt to establish clusters for the food industry will create a number of opportunities. These include:

(a) Development of food industry clusters would strengthen Nigeria's food industry by making it strong enough to produce made-in-Nigeria semi-finished products and finished products such as fruit juices, dairy products, cornflakes, milk, packaged eggs and beverages, thereby enhancing the industry's competitiveness. Other associated opportunities include reduction of imports, conservation of wasted foreign exchange, import substitution, avoidance of dumping and control over the quality of food consumed by the public.

(b) Establishment of food industry clusters is a proactive strategy for harnessing the potentials of the Nigerian food industry. The food clusters, when established, would afford interaction and collaboration among farmers, food processing and packaging companies, marketing agents and distributors/retailers to pursue mutually beneficial interests.

(c) Food industry clusters could serve as an effective mechanism for attaining food sustainability, that is, attainment of cheap, quality and regular processed food for Nigerians in the face of hunger, endemic poverty and extreme deprivation. Other inherent opportunities in food clusters include the prospect of stimulating more employment, wealth creation, growth of local technology, poverty reduction and sustainable economic development.

(d) When food industry clusters are established, Nigerians as entrepreneurs will be well positioned to take advantage of investment incentives offered by the National Investment Promotion Council (NIPC) with a view to acquiring the required machines and equipment for processing the nation's abundant food resource endowments into intermediate raw materials or finished goods for local consumption and export to earn foreign exchange. Annually, the nation's rich vegetables, fruits, cereals, tubers and grains are wasted because of poor processing and preservation methods.

Forward Integration Cluster in the Agriculture and Food Value Chain

The forward integration cluster in the food industry entails transformation of raw materials from the farms or agro-allied companies into semi-finished and finished foods ready for the supermarkets and open markets for onward dispatch to the final consumers. A typical forward integration cluster in the agriculture and food value chain is depicted in Fig. 4.1 below.

In Fig. 4.1 above, the products of companies in the agriculture and food industry clusters such as seeds, fertilisers, crop protection chemicals, food ingredients, agricultural services and so on are utilised by the farmers at the second stage in the value chain for producing agricultural crops, meat and dairy products. At the third stage, the outputs of the farmers are sold to traders, who process them into semi-finished products (like crops, meat and biofuels) which are supplied to the food company for further processing. At the fourth stage, the food companies process the semi-finished supplies into finished products such as packaged meat, dairy products, snacks and beverages, which are sold to retailers in the various supermarkets, hypermarkets and corner shops. At the fifth stage, the retailers sell the finished products in smaller units to the final consumers in the neighbourhood.

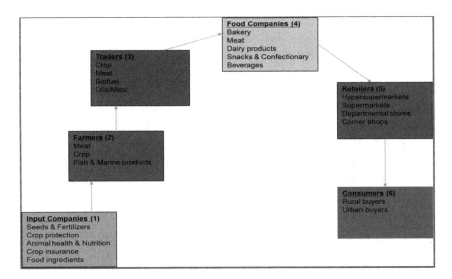

Fig. 4.1 Agriculture and food value chain (*Source*: Adapted from: Food Value Chain KPMG (2013))

Challenges of Food Industry Clusters

In spite of the limitless opportunities in cluster development, there are obvi-
ous challenges which must be addressed when they surface or avoided out-
right. The first challenge that the proposed food industry clusters are likely to
encounter is the inability to gain international competitiveness. Existing clusters in Nigeria have not gone beyond producing goods for local markets. This
challenge of poor competitiveness is traceable to weak institutional backing
and policy inconsistency. Nigerian Institute of Food Science and Technology
(NIFST) should therefore take cognisance of this fact in its resolve to pursue
clusters development in the food industry. Secondly, establishing clusters in
the food industry poses a big challenge as such projects require cheap and
reliable infrastructural backbones and an enabling business environment to
reap economies of large-scale production. Unfortunately, Nigeria has unreliable power/electricity supplies, bad roads and highways increase the cost of
transportation, the water supply is often irregular, and multiple tax systems
discourage investment in the industrial sector. Poor infrastructure and an
unfriendly business environment could mar the beautiful proposal of food
industry clusters. The third challenge is situated within the confines of the
weak regulatory environment. In Nigeria the civil and commercial laws are
weak, and enterprises cannot thrive in an economy where the civil and commercial laws are weak, inconsistent and anti-business. Without a sound regulatory environment, the clusters, instead of pursuing collaboration, may be
engrossed in cut-throat competition through price wars and cost-cutting as
well as disregarding environmental and labour standards to gain a competitive edge over other companies. Another critical challenge that food industry
clusters may face is outdated and environmentally hazardous technologies. It
is a fact that shortages in infrastructure and basic services would inhibit and
limit clusters' ability to produce the quality products and services required
to take advantage of emerging market opportunities locally and internationally. Finally, the challenge of finance must not be underestimated, because
Nigerian commercial banks are reluctant to give loans to small businesses
and new spin-offs without the required collateral securities, whereas the
model clusters across the globe thrive because of unhindered access to financial resources from banks and other financial institutions in the form of loans
and joint venture partnerships.

Recommendations and Policy Prescriptions

From the foregoing discourse, it is clear that clusters are important intervention projects required to accelerate industrial development in Nigeria. The following policy prescriptions are critical for leveraging clusters as mechanisms for industrial and technological development in Nigeria.

Firstly, there is an urgent need to increase awareness of clusters development through workshops, stakeholders' meetings, retreats and public lectures on the meaning and essence of clusters and procedures/modalities for establishing and managing clusters in the food industry.

Related to the first recommendation above, there is a need for the Ministry of Science and Technology and NIFST to establish food clusters in Nigeria through a private–public partnership (PPP), because most government-led programmes for industrial development have been ineffective in actualising their set objectives.

Thirdly, it is suggested that clusters development, especially the government-led model, should provide organised, high-quality entrepreneurship training and capacity-building workshops for small and medium enterprises (SMEs) operating in the various sectors of the food industry and other industries, through provision of appropriate technologies and infrastructural facilities to designated skills acquisition centres (SACs) in the industrial cluster for the purpose of promoting greater cluster competitiveness.

For long-term sustainability and competitiveness, it is recommended that there should be periodic partnership dialogue among all cluster companies and participants for ideas/knowledge sharing, risk pooling, strategic networking and government engagement for mutually beneficial policies/programmes in the clusters.

It is one thing to establish food clusters; it is another thing to have effective coordination in the industry concerned. It is therefore suggested that effective coordination is needed in the food industry in order to achieve the set objectives discussed above. Particular attention should be paid to business communication, leadership and conflict management, which are all critical issues for building sustainable cluster synergy.

Lastly, before venturing into food industry clusters development, there is a need for macroeconomic and political stability in terms of stable and sound policies on clusters, an effective and transparent regulatory framework and institutions under the Ministry of Science and Technology, improved infrastructure, sustainable rules and incentives for competition, friendly tax policies, a fair legal system, and security for lives and property in the industrial clusters.

References

Amaefule, E. (2012). FG approves 9,555 industrial clusters. *The Punch Newspaper*, November 11 Edition. Available: http://www.punchng.com/business/fg-approves-9555-industrial-clusters/ (Acceesed 4 Aug 2015).

Amobi, I. C. (2006). *Unleashing of industrial clusters for growth and prosperity in South East Nigeria*. Lead presentation at the Enugu Forum Seminar October, 2006.

Boja, C. (2011). Clusters models, factors and characteristics. *International Journal of Economic Practices and Theories, 1*(1), 1–43.

Cai, H., Todo, K., Zhou, L. A. (2007) Do multinationals' R&D activities stimulate indigenous entrepreneurship? Evidence from China's "Silicon Valley". NBER Working Paper No. 13618.

Department of Trade and Industry. (1998). *Our competitive future: Building the knowledge driven economy*. Cm4176. London: HMSO.

Ellison, G., & Glaeser, E. L. (1999). The geographic concentration of industry: Does natural advantage explain agglomeration? *American Economic Review, 89*, 311–316.

Glaeser, E. L. (Ed.). (2010). Agglomeration economics. Chicago: University of Chicago Press.

Iwuagwu, O. (2011). The cluster concept: Will Nigeria's new industrial development strategy jumpstart the country's industrial takeoff? *Afro Asian Journal of Social Sciences, 2*(2.4) Quarter IV, ISSN 2229-5313.

KPMG. (2013, November 8). *Food value chain KPMG*. Available: http://talkaboutfoodjb.com/?attachment_id=358 (Accessed 31 July 2015).

Kuah, A. T. (2002). Cluster theory and practice: Advantages for the small business locating in a vibrant cluster. *Journal of Research in Marketing and Entrepreneurship, 4*(3), 206–228.

Martin, R., & Sunley, P. (2003). Deconstructing clusters: Chaotic concept or policy panacea? *Journal of Economic Geography, 3*(1), 5–35.

Mazrui, A. A. (1986). *The Africans: A triple heritage*. London: BBC Publications.

Mueller, R. A., Sumner, D. A., & Lapsley, J. (2006). Clusters of grapes and wine. In *Third international Wine Business Research conference, Montpellier, France*.

Nigeria Vision 2020. (2009). *Economic transformation blueprint*. Nigeria: Federal Republic of Nigeria.

Porter, M. E. (1990). *The competitive advantage of nations*. New York: The Free Press.

Porter, M. E. (1998). Clusters and the new economics of competition. *Harvard Business Review, 76*(6), 77.

5

Understanding How Failing a Job Interview May Be a Source of Innovation: The Case of WhatsApp Founders

Alain Ndedi and Kelly Mua Kingsley

Introduction

Over the past five years, many Internet and smartphone users have become familiar with the name WhatsApp without imagining that a couple of years earlier, the founders of this famous brand failed a job interview at Facebook. Because often after a failure people lose direction, and are not able to bring forward something new or bright, this chapter guides the reader to the opposite direction by bringing out innovation, and of course creativity, as tools for achieving success. However, innovation requires focus. Clearly some people are more talented innovators than others, but their talents lie in well-defined areas. Innovation requires knowledge, ingenuity and, above all, focus from the person wishing to benefit from it.

A. Ndedi (✉)
Saint Monica University, Comerci, Douala, Cameroon

K.M. Kingsley
Harvard Kennedy School of Government, Cambridge, MA, USA

© The Author(s) 2017
A. Ahmed (ed.), *Managing Knowledge and Innovation for Business Sustainability in Africa*, DOI 10.1007/978-3-319-41090-6_5

In innovation, as in any other endeavour, there is talent, there is ingenuity and there is knowledge. But when all is said and done, what innovation requires is hard, focused, purposeful work. Did the founders of WhatsApp go through these steps? If diligence, persistence and commitment are lacking, talent, ingenuity and knowledge are of no avail.

Because innovation is conceptual and perceptual, would-be innovators must also go out and look, ask and listen. The WhatsApp founders' failure gave them the opportunity to go out, listen to what was being done in their various fields and come up with the idea of WhatsApp. Successful innovators use both the right and left sides of their brains. They work out analytically what the innovation has to be to satisfy an opportunity.

This chapter explains that what is remarkable about WhatsApp's rise to success is the story of founders Jan Koum and Brian Acton. They were no strangers to failure, yet their incredible journey speaks volumes about the value of tenacity and vision. Today, Jan and Brian's app (WhatsApp) is the most valuable messaging platform on the planet, but they experienced their fair share of rejection by top tech companies, including the one that eventually bought their service, Facebook. The chapter explains the various steps one needs to follow after a failure to learn from this misfortune and move forward with one's life. The chapter discusses the WhatsApp founders' history, as well as the link between creativity, frustration and innovation that is at the origin of most incremental and breakthrough inventions.

Summary of WhatsApp History

The company WhatsApp Inc. was founded in 2009 by two Americans engineers, Brian Acton and Jan Koum, both former employees of Yahoo!. After Koum and Acton left Yahoo! in September 2007, the duo travelled to South America as a break from work (WhatsApp website, 2014). According to Forbes (2015), in June 2009, Apple launched push notifications, letting developers ping users when they were not using an app. Koum updated WhatsApp so that each time the user changed their status, it would ping everyone in the user's network. WhatsApp 2.0 was released with a messaging component and the number of active users suddenly swelled to 250,000. Koum visited Acton, who was still unemployed while managing another unsuccessful start-up, and Acton decided to join the company. WhatsApp was switched from a free to a paid service to avoid growing too fast, mainly because the primary cost was sending verification texts to users. In December 2009, WhatsApp for the iPhone was updated to send photos. By early 2011, WhatsApp was in the top 20 of all apps in Apple's US App Store. Koum then hired an old friend who lived in Los Angeles, Chris Peiffer, to make the BlackBerry version, which arrived two months later (Forbes 2014).

Initial Capital to Launch the Company

Following his departure from Yahoo!, Koum relied on his US$400,000 in savings. By February 2013, WhatsApp had a staff of 50 people. Sequoia Capital invested US$50 million in the company, valuing WhatsApp at US$1.5 billion. In April 2011, the founders (Jan Koum and Brian Acton) agreed to take another US$7million from Sequoia Capital on top of their US$250,000 seed funding, after months of negotiation with Sequoia. Later, Acton persuaded five ex-Yahoo! friends to invest US$250,000 in seed funding, and as a result was granted co-founder status and a stake, who officially joined the company on November 1, 2011 (Forbes 2014).

Failure Leads to Innovation

Before explaining the process of innovation leading to something novel, it is important to develop the link between creativity and innovation—creativity leading to innovation.

Failure in the Creative Process

Webster (1976:54) defines creativity as the ability to bring something new into existence.

There are many aspects of creativity, but one definition would include the ability to take existing objects and combine them in different ways for new purposes. Thus, a simple definition of creativity is the action of combining previously uncombined elements. Another way of looking at creativity is as playing with the way things are interrelated. Creativity is the ability to generate novel and useful ideas and solutions to everyday problems and challenges (Webster 1976). Thus, while entrepreneurship is about making things happen and deals with the practical challenges of implementation, creativity is the capacity to develop new ideas, concepts and processes (Miller 1999).

According to Amabile (1998), in management, creativity occurs at the strategic level in developing alternative approaches to business processes, such as strategy formulation and organisational change, and at the operational level in the development of new products and technological innovation. In short, it is the desire to think outside the box and challenge conventional wisdom and ways of doing things within or outside established organisations.

Amabile (1998:77) suggests that there are three components of successful creativity in organisations: expertise, motivation and creative thinking skills.

Expertise encompasses what a person knows and can do. It defines the intellectual space that he/she uses to explore and solve problems. Motivation can be extrinsic (desire to achieve company rewards and awards) or intrinsic, with the latter being the most critical. Intrinsic motivation refers primarily to passion and interest, or the person's internal desire to do something. The person is driven by the challenge and joy of accomplishment. According to Ndedi (2012), creative thinking skills refer to the particular way individuals approach problems and solutions and the techniques they use for looking at a problem differently, seeking insights from other fields of endeavour, challenging, assumptions and so forth. Creativity involves a paradox, a dilemma or an unknown or unprepared for situation.

De Bono (1990) introduces and describes lateral thinking as a contrast with vertical logical thinking. In the process of lateral solving, it is unnecessary to be right at every step, and the process permits a delay in judgement to allow the interaction of ideas to occur.

The Creative Process

As has been explained in the previous paragraphs, to benefit from failure, it is important to positively use the frustration that occurs after a misfortune. Figure 5.1 has a step called 'frustration' during which the entrepreneur can either survive or be broken. If the latter occurs, the person has lost control of his/her life and is unable to imagine another future or another word other than failure. Definitively, Jan Koum and Brian Anton experienced frustration, but the way they managed their frustration enabled them to move forward with their lives.

According to Kuratko and Hodgetts (2004), the creative process has four steps:

Preparation

Frustration

Incubation

Illumination

Elaboration

Fig. 5.1 The creativity steps according to Morris and Kuratko (*Source*: Adapted from Morris and Kuratko (2002:107))

The accumulation of background and knowledge is the first step in the development of creativity. During this phase, the potential entrepreneur gathers the information that will be useful to him/her in the future. The experience accumulated by the founders of WhatsApp at Yahoo! gave them the expertise necessary to think outside the box when confronted with an issue or problem. This is what happened to them following their failure to join Facebook and other failures encountered during that period.

The next step in the creative process is the frustration. After failure, a person is frustrated with what has happened. The incubation process is therefore necessary to move forward. The incumbent must take some time off and try to view the world differently. During this stage, a potential entrepreneur or innovator must create his/her own world in order to explore and gauge alternatives not only for his/her own life, but also for problems in the surrounding environment.

The illumination step is the most important level in the creative process. In this phase, a potential entrepreneur has numerous ideas that need to be evaluated and implemented. The last step, the evaluation and implementation, requires a great deal of courage, self-discipline and perseverance.

In sum, creativity involves a process of being sensitive to problems, deficiencies, missing elements and disharmonies; identifying the difficulties; and searching for solutions, making guesses or formulating hypotheses about the deficiencies. In January 2009, without doubt, Jan Koum of WhatsApp went through this, identifying difficulties when he purchased an iPhone and realised that the App Store was about to spawn a whole new industry of apps.

Innovation

According to Drucker (1984, 1985, 1994), the most innovative business ideas come from methodically analysing seven areas of opportunity. Some of them lie within particular companies or industries, and some in broader social and demographic trends. Innovation is the specific function of entrepreneurship, whether in an existing business (intrapreneurship), a public service institution (public entrepreneurship) or a new venture started by a lone individual in the family kitchen. It is the means by which the entrepreneur either creates new wealth-producing resources or endows existing resources with enhanced potential for creating wealth. After taking a year off to travel in South America, both Brian and Jan applied to Facebook, and were promptly rejected. It was during that fateful year that Jan was inspired to create WhatsApp, a simple platform-agnostic messaging app that would allow any Smartphone user to text without incurring SMS fees. Brian, who was an early employee at Yahoo!, had also invested and lost millions in the dot-com boom of the early 2000s, but rebounded by joining Jan in building a start-up from scratch with a unique business philosophy.

There are innovations that spring from a flash of genius. Most innovations, however, especially the successful ones, result from a conscious, purposeful search for innovation opportunities, which are only found in a few situations. Four such areas of opportunity exist within an existing industry: unexpected occurrences (for example, failure), incongruities, process needs, and industry and market changes. Three additional sources of opportunity exist outside a company in its social and intellectual environment: demographic changes, changes in perception and new knowledge. It is true that these sources overlap, different as they may be in the nature of their risk, difficulty and complexity, and the potential for innovation may well lie in more than one area at a time. But together they account for the great majority of all innovation opportunities.

This chapter focuses on the unexpected failure that may be an equally important source of innovation opportunities. Unexpected successes and failures are such productive sources of innovation opportunities because most businesses dismiss them, disregard them and even resent them. In recent years, Jan Koum and Brian Acton, two former Yahoo! employees, failed a job interview at Facebook, but did not close their minds to new ideas (Rowan 2014).

According to Olson (2015), in January 2009, after Koum purchased an iPhone and realised that the App Store was about to spawn a whole new industry of apps, he started visiting his friend, where the three would discuss how having statuses next to individual names of the people, but this was not possible without an iPhone developer. However, early versions Of WhatsApp kept crashing or getting stuck and at a particular point, Koum felt like giving up and looking for a new job, upon which Acton encouraged him to wait a few more months. (Olson, 2015)

To be effective, an innovation has to be simple, and it has to be focused. It should do only one thing. The founders' insistence was on focus: All software bloats to the point when it sends and receives email. The difficult part for them was adding features without making the product more complicated. They didn't want to build a hook-up app with which one could find someone weird to talk to. The app was about intimate relationships. New features are added only after intense discussion and experimentation, and a conviction that execution will simplify rather than bloat the service.

Summary

People may lose direction after they experience failure, but innovation requires focus. Clearly some people are more talented innovators than others, but their talents lie in well-defined areas. Innovation requires knowledge, ingenuity and, above all else, focus from the person wishing to benefit from it. In innovation, as in any other endeavour, there is talent, there is ingenuity and there is knowledge. But when all is said and done, what innovation requires is hard, focused, purposeful work. Because innovation is conceptual and perceptual, would-be innovators must also go out and look, ask and listen. Successful innovators use both the right and left sides of their brains. They work out analytically what the innovation has to be to satisfy an opportunity. Then they go out and look at potential users to study their expectations, their values, their failures, their successes and their needs. As has been explained in this chapter, what remains remarkable about the app's rise to success is the story of its founders. Jan Koum and Brian Acton were no strangers to failure, and their incredible journey speaks volumes about the value of tenacity and vision in life. (Satariano, 2014). Today, as noted by Nguyen (2014), Jan and Brian's app is the most valuable messaging platform on the planet, but they have experienced their fair share of rejection by top tech companies, including the one that eventually bought their service, Facebook.

References

Amabile, T. (1998). How to kill creativity. *Harvard Business Review, 76*(September–October), 77–87.

De Bono, E. (1990). Lateral Thinking for Management: A Handbook. Penguin UK (July 1990).

Drucker, P. F. (1984, January/February). Our entrepreneurial economy. *Harvard Business Review*, pp. 59–64.

Drucker, P. F. (1985). *Innovative and entrepreneurship practice and principles.* New York: Harper & Row, Publishers..

Drucker, P. F. (1994). *Innovation and entrepreneurship.* Oxford: British Library Cataloguing.

Forbes. (2014). *Looking inside the Facebook–WhatsApp megadeal: The courtship, the secret meetings, The $19 billion poker game.* Retrieved from http://genius. com/Jim-goetz-jim-goetz-and-jan-koum-at-startup-school-4sv-2014-annotated, (January 10th, 2015).

Forbes, (2015). Inside The Facebook-WhatsApp Megadeal: The Courtship, The Secret Meetings, The $19 Billion Poker Game. Available at http://www. forbes.com/sites/parmyolson/2014/03/04/inside-the-facebook-whatsapp-megadeal-the-courtship-the-secret-meetings-the-19-billion-poker-game/#791ab4542f20. Accessed on the 22nd January 2016.

Kuratko, D. F., & Hodgetts, R. M. (2004). *Entrepreneurship: Theory, process & practice.* Mason: South-Western Publishers.

Miller, C. W. (1999), Flash of brilliance. Reading, Massachusetts, Perseus Books.

Morris, M. H., and Kuratko, D. F. (2002). Corporate entrepreneurship: Entrepreneurial development within organizations, Orlando, FL: Harcourt College Publishers.

Ndedi, A. A. (2012), Principles on Corporate Entrepreneurship and Strategy. LAP

Nguyen, N. (2014). *The founders of WhatsApp prove perseverance wins.* Available at: http://www.popsugar.com/tech/WhatsApp-Founders-Jan-Koum-Brian-Acton-34113022 (Accessed on the 25th December 2015)

Olson, P. (2015). *The rags-to-riches tale of how Jan Koum built WhatsApp into Facebook's new $19 billion baby.* Retrieved from http://www.forbes.com/sites/parmyolson/2014/02/19/exclusive-inside-story-how-jan-koum-built-whatsapp-into-facebooks-new-19-billion-baby/#2715e4857a0b13af3bc94ffb

Rowan, D. (2014). *WhatsApp: The inside story.* Retrieved from http://www. wired.co.uk/news/archive/2014-02/19/whatsapp-exclusive

Satariano, A. (2014). *WhatsApp's founder goes from food stamps to billionaire.* Retrieved from http://www.popsugar.com/tech/WhatsApp-Founders-Jan-Koum-Brian-Acton-34113022 (Accessed 10 Jan 2016).

Webster, F. A. (1976). A model for new venture initiation: A discourse on rapacity and the independent entrepreneur. *The Academy of Management Review, 1*(1), 26–37.

Part III

Education

6

Impact of Education Quality on Sustainable Development in Africa

Adil A. Dafa'Alla, Elmouiz S. Hussein, and Marwan A.A. Adam

Introduction

Africa is a continent in crisis. Despite being rich in natural resources, it is blighted by widespread poverty, corruption, bad governance and a very low standard of living in many countries. The contribution of Africa to global research and the global economy is very low, as is evident in all statistics coming from reputable international organisations such as the United Nations Development Programme (UNDP), the United Nations Economic Commission for Africa and the World Economic Forum. In Dafa'Alla et al. (2015, 2016), we presented the meaning, goals and objectives of education as a human right and argued that, realistically, the existing or prevailing social, political and economic conditions of life

A.A. Dafa'Alla (✉) • E.S. Hussein
AIRBUS, Bristol, UK

M.A.A. Adam
Sudanese Knowledge Society, Khartoum, Sudan

© The Author(s) 2017
A. Ahmed (ed.), *Managing Knowledge and Innovation for Business Sustainability in Africa*, DOI 10.1007/978-3-319-41090-6_6

are taken into consideration and largely determine the aims of pragmatic education. This is particularly true for developing countries, which need to optimise their resources in order to serve their national development plans and goals as best as they can. Our aim in this chapter is to investigate the role of education in achieving sustainable development, and whether it can reasonably be expected to improve the state of underdevelopment from which Africa suffers.

Sudan is considered as representative of many African countries that have emerged from the colonial phase and are still trying to find their footing in the modern world, with varying degrees of success. Like many African countries, Sudan also inherited a British colonial education system that was designed to prepare the Sudanese only for taking up certain subordinate positions in government offices (Mohamed 2005). It was not intended to develop among the people capacities to take leadership and initiative in different walks of life. Hence, the aims and objectives of the education system were adjusted after independence to put more emphasis on promoting education to serve the development needs of the country economically, technologically, culturally as well as socially. Accordingly, in this chapter we will review the performance of the education system in post-independence Sudan in order to understand and relate major reforms that took place during this period and assess their impact on the economic performance of the country. We will then generalise and apply lessons learned from the Sudanese experience to the problem of underdevelopment in the whole continent of Africa.

Literature Review

It is not the intention of this section to cover the literature on education in general. Rather, it will review three important themes central to the objectives of the chapter, namely the evolution of the concept of education as a human right, the importance of the link between education aims and objectives and the national development plan (NDP), and modelling education as a 'system' using an engineering methodology approach, as found in the literature.

The United Nations Educational, Scientific and Cultural Organization (UNESCO) made an effort to harmonise national education systems with international education strategies and visions. These strategies evolved from workforce and socio-economic development drivers to more humanistic ones. In 1972, UNESCO formulated the vision of 'Learning to be', a concept of lifelong education that meets the challenges of a rapidly changing world (Faure et al. 1972). This vision was seen as necessary because of its advantages of flexibility, diversity and availability at different times and places. It also went beyond the traditional distinction between initial schooling and continuing education to suggest lifelong education as the master concept for educational policies. Additionally, UNESCO's report (Faure et al. 1972) aimed towards developing a scientific humanism, creativity, social commitment, complete development and learning society. This was followed by a global commitment during the World Conference on Education for All at Jomtien, Thailand to make primary education accessible to all children in order to massively reduce illiteracy before the end of the decade (UNESCO 1990). At this conference, a clear tie between human development and contemporary global challenges was established, and this became the driver of the recommended Global Education Action Plan for the 1990s. The focus on universal access to learning and equality in education was fostered by the Dakar Action Framework to establish tight monitoring, evaluation and global commitment to Education for All, which were summarised in the six goals of the Dakar Declaration to be achieved by 2015 (UNESCO 2000). This declaration amounted to establishing education as a human right. Delors et al. (1996) revisited the global education vision in their report 'Learning: The Treasure Within', in which they advocated a shift of focus from the local community to a world society, from social cohesion to democratic participation, from economic growth to human development, and from basic education to universities. This, together with fostering the four pillars of learning to know, learning to do, learning to live together and with others, and learning to be, was a main vision shift, which suggested a strategy backdrop of lifelong learning.

Although there is clear evidence that education has a positive impact on national development, it remains less clear how this impact manifests itself. The Human Development Report (UNDP 1990) identified education as one pillar to enlarge people's choices. The social and economic development of nations is fundamentally an education process in which people not only improve their individual capacity but also learn to create new institutions, utilise new technologies, cope with the environment and alter their patterns of behaviour. As such, education becomes a catalyst for the closely interrelated economic, social, cultural and demographic changes that become defined as national development aims (Adams 2002). Therefore, education strategies must be at the core of any NDP, which, besides social and economic development, must pay attention to diversity, nation building and equality in access to education services. Uneven education distribution will deepen and legitimise social and wealth divisions in society. While building and strengthening national culture and diversity, the NDP must also balance the other sides of living in a global, borderless and connected environment. Hence, the challenges of globalisation will, in turn, be reflected in the complexity of education strategy, policy and plans.

Besides the necessity of integrating the strategic plan of education into the NDP, the quality of education must be maintained and improved continuously. One paradigm that enhances the design, evaluation and evolution is to treat education as a system using an engineering methodology approach. Different authors, such as Sinha and Satsangi (1972) and Miokovic et al. (2011), have applied this approach successfully to different aspects the education system in different countries. However, in order to apply the approach to analyse the whole education system, rather than just one specific aspect, it is desirable to use a simple system that can be easily analysed and understood by all stakeholders in the educational process; some of them are not necessarily specialists in the field. This will extend the benefits of the engineering system approach as well as pave the way for developing effective tools for monitoring education system performance. Such an approach was used by Dafa'Alla et al. (2015, 2016), who modelled education as a simple engineering system of processes. The system, which is supposed to satisfy certain measurable key performance indicators (KPIs), identifies the individual as input and the qualified trained graduate as product. In this sense, the education system is purposefully designed to serve the objectives of the national development plan in any specific state or country. Consequently, they modelled the education generically as a closed loop system that is fed and driven by the society and pays back its return to the society, as shown in Fig. 6.1. The flow chart shown in the figure summarises the various elements of their generic educational model together with its dependencies and interfaces. The model provides a natural means to measure its performance. The ability of the system to meet the demand of the labour market was the primary KPI through which the success of the education system could be measured against its general objective of serving the goals of the NDP. Additionally, the well-being of society and hence the standard of living of its members is a reflection of the success of the system. However, the education system, though instrumental, is not the only factor in determining such a complex goal. Other factors, such as type of governance, good planning, secure funding, efficient management and

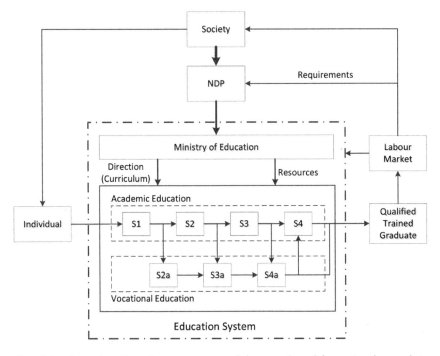

Fig. 6.1 Generic education system model as a closed loop to the society (Dafa'Alla et al. 2016)

so forth also play significant roles. Accordingly, the well-being of society and standard of living could only be considered as a secondary KPI. The model of Dafa'Alla et al. (2015, 2016) is generic and can thus be applied to and used for the evaluation and assessment of the education system in any developing country.

Evaluation and Critical Assessment of the Education System in Sudan

A good historical perspective on educational development in pre-independence Sudan since the year 1820 was presented in Mohamed (2005), while a thorough discussion of the education in Sudan and its evolution in the context of economic and administration evolution for the pre-independence period of 1898–1956 was given by Professor Mohamed Omer Bashir (1983). This section is intended to highlight and evaluate the education system and its contribution to the well-being of Sudanese society in the post-independence period only. Like other African countries, Sudan has inherited a deficient education system that was designed to satisfy the needs of the British colonial power rather than meet its own national and global objectives. Vocational efficiency was one of the urgent problems of post-independence Sudan. There was a need to improve productive efficiency and to increase the national wealth and thereby raise the standard of living. Together with the general national aims of the country, these objectives were translated into a national development plan that stressed Sudanese values, defining its identity, building the infrastructure and accelerating development. Therefore, there was an urgent need immediately after independence to review and amend the education system, its aims, goals and objectives against the new direction set for the country at the time. The new system should bring forth vocational efficiency, develop personality or character, educate for leadership, increase national productivity, achieve social and national integration, accelerate the process of modernisation, and cultivate social, moral and spiritual values. In other words, the functional role of education as a driver for social change and progress was emphasised. However, these new objectives were not set in stone and were subject to changes throughout the country's post-independence history.

In our complementary study (Dafa'Alla et al. 2015, 2016), using Sudan as a case study, we developed and applied the generic education model to review the performance of the education system in detail and identify deviations with time due to education reforms through three distinct political phases in the post-independence history of the country. While the initial post-independence phase, Phase 1 (1956–1969), was characterised by a stable education system that was run smoothly, efficiently and successfully with clear objectives linked to the NDP, the following two phases, Phase 2 (1969–1989) and Phase 3 (1989–2016), were characterised by major reforms that were driven by ideological philosophy and political aims without adequate consultation and were rushed through in extremely short time frames. It was shown that this was a deadly combination that brought both the system and the country to a state of crisis. This manifested itself in skills gaps in the labour market and, together with other factors, was reflected in a weakening economy and an ever-declining standard of living in the country, leading to mass emigration—a situation characteristic of many African countries. The system has simply failed to satisfy both its primary and secondary KPIs (see Dafa'Alla et al. 2016 for a detailed evaluation).

The aim of modern education is individual development as well as social advancement. It emphasises the total development of an individual, including intellectual, social, moral, aesthetic, cultural and physical development. The spirit of modern education was clearly captured in the education system in post-independence Sudan. However, according to Mohamed Khair Othman, nearly all post-independence governments failed to care about the nationalism of education and restricted it to the domains of general and educational bureaucracy, allowing education to proceed through inertia alone, with no strategic objectives or scientific planning (Othman 2015). Accordingly, he stressed that it is important for education to take a national role in emphasising citizenship, engagement in democracy and breaking down the boundaries between people where they live, work and interact. Nevertheless, immediately following independence, a very well designed, funded and run education system was adopted to attain the social and economic development dictated by the newly established NDP. The system produced the trained teachers to run it as well as the qualified cadre to meet the demand of the labour market and aid the execution of the NDP for the benefit of the whole society.

To this end, the education system during the initial post-independence phase, Phase 1, met its overall objectives quite satisfactorily. However, it was not free from criticism. For example, Mohamed Khair Othman argued that the British colonial power had created a defective education system in pre-independence Sudan, which led to the phenomenon of educational injustice in the southern part of the country (Othman 2015). He blamed the Sudanese elites for not paying enough attention at the time of independence to this phenomenon, which created an uneven distribution of educational opportunities between the north and south, and questioned how it began and who was responsible for it. This created the longest and most dangerous dichotomy of educational opportunity between the two parts of the country (Othman 2015) and arguably was used politically to justify the separation of the south later on. Likewise, the competitive nature of the system and the teaching philosophy, which was based on filling the individual with knowledge and information that would be tested regularly and rigorously to ensure that the preset standard was achieved, was at odds with modern education philosophy, which is based on self-learning while the role of the teacher is to secure and manage the environment in which the individual is encouraged to develop their faculties in their own way according to their own abilities, talents and interests. There is an implied assumption here that there is enough variety among the population to ensure that all the skills required by the labour market will be naturally met without further steering from the authorities. Such modern practices were used in different parts of the developed world with varying degrees of success. For example, the education system in Finland was completely liberal, with absolutely no testing during the mandatory education stages, which cover the whole childhood period of the candidate. Following the self-learning philosophy, the children in Finland were encouraged to pursue their own interests under the supervision of highly trained teachers while progressing through the various education stages based on their age only without any consideration of ability. The system was reported to be extremely successful and was known to produce some of the best graduates in the world. The British system, on the other hand, while not far removed from the Finnish one, does include some testing at Key Stage 2 for 10–11 year-olds, the SATS test, which takes place between the primary and secondary stages at national level. As age is the only factor considered for a pupil's progression from one stage to the other, results of the SATS test are not decisive for the progression of the pupil from the primary to the secondary stage of the mandatory education. The only purpose of the test is to serve as a dipstick to measure the performance of individual schools, rather than pupils, against a preset national standard. However, despite the larger population of the United Kingdom relative to Finland, the country is now suffering from a skills gap of about 1.5 million jobs (Winterbotham et al. 2014), the majority of them in the fields of health and technology, which are filled to some extent by immigrant workers (Lewis 2014). Indeed, a survey conducted by the Confederation of British Industry (CBI) found that a quarter of employers who need technicians qualified in science, technology, engineering or mathematics already reported difficulty recruiting, and a third anticipated problems in the next three years (Groom 2014). This shows that the level of success of the Finnish system cannot be readily replicated elsewhere. It could also indicate the presence of other forces in the society acting in a different direction, in a manner strong enough to invalidate the assumption that natural variety among a population would automatically ensure satisfying the needs of the labour market, as implied in the self-learning theory cited above. Indeed, when it comes to developing countries in general, and the underdeveloped, such as in Africa, in particular, tighter control and balance between complete freedom of choice and meeting the needs of development plans is highly desirable. The balance can only be dictated by the development stage of the country. Clearly, this approach helped the education system in Sudan to perform well in its initial phase following independence and is still recommended for the country now, as the challenges facing the country still persist. Once the development plan is running smoothly and efficiently, the system can then be relaxed gradually and proportionately.

However, largely thanks to major reforms introduced to the education system on the hoof, with no proper thinking or acceptable level of public consultation following the change of political regimes in May 1969 and June 1989 respectively, the performance of the education system and hence its ability to meet the demands of the labour market and NDP were gradually eroded. The first major reform introduced in Phase 2 following the Socialist Pro-Arab Nationalism military coup of May 1969 attacked the architecture of the education system and hence the national curriculum without enough planning or even proper thinking about the consequences. The education system ladder was changed from three four-year stages to a six-year primary stage followed by two three-year general and high secondary stages, with new subjects introduced in the intermediate stage. The motive behind the change was mainly ideological and driven only by political considerations. The funding was inadequate, the implementation was poor and the result was a deterioration in the quality of the education standard. In fact, education was not the only facet of life that was adversely affected during that phase. Corruption was rife, the economy was weakening and the standard of living was continuously declining as governance lacked stable direction. Admittedly, these factors are interdependent, and the situation is too complex to blame one of them in isolation or even to quantify its share of the blame. However, the role of education is too significant to ignore. The performance of the education system during Phase 2 was weak and its ability to meet the NDP objectives through satisfying the demand of the labour market was clearly inadequate.

The impact of the second major reform, which followed the Islamist military coup of 1989 at the beginning of Phase 3, was even more devastating for education than its predecessor. The change this time attacked both the structure and the architecture, including the goals and aims, of education in the country. The three-stage main education ladder was replaced by a two-stage one consisting of an eight-year foundation stage and a three-year secondary stage, hence erasing one year from the ladder. Furthermore, new subjects were introduced to reinforce the country's new identity as defined by the regime, at the expense of the functional and vocational aims of education. It was ideologically driven and aimed at remoulding the identity of the Sudanese people. Education was seen as the tool to bring about this identity change. Hence, the vocational efficiency character of the education was replaced by one that emphasised the character building and individual development role of education. This structural change was enforced by changing the architecture of the education system and introducing new subjects to the national curriculum. Consequently, the alignment between the academic and vocational streams of education was muddled, and target market niches for each stream were blurred as colleges and polytechnics were converted into universities offering both Diploma certificates and university degrees (c.f. Dafa'Alla et al. 2015 , 2016). This move was also criticised by Habib (2004) in his critical assessment of planning technical education in Sudan, as it 'distorted the distinguished identity of the existing technical institutes and colleges' and was done without a proper consultation process: What role will these new degree graduates play? Is there any demand for them? Who is going to fill the roles that the old colleges and polytechnics used to, and how can the labour market deal with them? This was confusing to the labour market and also created a skills gap which is difficult to fill. It was a radical change to the system that has resulted in de-linking the education system and the declared objectives of the NDP and has brought chaos to the labour market. It is not surprising, therefore, that the 2011 Sudan Labour Force Survey (SLFS) has revealed an unemployment level of 50 % among the working age population, a quarter of them with a university/tertiary education qualification (International Labour Office 2013)!

It should also be noted here that both of the major reforms discussed above were introduced and implemented in record short periods of time of less than six months each. This rush introduced implementation problems and mistakes that required many years, typically more than 20, to repair. Indeed, there is talk in Sudan about changing the current eight-year foundation education stage into a nine-year one. On the one hand, this proposal is an admission of the problems introduced by the latest reform and, on the other hand, it will introduce its own new challenges of a different nature, such as dealing with children of the extreme age range of 7–16 years in the same school building and environment, let alone the usual problems of any architectural change, such as invalidating the existing curriculum due to the change of the educational period from eight to nine years! Equally significantly, such a change will not address the problems of teacher training or linking the system back to the NDP. Note that, like the rest of the workforce in Sudan, the teaching profession has recently suffered from uncontrolled mass emigration of qualified and well-trained teachers at all educational stages. Low morale, low payment and the deteriorating economic situation leading to the lowest-ever standard of living were among the main factors for the emigration of teachers. Interestingly, the last batch of teachers who served in Phase 2 will retire naturally by the year 2016. Hence, any attempt to repair the system by reverting back to its predecessor will be hampered by the loss of their invaluable experience.

Also, both reforms introduced accelerated expansion to the education establishments. The first reform in Phase 2 accelerated the expansion of the state-funded main education schools, while the second one in Phase 3 expanded university education and the role of the private sector in the field of education. Neither of the two was adequately funded nor rigorously monitored. In fact, instead of increasing the expenditure on education in order to meet and fund the expansion, UNICEF (2008) revealed that education expenditure in Sudan dropped from 4 % of the gross domestic product (GDP) and 15 % of total government expenditure in the early 1980s to around 1 % and 3 % respectively in the 1990s. As a result, schools suffered from teacher shortages and were starved of resources and educational aids. School buildings were run-down, if not collapsing, as funding for schools maintenance and operation became scarce. Consequently, schools needed to generate their own income through private admissions, levying parents and raising public donations in order to survive. No wonder teachers' morale was low!

Likewise, the enlargement of the role of the private sector was another missed opportunity. Instead of following the South Korean example of utilising the monitored private sector to help expand higher education and hence allow government to free invaluable resources to expand main education, particularly primary, in order to achieve their goal of Basic Education for All and steer the education system to serve their Knowledge-Based Economy, as noted by Chen (2007), the private educational institutions in Sudan were managed as commercial enterprises, rather than educational establishments, with particular emphasis on teaching medicine. Interestingly, foreign secondary certificates, such as the international Oxford, American and Gulf certificates, were downgraded relative to their Sudanese counterparts and hence forced the children of the Sudanese diaspora, despite proving themselves academically, to apply for private, rather than general, admission in the Sudanese state and private universities. This was interpreted by them as an attempt to boost the private sector rather than a fair reflection of the academic standard of their certificates. However, in summary, this uncontrolled, ill-thought-out and underfunded expansion of main and higher education during Phases 2 and 3 has resulted in a bad trade of quality for quantity. The result was the lowering of the education standard and mass graduation without a proper link to the demands of the labour market.

The discussion above clearly shows that the damage inflicted on the education system in post-independence Sudan is both visible and deep. Indeed, the figures for 2014 released by the Ministry of Cabinet Central Bureau of Statistics (MICS) show that only 36.4 % of children of school-entry age entered the first grade of primary school (a drop of 3 % relative to 1970) and 28.4 % of children of secondary-school age were attending secondary schools or higher (MICS 2015). This speaks volumes about the dilemma faced by education in Sudan. The economic indicators for Sudan are in equally bad shape. The GDP growth rate has dropped by over 53 %, and the consumer price index increased by 266 % between the years 2006 and 2013, according to the African Statistical Book 2014 published by the UN African Centre for Statistics (UNECA et al. 2014). Simply put, these figures show that the education system has lost its way and so has the country.

Education, Innovation and Sustainable Development in Africa

As stated earlier, Sudan is used herein as a typical example of an African country and the ills of its education system are not unique. Indeed, the educational statistical data for Africa published by the UN African Centre for Statistics (UNECA et al. 2014) show that Sudan's statistical figures are not far removed from the African average. Also, the backward economic situation and poverty is a common African issue. This in itself is a reflection of the state of the education system in the continent. Therefore, it is not a coincidence that the contribution of Africa, as a whole, to the world scientific research literature is next to nil.

Remember that education drives national prosperity and sustainable development. China, India, Malaysia, South Korea, Singapore and the other Asian Tigers all have used technology, widespread industrialisation and education to escape the trap of poverty and build world-class economies. Human resources development is the single-most important factor responsible for South Korea's release from the vicious cycle of poverty and underdevelopment from which it suffered for many decades (Eltayeb 2006). With its scant natural resources, human resources development played a vital role in modern South Korea's development. Clearly South Korea has emerged as an exemplary showcase for national development powered by human resources development (Eltayeb 2006). Likewise, Singapore is a city-state with not much land area that is not particularly rich in natural resources. It won its independence from British colonial power in 1965 and has a population of only 5.4 million as per the 2013 census. Singapore obtained its independence 18 years after Pakistan, has no natural resources and has a mere 3 % of Pakistan's population, but it has a GDP roughly 20 % higher in nominal terms than Pakistan's and a literacy rate of 96 % (Amanulla 2012). It all stems from the innate power of education. Education drives progress. Education drives intellectual capacity-building, which drives the ability to know right from wrong, which in turn drives the overall governance of a country. Education enhances the ability to think and decide which, in turn, gives the masses the ability to elect qualified people. Education drives innovation, values, the ability to see the future and solution-based thinking, which in turn drives economic growth. In a recent study it was shown that a 20–30 % increase in literacy produces an 8–16 % gain in GDP, while teaching mothers to read can lead to a decrease in infant mortality of up to 50 % (Amanulla 2012).

Benchmarking Africa's education systems against their peer continent Asia in terms of how education drives development can also provide useful insights. Figures 6.2, 6.3 and 6.4 depict relationships between accessibility to education (as measured by the average number of schooling years among the population) and quality of education system on the one side, and sustainable development indicators, such as human development, ability to innovate and economic competitiveness for African and Asian countries, on the other, based on data extracted from UNDP (2015), WIPO (2015) and World Economic Forum (2016) respectively. For the sake of presentation clarity, not all countries are labelled in these figures. The clear strong correlations reflected in the figures indicate

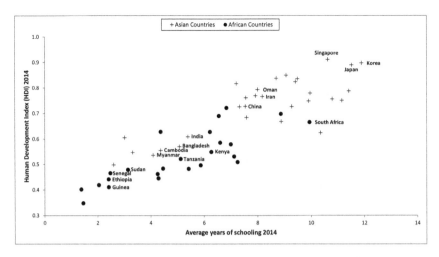

Fig. 6.2 Correlation of human development and average years of schooling for Africa and Asia (*Data source*: UNDP 2015)

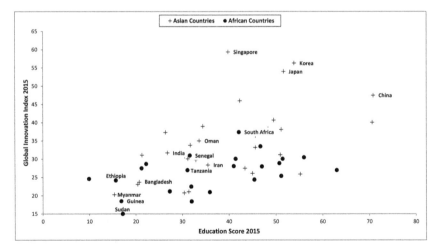

Fig. 6.3 Correlation of global innovation and education quality for Africa and Asia (*Data source*: WIPO 2015)

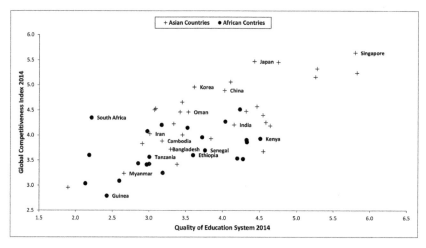

Fig. 6.4 Correlation of global competitiveness and education quality for Africa and Asia (*Data source*: World Economic Forum 2016)

that the longer the members of the society stay in good-quality education, the more developed the individuals will be, the greater the ability of the population to innovate and the better the chance for the country to gain economic competitive advantage in a sustainable development environment. Additionally, the figures also reveal that, while the African countries are generally lagging their Asian peers in terms of human development, innovation and economic competitiveness, the countries with the poorest education quality in both continents are clustering close to the bottom end of the curves. Sudan, which is used as a case study in this paper, scores among the poorest, while Singapore and South Korea are in leading positions. This clearly supports the argument made above, that countries that have built education-based economies to guide their development plans are not only standing out relative to other countries in Africa and Asia but, indeed, comparing favourably with the best in the world, such as Japan and China, as the figures show.

Hence, although weak education cannot be solely blamed for all the ills of the African continent, it must be considered a factor of significant importance. Other factors, such as corruption; type of governance; lack of good planning, secure funding and efficient management; and so on are also contributory factors, as noted above. However, education that builds capacity and fosters innovation is a means to catching up with lost opportunities, building an 'innovation-based economy' and realising the African dream. Africa is a continent emerging from centuries of colonisation and still finding its footing in the modern world. However, it is not a poor continent—it is a backward one. It has a wealth of natural resources, such as minerals (including diamonds, gold, copper and more), huge reserves of oil, forestry and agricultural products (timber, cotton, tea, cocoa, wheat, etc.) as well as livestock—all in abundance. However, as the late President Kenneth Kaunda of Zambia once put it, no country can depend on exporting raw materials and importing all its needs of processed goods to escape the trap of poverty.

The international community has given Africa lots of aid, particularly to help it face natural disasters. However, it is now generally accepted that this 'charity-based aid' is not helping Africa to escape the poverty trap, let alone to build its own capacity and develop its own resources. Sharma (2009) revealed that more than $50 billion of foreign aid is given to African countries every year to address poverty on the continent. Although this may seem generous and, to some, a solid strategy to treat Africa's ailments, he questioned whether this aid is helping or hurting Africa. Indeed, Dambisa Moyo, a Zambian economist with a background that includes Harvard, Oxford and Goldman Sachs, says just the opposite. In her book *Dead Aid: Why Aid Is Not Working and How There Is Another Way for Africa*, Moyo claimed that foreign aid has been 'an unmitigated political, economic and humanitarian disaster'. She strongly argued that 'charity-based aid' cannot provide long-term sustainable development for Africa. She added that the $60 trillion of this aid that has been given in the past 60 years is not working, evident from the fact that the number of Africans who live on less than $1 a day has doubled in the last 20 years. And most foreign government aid, she argued, had been pocketed by corrupt politicians (Moyo 2010).

Levels of corruption and bad governance are obviously huge concerns that need to be tackled in Africa; however, the underlying issue, in our opinion, is much deeper and rests in the fundamentals and the philosophy of aid-giving itself. Yes, food aid, emergency disaster relief and fighting endemic diseases in Africa need immediate action in the short term;

however, they are neither the long-term problems of poverty and under-development in Africa nor the cause of Africa's lack of real contribution to the world economy. The general wisdom says 'give the poor a fish, they will eat for a day; give them a fishing rod, they will eat for life'. The root cause of African backwardness is that Africans do not possess the fundamental tool required to develop their countries and lift them out of poverty. This tool is good-quality education, as argued above. What is required is an innovative education system that promotes innovation, fosters local talent and spearheads sustainable development. There are immense possibilities for greater and more widespread change with the use of present-day technological advancements as well as with the implementation of innovative educational programmes. The challenge is to ensure that innovation plays a constructive role in improving educational opportunities for billions of people who remain underserved in a rapidly developing world (Kuboni et al. 2006). Providing education in new and unconventional ways is only one of a number of solutions, but it is through innovation that we can meet the challenges of improved efficiencies, lower costs, increased accessibility and greater success in achieving sustainable development goals through education. This has happened in the many examples quoted above and it can happen in Africa. The question is how to bring it about in a continent handicapped by corruption, poverty, bad governance and national debt.

In previous papers, namely Dafa'Alla et al. (2015, 2016), we argued that the education system in Sudan has lost its way. Hence, an 'Action Plan' to repair the situation is urgently needed. The design, implementation and funding of the education system is a complex problem. Likewise, introducing radical changes to it is a complex process that requires deep thinking and wide consultation, as it is linked to the NDP and has repercussions for all facets of life. Hence, major reforms to the system should not be taken lightly or based on a unilateral decision by any group or party. Wide societal debate and consultation should take place before changes are introduced. In other words, changes to the education system should be taken out of the political arena and only be introduced by national consensus. We called upon all concerned and all interested parties to engage constructively and participate in outlining the required Action Plan to get the education system, and hence the country, back on track. It is our aim in this chapter to widen this call to include the whole African continent. This can be facilitated by calling for an African conference on education under the slogan 'Education, Innovation and Sustainable Development' to set the African goals and targets for education at a high level and to come up with an 'Action Plan for Education in Africa' as an outcome of the conference. Then, each country can adopt and adapt these general goals and guidelines to suit their own national targets and development phases. A maximum degree of harmonisation can thus be achieved regarding vocational and functional education aims, while a high degree of flexibility can be granted for others, such as cultural and character formation aims. A 'High Bureau' affiliated to the African Union could then be set up to oversee the implementation process.

From our perspective, the whole world will benefit from a vibrant African continent that is playing its full role and contributing its full share to world prosperity. The world needs the virgin natural resources of Africa to keep functioning, and Africa needs the rest of the world to trade with and develop its resources. Hence, the whole world needs to come to the rescue of Africa and help it, not to feed its population, but to build its education system. Clearly, Africa is not in a state to fund this change at present, and this is where the international community under the auspices of the United Nations and its agencies, such as UNESCO, can help. If there is a will, the world can easily divert some of the 'charity-based aid' it is quite happy to pay annually to implement this Action Plan for Education in Africa as a solution to the long-term problems of Africa and a means to put Africa back on the world map. The African Union can act as the custodian to the plan, call for and organise the conference, and ensure links with other international organisations.

However, in addition to the fact that quality education is synonymous with sustainable development and the importance of linking the education system to the NDP, there are another two main lessons to be learnt from the Sudanese experience cited above in this regard. First, the education system has to be indigenous to its environment, as one of the main weaknesses in the experience of Sudan during Phase 2 was that it copied large parts of the education system from the Egyptian one (c.f. Dafa'Alla et al. 2015, 2016). The second important lesson is to take the educational reforms out of the political arena, and hence the competition among politicians, and only introduce them by national consensus (c.f. Dafa'Alla et al. 2015, 2016). This is particularly important in Africa, where regime change is a regular occurrence and corruption and bad governance will undoubtedly hinder the implementation of any plan, no matter how good it is. Therefore, we should stress here that the proposed Action Plan should not be a mere copy of a European or American system. It has to be an indigenous African plan, dealing with local African issues and hence engineered by African intellectuals in consultation with their community groups and stakeholders and in reaction to the needs of their own masses without political interference. Otherwise it will not work.

Conclusions

Good-quality education and sustainable development are synonymous. Education drives innovation, values, the ability to see the future and solution-based thinking, which in turn drives economic growth and sustainable development. This has been clearly demonstrated in many emerging economies worldwide.

Although weak education cannot be solely blamed for all the ills of the African continent, it must be considered a significant factor in the state of underdevelopment from which it suffers. This was clearly demonstrated in the case of Sudan, as an example typical of the African continent.

A critical review and assessment of the education system in post-independence Sudan was undertaken here. The review considered three significant phases in the history of education in post-independence Sudan in which the education system experienced major reforms: Phase 1 between 1956 and 1969; Phase 2 between 1969 and 1989; and Phase 3 from 1989 to 2016.

The link between significant political events in the country and major reforms to the education system was evident. While the initial post-independence phase was characterised by a stable education system that was run smoothly, efficiently and successfully, with clear objectives linked to the NDP, the following two phases were characterised by major reforms that were driven by ideological philosophy and political aims without adequate consultation and rushed through in extremely short time frames.

These reforms contributed to the deterioration of the quality of education in Sudan and gradually de-linked the education system from the objectives of the NDP. The current system resembles a ship sailing in rough seas without a captain.

The damage inflicted on the system throughout the years was wide, deep and fundamental, and it is now in a state of crisis. This manifested itself in a skills gap in the labour market and, together with other factors, was reflected in a weakening economy and ever-declining standard of living in the country leading to mass emigration. The system has failed to satisfy both its primary and secondary KPIs. The case of Sudan is reminiscent of many African countries.

The problem of development in Africa has repercussions worldwide; therefore, it is beneficial for the whole world to ensure that Africa is playing its full role in world prosperity. Hence, this chapter calls for an African conference on education to address education as the root cause of the lack of sustainable development in Africa. The objective of the conference should be to set African goals and targets for education and to draw up an 'Action Plan for Education in Africa' that supports the building of an 'innovation-based economy' as an outcome.

The plan should reflect African values and development needs. It should be an indigenous African plan, dealing with local African issues and therefore engineered by African intellectuals in consultation with their community groups and stakeholders and in reaction to the needs of their own masses, without political interference.

The African Union should adopt the plan, act as its custodian and oversee the implementation phase, with support from the international community through the United Nations and its agencies. Diverting some of the annual charity-based aid to Africa was seen as a means to fund the plan.

It was suggested that the conference would be held under the slogan 'Education, Innovation and Sustainable Development' and should produce an 'Action Plan for Education in Africa' that is capable of repairing the damage and putting the education system, hence Africa, back on the world map.

Acknowledgement The authors are extremely grateful to Drs Badr Eldin Ahmed Dafalla, Magid Mustafa Elsayed and Awad Elkarim Ahmed Dafalla for revising and commenting on the manuscript. Their invaluable comments were incorporated in the manuscript as appropriate.

References

Adams, D. (2002). *Education and national development: Priorities, policies and planning.* Mandaluyong City: Asian Development Bank Publication.

Ahmed, A. (Ed.). (2015). *Connecting universities with the discourse of sustainable inclusive growth in Sudan.* Brighton, UK: Book published by WASD. ISBN 978-1-907106-36-1.

Amanulla, S. (2012). Education drives national prosperity. Article published in "The Express Tribune" Magazine of Pakistan on 26 March 2012. http://tribune.com.pk/story/354878/education-drives-national-prosperity/

Bashir, M. O. (1983). *Education development in the Sudan 1898–1956* (2 ed.). Beirut: Book in ARABIC published by Al-Jeel publishing house.

Chen, D. (2007, December 13). Korea as a knowledge economy: An overview. In *Dissemination Seminar: Korea as a knowledge economy evolutionary process and lessons learned.* World Bank Institute, Washington, DC.

Dafa'Alla, A. A., Hussein, E. S., & Adam, M. A. A. (2015). Critical review of the education system in the Sudan from independence to date. In *Proceedings of 2nd Sudanese Diaspora international conference,* University of Sussex, Brighton, UK, 11–12 June 2015, Also see Allam Ahmed (Editor), (2015), *Reconnecting Universities with the discourse of Sustainable Inclusive Growth in Sudan,* Book published by WASD, Brighton, UK, ISBN 978-1-907106-36-1.

Dafa'Alla, A. A., Hussein, E. S., & Adam, M. A. A. (2016). Education in post-independence Sudan: A critical assessment. *International Journal of Sudan Research, 6*(1), pp. 1–19.

Delors, J. et al. (1996). *Learning: The treasure within.* UNESCO Report, Paris. ISBN 92-3-103274-7.

Eltayeb, E. I. (2006). Vocational education training, A Sudanese–Korean co-operation target. *Journal of the Sudan Engineering Society, 52*(45), 49–56.

Faure, E. et al. (1972). *Learning to be: The world of education today and tomorrow.* Report UNESCO, Paris. ISBN 92-3-101017-4.

Groom, B. (2014). Businesses warn UK schools over growing skills gap. Article in the Financial Times Business & Economy Page on July, 4th, 2014. Also found http://www.ft.com/cms/s/0/c5d43630-02b7-11e4-8c28-00144feab7de.html

Habib, B. O. (2004). *Planning technical education in the Sudan – A critical assessment.* M.Sc. Thesis, Development Studies and Research Institute, University of Khartoum, Sudan.

International Labour Office. (2013). *Sudan labour force survey, SLFS, 2011 – Final report,* Published by the Directorate General of Planning and Monitoring, Ministry of Human Resources Development and Labour, Sudan Government.

Kuboni, O., Kinshuk, L. H., Mackintosh, W., Victor, L., Webb, R., & West, P. (2006). *Innovation in education and development.* Presented at the fourth pan-commonwealth forum on open learning (PCF4) on achieving development goals: Innovation, learning, collaboration and foundations, Sunset Jamaica Grande Resort, Ocho Rios, Jamaica, 30 October–3 November, 2006. Available online http://pcf4.dec.uwi.edu/innovation.php

Lewis, G. (2014). *Employers hire migrants to fill UK skills gap, finds BBC.* A BBC report on Nov, 24th, 2014. Also found http://www.cipd.co.uk/pm/peoplemanagement/b/weblog/archive/2014/11/24/employers-hire-migrants-to-fill-uk-skills-gap-finds-bcc.aspx

MICS. (2015). *Sudan multiple indicator survey 2014 – Key findings 2015.* A publication of the Ministry of Cabinet Central Bureau of Statistics (MICS), Sudan Government.

Miokovic, I., Aksamovic, A., & Hebibovic, M. (2011). Education system as an adaptive system of control with reference model. In *MIPRO, 2011 Proceedings of the 34th international convention.*

Mohamed, D. S. (2005). *Development of education in the Sudan in the period 1956–1970.* M.Sc. Thesis (in Arabic) presented to the Faculty of Higher Studies, University of Khartoum, Sudan.

Moyo, D. (2010). *Dead aid: Why aid is not working and how there is another way for Africa.* A book first published by Allen Lane in 2009 and 2nd edition by Penguin Books in 2010. ISBN: 9780141031187.

Othman, M. K. (2015). *Introduction to Bakht al-Ridha and other articles.* Khartoum: Published in Arabic by Madarik publishing house.

Sharma, M. (2009). *Is AID helping or hurting Africa?.* An Article in the "Global Envision", published in 20 Apr 2009. http://www.globalenvision. org/2009/04/20/foreign-aid-helping-or-hurting-africa

Sinha, A. K., & Satsangi, P. S. (1972). A network system model for an institute of higher education. *India, IEE-IERE Proceedings, 10*(6), 200–209.

UNDP. (1990). *Human development report.* hdr.undp.org/en/reports/global/hdr1990

UNDP. (2015). *Human development report.* http://hdr.undp.org/en/data

UNESCO. (1990). *Meeting basic learning needs: A vision for the 1990's.* Background Document of World Conference on EFA, Jomtien.

UNESCO. (2000). *Dakar framework for action: Education for all: Meeting our collective commitments.* UNESCO Publication ED-2000/WS/27, Paris. http://unesdoc.unesco.org/images/0012/001211/121147e.pdf

UNICEF. (2008, May). "UNICEF data: Monitoring the situation of children and women" statistical information commissioned by the Division of Policy and Practice, Statistics and Monitoring Section, www.childinfo.org. Reproduced in http://www.childinfo.org/files/MENA_Sudan.pdf

United Nations Economic Commission for Africa (UNECA), The African Union Commission (AUC) and The African Development Bank (AfDB). (2014). *African statistical yearbook 2014.* Published by the UN African Centre for Statistics. Also available http://www.uneca.org/publications/african-statistical-yearbook-2014

Winterbotham M., Vivian D., Shury J., Davies B., & Gennakik, J. (2014). *Evidence report 81 on UK commission's employer skills survey 2013: UK results.* Survey commissioned by UK Commission for Employment and Skills (UKCES).

World Economic Forum. (2016). *The global competitive report 2015–2016.* http://reports.weforum.org/global-competitiveness-report-2015-2016/. Accessed Jan 2016.

World Intellectual Property Organisation (WIPO). (2015). *Global innovation index 2015.* https://www.globalinnovationindex.org/content/page/GII-Home

7

Use of Mind Mapping (MM) as an Unconventional Powerful Study Technique in Medical Education

Introduction and Objectives

An Overview of the Problem

Medical students everywhere are overloaded with an excessive quantity of information, with a restricted amount of time to learn and remember all the information and to utilise it immediately. Consequently, many medical students struggle with their individual capability to meet the demands of medical programmes, courses and syllabuses and thus are not successful at examination time (Yussof and Baba 2013; Anderson and Graham 1980).

Many medical educators throughout the world use the traditional method—PowerPoint slides—as the chief information distribution

N.A. Khalifa (✉)
Clinical Nutrition Department, Faculty of Applied Medical Sciences, King Abdulaziz University, 54539, Jeddah 21524, Saudi Arabia

© The Author(s) 2017   **119**
A. Ahmed (ed.), *Managing Knowledge and Innovation for Business Sustainability in Africa*, DOI 10.1007/978-3-319-41090-6_7

platform in their lectures. PowerPoint is described by Garber (2001) as the use of slides, disordered with text, often with unconnected additions, leading to little expressive learning and student dullness. As a traditional method, PowerPoint presentations can be developed, but there is a drawback to this educational method. Lectures and text slides are linear representations that cannot express the rich interrelations among medical ideas and concepts. This results in linearity more than connectivity, less critical thinking and less expressive learning, which are important in the education and development of future medical practitioners.

The quick, sustained transformations in medical science, and the need for future medical practitioners to remain capable, requires an alteration in the educational techniques by which medical students are trained. Lately, the number of studies on learning methodologies used in medical education that might help students study and ultimately integrate information has increased (Dolmans et al. 2005; Kim et al. 2006; Zajaczek et al. 2006). Different authors have documented the need for alternate methods of teaching and learning that will empower medical students to recall enormous amounts of information, develop critical thinking skills and resolve a range of complicated clinical problems.

Pudelko (2012) reported that mind mapping (MM) is a multisensory, non-linear teaching and learning approach that has recently surfaced in higher education as a means to support students' critical thinking and encourage a deeper level of integrated information.

While the MM teaching and learning strategy has appeared in the literature, its usage by medical educators in Sudan is unknown. As Sudanese medical educators, fostering an environment that improves students' critical thinking and their ability to master the quantity of information required to succeed in medical institutions in Sudan is one of our principal roles.

Definition and Tools of MM

Tony Buzan, the inventor of mind mapping, defines MM as a powerful graphic technique that acts as a master key to unlock the brain's potential by creating a visual display of a concept using mind mapping tools that include images, keywords, lines and colours in a distinct, uniquely powerful, structured manner. MM can be used in all aspects of life where critical thinking and enhanced learning will boost human performance.

The Key Elements of Mind Maps and Evidence Supporting MM

Many studies emphasise the usefulness of MM in many kinds of occupations including research, teaching, learning, unifying, problem-solving and so forth. Mind maps are built on several key elements, which have been verified to play an important function in liberating thinking capacity.

Radiant Structure

Anokhin (1973) reported that the brain works on the basis of association and is capable of connecting thousands of ideas. Mind mapping is a pattern of radiant thinking application, which stimulates all parts of the brain that work in communication, starting with a central thought that radiates to infinite space, as opposed to the normal linear method of thinking, which restricts thinking and information retention and recall (Buzan and Buzan 1994). The radiant structure of the mind map encourages longer continuous thinking as it is much simpler to find new connections between the branches of the mind map, resulting in a natural flow of thinking that tries to fill in the blank spaces.

Basic Ordering Ideas (BOIs)

Basic Ordering Ideas (BOIs) is well defined as the initial - level topics that come out from the mind map central idea like headings of chapter in a written book on certain subject. BOIs consider as the main concepts that assist to create the utmost number of associations as putting and arranging thoughts. Ideally, the initial - level topics should be wide-ranging to provide for a greater range of associations. The author of the Mind Mapping Software Blog (2008) Chuck Frey considers good BOIs for adjustment of the MM quality.

Single Keywords

A keyword is generally a word that will produce as much correlated meaning as possible. In MM keywords open up thinking and stimulate the mind to see more details that were previously unseen. By trying to choose a word that most suitably conveys a subject, the brain is forced to think more actively rather than only gathering or repeating information. A study done by Howe (1970) on note-making and note-taking reported that keyword notes given to students were more efficient in terms of understanding and recall than complete sentence summaries or text notes. Keywords generate many associations.

Interesting Colour

Colour is one of the most forceful and entertaining parts of MM. It recovers memory, excites creativity and influences how one communicates with others. Psychologists have discovered that colour helps one process and store images more competently than colourless (black and white) scenes, and to better memorise them as a result (Journal of Experimental Psychology 2002).

Influence of Images and Icons

Images are an excellent memory aid. Our ability to remember images is far better than our memory for words. A study by Anglin et al. (2004) confirmed the power of pictures, while one by Haber (1970) also supports the value of imagery. McArdle (1993) found that adding visuals such as photos or maps to a presentation increases the amount of information recalled by as much as 55 %. Mind mapping stresses pictures, visual imagery, drawings, doodles and symbols. Using imagery arouses the brain's imagining and visualisation capacity, which produces huge creativity benefits and improves the memory's storing and recalling abilities.

Icons impart clearness and appropriate meaning to topics and are promptly understood by the brain. Small visual symbols such as triangles, circles, ticks and crosses strengthen the benefits of using imagery in mind maps, for example denoting category, hierarchy, priority, status and so on.

Relationship Arrows

Association arrows explicitly link different topics together throughout the map and present multidimensional direction to thoughts, thus promoting different and extremely creative thinking (White and Gunstone 1992).

Emphasising (Chunking)

Emphasising, or chunking, is a technique used in mind mapping to gather and emphasise the main branches within a boundary to make specific topics or ideas in the mind map visually noticeable alongside the rest of its content, thus making these ideas simpler to memorise and connect to others. According to Frey (2008), short-term memory is usually only effective in storing seven items of information, and chunking can aid in using this storage space more competently.

Whole Brain Thinking

Using all of the above mind mapping elements produces a functional arrangement of a range of cognitive purposes and processes in a way that uses both the right and the left sides of the brain. The two brain sides cognitive function is primarily discover by Sperry (1968), who set that the thinking cap of the brain (Cerebral Cortex) is separated into two main hemispheres that perform a range of intellectual tasks (cortical skills). The right brain works using images in a non-verbal way and takes over in dealing with emotion, colour, form and shape, rhythm, and perceptive information. The right brain processes information rapidly, in a non-linear and non-sequential style. The left brain is found to work in a linear way, recording things in a consequential order. It is related to analytical thinking and logic, dealing with naming and classifying language, things, reading, writing, mathematics and representative inference together with

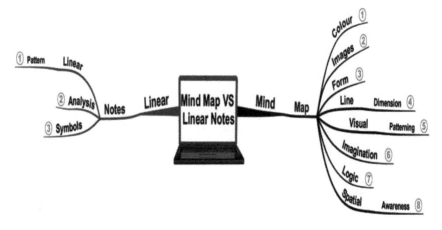

Fig. 7.1 Mind map vs linear note (devised by author)

seeing things in black and white. An individual's mental ability is based on how they use their brain. Mind mapping is one approach to using both sides of the brain (ambidextrous). When using MM, thoughts are diffused and stream between lines and relations, which is linked with imagination and creative thinking as opposed to the linear approach (Fig. 7.1).

Research Studies on MM in Education

Mind maps have been shown to be a simple but powerful technique for learning and have had surprising success in education all over the world in the 40 years since Tony Buzan first invented the method. The techniques of MM have been embraced by students of all ages to help them understand, generate ideas, revise and recall information related to their subjects. Important studies have shown the potential of MM as a powerful tool for learning and teaching.

Promote Creativity

A study by Al-Jarf (2009) showed that the spatial layout of a mind map provides a better overview that makes new associations more noticeable and generates an unlimited number of ideas, thoughts and associations related to any subject. Mind mapping software offers prominent advance for enhancing the aptitude of anyone to MM yield ideas as it is built over several key parts, which have been verified to play an essential function in releasing thinking capacity. Mind Map unify ideas by thinking with greater clarity to learn associations between ideas and put an innovative viewpoint on things and seeing all the correlated issues and study alternatives in bright of the large image Visualize ideas' by creating a visual display of a concept through using MM tools, which include images, key words, Lines, and colors, in a powerful structured manner. The subjects in the study confirmed that the MM tools stimulated creative thinking and enabled them to more rapidly conceive and shape ideas for their writing.

Augment Memory

Compared to conventional learning methods and note-taking, the cortical skills of mind mapping have been shown to significantly increase information recall. A study by Wickramisinghe et al. (2007) revealed that a majority of medical students using MM found it more useful for memorising information in a structured way compared to their former study methods.

Toi (2009) confirmed that MM can help children remember words more easily than using lists, with up to 32 % improvement in memory. Additionally Farrand et al. (2002) found that mind mapping improved medical students' long-term memory of precise information by 10 %.

Boost Teaching Confidence

Boyson (2009) found that using MM for lesson preparation helped teachers develop lessons plans and teaching methods, and improved their recall of the subject material. This can enhance teaching confidence and help smooth management of classes and boost teaching confidence.

Mind Mapping was found to be a valuable approach for presenting novel concepts, attract a whole-class concentration, and assist in people in planning and build up projects and assignments more efficiently (Goodnough and Long 2002).

Learning Process Empowering Medical Education

The first study regarding the potential utility of MM in medical education was conducted by Farrand et al. (2002). They examined the advantages of the mind map learning technique compared to traditional note-taking for medical students' long- and short-term recall of written information. The investigators found that the mind map technique significantly improved long-term memory of information.

D'Antoni and Pinto Zipp (2005) reported that of 14 physical therapy students studied, ten found that MM helped them arrange and assimilate the material presented in their course. Many of the study participants enjoyed being creative when making mind maps, employing a variety of designs, symbols, colours and keywords.

A study of undergraduate medical students to determine the efficiency of using MM to improve reliable recall from written information concluded that MM was a competent study technique when applied to written material and improved recall of information and memory (Farrand et al. 2002).

Willingham (2007) reported that; critical thinking happens when students enters behind the surface structure of a problem and knowhow the problem can be explained, and possesses the content knowledge important to solving the problem.

The extra capacities of pictures and colors that are uniquely to mind maps does not enable just memory but also deliver a wide range of medical students to distinguish the intra and inter relationships between thoughts, which exposes the way of real-world thinking prevalent in the clinical location. Srinivasan M et al. (2008).

Spencer et al. (2013) published a study entitled 'Radiant Thinking and the Use of the Mind Map in Nurse Practitioner Education', which stated that the MM graphical method increases the visualisation of relationships and connections between thoughts, which helps in information attainment, data holding and inclusive comprehension.

Descriptive unpublished data on the use of MM in note-making (teaching) and note-taking (learning) in a general pathology course for students in a clinical nutrition department shows that using MM resulted in high grades among student (23.8 % received A+, 19 % A, and 21 % B+) (Fig. 7.2)

Presentation Effectiveness

A study done by Mento et al. (1999) on a number of managers using mind mapping, showed a successful way in remembering and managing

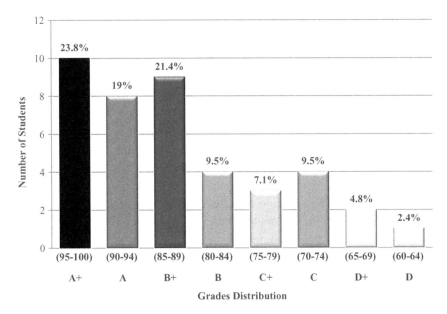

Fig. 7.2 Pathology final exam result for second-year clinical nutrition students who used mind mapping in education (devised by author)

information, which are held and kept in connected and organized manner rather than linear.

Project Preparation

Holland et al. (2003/2004) reported that Mind Mapping is consider as forceful approach that help in designing and planning projects and improve the written skills of assignments. Contributors will be capable to of planning and organizing their thinking for any type of project.

Writing Improvement

Written work based on the use of MM was well schematised and linked ideas with more associated detail. It improved the work of students at all stages as they became more imaginative in creating and combining ideas for their writing (Al-Jarf 2009).

Thoughts Organisation

A Mind Map is considered as brain storming showed in one picture therefore it assist in thinking with greater clarity to discover connections between ideas and characters and find keys to problems by places a innovative viewpoint on things and seeing all the correlated issues and study alternatives in bright of the large image. This had been approving by results of Mueller et al. (2002) study which expressive how the use of Mind Maps to suggest patient care at Front Range Community College settled an increased critical and inclusive thinking.

Although the MM teaching and learning technique has appeared in the literature, its use in Sudanese medical education is unknown. While computerised databases are ingenious and useful, **NO** data was found in a search for the current literature review (Use of mind mapping in medical education in Sudan).

Specific Purpose of the Literature Review

The purpose of this literature review is to present evidence of MM's effectiveness in improving research and education (teaching and learning), and to progress understanding about using MM to improve students' critical thinking and their ability to handle the quantity of information necessary to succeed in Sudanese medical institutions.

Methodology

Literature Searching

- **Targeted Search**
  The literature was obtained through library databases (PsychINFO, PubMed, MEDLINE PsychINFO and EMBASE). It includes both empirical and conceptual published literature on the definition, characteristics and uses of MM in medical education up to April 2016.

- **Search Strategy**

  The search strategy primarily involved looking for the following keywords and phrases: mind mapping, medical education, critical thinking, visual education, and Sudan. The reference lists from reports and published studies were searched for more sources. A number of electronic journals specialising in medical education, Tony Buzan's website (ThinkBuzan.Com), and scientific studies and research on MM were examined. The general search mechanism revealed information from consultation papers, discussion papers and opinions of medical educators, and all which were examined for evidence related to the present integrative literature review objectives.

Selecting the Articles and Review Resources

Inclusion Criteria: the inclusion criteria include articles (reviews, use of mind mapping in learning, teaching, critical thinking and outcomes required), chiefly in Sudan.

Topics of Interest: topics of interest are: mind mapping learning and teaching types, Sudanese medical education system.

Evaluating the Evidence: final selection of articles was done by thorough review of each studied article by two persons to minimise omissions and errors.

Discussion

Medical educators face many challenges in preparing students to recall huge amounts of content and to develop associations between concepts, especially with the rapid growth and transformation of clinical practice and medical education. Medical educators are responsible for preparing graduates who are skilled in analytical reasoning and problem-solving in a variety of clinical practice locations, which requires them to use teaching strategies that improve communicative learning instead of depending on traditional methods involving rote memorisation.

The medical educator must generate magnificent learning experiences for the enhancement of critical thinking in order to improve students' effectiveness as evidence-based independent clinicians.

The evaluation in this study focuses on the usefulness and creativeness of one teaching approach, mind mapping, compared to more traditional methods. A study by D'Antoni et al. (2005) identified MM as a credible teaching and learning approach that actively engages the mapper (learner) in assimilating material in a non-linear, meaningful way, which boosts critical thinking.

The combination of images and words makes mind maps a rich optical channel for pioneering and imaginative vision. Visual presentations are more effective than verbal presentations. The presenters who used visual language were stronger, more exciting, brief, specialised, reliable and better prepared. These findings agree with the results of Howe (1970), which showed that keywords were more efficient by far than sentence summary notes or whole text notes in terms of recall.

Farrand et al. (2002) stated that MM is a successful study method when applied to written material and is likely to motivate a greater level of managing for memory creation.

Mind Mapping increases the mind's potential for entire brain thinking by using both cortical sides together—the left brain (numbers, linearity, logic, words) and the right brain (creativity, images, colour, curves, space)—which increases the brain's power. This is confirmed by the findings of Sperry (1968), who reported that the more assimilation there was between the left and right brain actions, the more the brain's performing turned out to be synergetic, which means that every cortical skill encourages the actions of other parts so that the brain is operating at its peak.

Medical educators should encourage the use of MM techniques for learning collaboratively, taking notes, brainstorming, presenting and organising ideas, and studying. Moreover MM can be used in problem-based learning, medical care process; identify disease causes, diagnoses and planning treatment.

Conclusions, Recommendations and Implications

Many studies have verified the effectiveness of MM in education. Mind maps can be used as a teaching method to improve critical thinking in medical education by inspiring students to link information across disciplines and recognise relationships among the clinical and basic sciences. The use of mind maps in medical education may benefit more students with diverse learning types. Mind mapping was found to be a useful tool for creative thinking and collaborating with others.

The literature review showed that Sudanese medical educators are not at present using Tony Buzan's mind maps as a method for conveying and assimilating information in medical education programmes. This primary data is the first of its kind on the potential usefulness of mind mapping in medical colleges in Sudan and can be used to explore plans to address the assumed obstacles.

Considerable work will be required to promote mind mapping as a tool that can promote critical thinking skills. Informing higher education officials about the MM approach and what it can achieve may lead to their support for the use of MM as a learning and teaching approach within medical education and health care programmes in Sudan

Nevertheless, before mind maps become generally accepted as a study technique, attention has to be given to ways of improving inspiration amongst users. Mind mapping is a stimulated technique for students to employ that can improve memory and help create a unique environment for managing information.

References

Al-Jarf, R. (2009). *Enhancing freshman students' writing skills with a mind mapping software.* Paper presented at the 5th international scientific conference, eLearning and software for education, Bucharest.

Anderson, J., & Graham, A. (1980). A problem in medical education: Is there an information overload? *Medical Education, 14*, 4–7.

Anglin, G. J., Hossein, H., & Cunningham, K. L. (2004). Visual representations and learning: The role of static and animated graphics. In *Handbook of research on educational communications and technology* (2nd ed.). Mahwah: Lawrence Erlbaum Associates.

Anokhin P. K. (1973). The forming of natural and artificial intelligence. *Impact of Science in Society, 23*(3), 32.

Boyson, G. (2009). *The use of mind mapping in teaching and learning*. The Learning Institute, Assignment 3.

Buzan, T., & Buzan, B. (1994). *The mind map book: How to use radiant thinking to maximize your brain's untapped potential*. New York: Dutton.

D'Antoni, A. V., & Pinto Zipp, G. (2005). Applications of the mind map learning technique in chiropractic education. *Journal of Chiropractic Education, 19*, 53.

Dolmans, D. H., De Grave, W., Wolfhagen, I. H., & Van Der Vleuten, C. P. (2005). Problem-based learning: Future challenges for educational practice and research. *Medical Education, 39*, 732–741.

Farrand, P., Hussain, F., & Hennessy, E. (2002). The efficacy of the "mind map" study technique. *Medical Education, 36*(5), 426–431.

Frey, C. (2008, December 18). *What are basic ordering ideas and how can they improve your mind mapping?* Mind Mapping Software Blog.

Garber A. R. (2001, April 1). *Death by power- point*. Available from: http://www.smallbusiness-computing.com/biztools/article.php/684871

Goodnough, K., & Long, R. (2002). Mind mapping: A graphic organizer for the pedagogical toolbox. *Science Scope, 25*(8), 20–24.

Haber, R. N. (1970). How we remember what we see. *Scientific American, 222*, 104–112.

Holland, B., Holland, L., & Davies, J. (2003/2004). *An investigation into the concept of mind mapping and the use of mind mapping software to support and improve student academic performance*. Learning and teaching projects 2003/2004 (pp. 89–94).

Howe, M. J. A. (1970). 'Using students' notes to examine the role of the individual learner in acquiring meaningful subject matter'. *Journal of Educational Research, 64*, 61–3. http://www.tonybuzan.com/about/mind-mapping/

Journal of Experimental Psychology. (2002). Learning, memory and cognition.

Kim, S., Phillips, W. R., Pinsky, L., Brock, D., Phillips, K., & Keary, J. (2006). A conceptual framework for developing teaching cases: A review and synthesis of the literature across disciplines. *Medical Education, 40*, 867–876.

McArdle, G. E. H. (1993). *Delivering effective training sessions: Becoming a confident and competent presenter*. Cengage Learning.

Mento, A. J., Martinelli, P., & Jones, R. M. (1999). Mind mapping in executive education: Applications and outcomes. *The Journal of Management Development, 18*(4), 390–416.

Mueller, A., Johnston, M., & Bligh, D. (2002). Joining mind mapping and care planning to enhance student critical thinking and achieve holistic nursing care. *Nursing Diagnosis, 13*(1), 24.

Pudelko, B., Young, M., Vincent-Lamarre, P., & Charlin, B. (2012). Mapping as a learning strategy in health professions education: A critical analysis. *Medical Education, 46*(12), 1139–1232.

Shone, R. (1984), Creative Visualization. New York: Thorsons Publishers Inc.

Spencer, J. R., Anderson, K. M., & Ellis, K. K. (2013). Radiant thinking and the use of the mind map in nurse practitioner education. *Journal of Nursing Education, 52*(5), 291–229.

Sperry. (1968). Split brain study 'hemisphere deconnection and unity inconscious awareness'. *American Psychologist, 23*, 723–733.

Srinivasan, M., McElvany, M., Shay, J. M., Shavelson, R. J., & West, D. C. (2008). Measuring knowledge structure: Reliability of concept mapping assessment in medical education. *Academic Medicine, 83*(1196), 1203.

Toi, H. (2009). *Research on how mind map improves memory*. Paper presented at the international conference on thinking, Kuala Lumpur.

White, R., & Gunstone, R. (1992). *Probing understanding*. New York: Falmer Press.

Wickramisinghe, A., Widanapathirana, N., Kuruppu, O., Liyanage, I., & Karunathilake I. (2007). Effectivness of mind maps as a learning tool for medical students. *South East Asian Journal of Medical Education, 1*(1) (inaugural issue).

Willingham, D. T. (2007). Critical thinking. Why is it so hard to teach? *Am Educator, 31*, 8–19.

Yussof, M., & Baba, A. (2013). Prevalence and associated factors of stress, anxiety and depression among prospective medical students. *Asian Journal of Psychiatry, 59*(2), 128–133.

Zajaczek, J. E., Gotz, F., Kupka, T., Behrends, M., Haubitz, B., Donnerstag, F., Rodt, T., Walter, G. F., Matthies, H. K., & Becker, H. (2006). eLearning in education and advanced training in neuroradiology: Introduction of a web-based teaching and learning application. *Neuroradiology, 48*, 640–646.

Part IV

Capacity Building and Human Capital

8

Design and Engineering Capacity Building for a Sustainable Development of African Economies: The Case of Algeria

Abdelkader Djeflat

Introduction

Over the past half century, important technologies increasingly have become associated with fields of applied science and engineering. As mentioned in several contributions (Bell 2007, Salter and Gann 2001), design and engineering (D&E) activities constitute what might be considered the 'core' of Science Technology and Innovation (STI) systems in advanced industrial economies. On the other hand, sustainable development rests on proper policies and adequate capabilities in STI. Sustainability can be achieved through the design of products that comply with environmental regulations through proper D&E capabilities. This simple reality has not been clearly perceived in African countries as it has in other parts of the developing world in recent years. This has led gradually to a wide gap

A. Djeflat (✉)
Maghtech – Clerse CNRS (UMR 8019), University of Lille, Lille, France
Oran University, Oran, Algeria

© The Author(s) 2017   **137**
A. Ahmed (ed.), *Managing Knowledge and Innovation for Business Sustainability in Africa*, DOI 10.1007/978-3-319-41090-6_8

between advanced and least developed countries (LDC) economies in terms of D&E capabilities. This is perhaps as important as the digital divide, which has been well covered in the literature yet has not attracted much attention from either policymakers or researchers. As Bell put it (2007), there are some indications that global inequalities with respect to the design and engineering component of STI systems in LDCs may be much greater than they are in connection with other components such as R&D.

From a different perspective, R&D and innovation systems have polarised the attention of researchers in LDCs, including in African countries, at the expense of D&E, and it is only recently that D&E has been at the heart of the innovation process. The commodity boom in African economies has brought massive imports of technology in various sectors of industry, broadly defined, as we will see. While the sustainability issue has appeared on the agenda, the learning potential of these international transactions has not always been properly grasped. Yet it would be of enormous importance if proper D&E policies were worked out. This unprecedented window of opportunity for learning via these channels will be lost if no action is taken and the level of awareness remains at its current level.

This chapter examines the current situation of D&E in African industry. To assess the real situation, we looked at a small sample of 20 Algerian firms from both the public and private sectors, including both small and big enterprises from various areas of industry. This exploration enabled us to identify some of the key issues and make some recommendations for policymakers, as well as to suggest some future areas of research. The first section addresses the concepts and tools of D&E, followed by a section that looks briefly at the situation of D&E in Africa. The next section analyses the function of D&E in Algerian industry. Finally, the last section concludes and makes some recommendations.

Concepts and Tools of Design and Engineering (D&E)

The proper definition of D&E is a key issue which needs to be clarified before we engage in an assessment. The design process is principally concerned with how things ought to be. It involves thinking ahead creatively in order to make a technical object that fits the requirements of users or clients. This process of creation often involves developing new combinations of existing technologies. The design problem-solving process evolves through a series of iterative and overlapping phases (stages): from problem identification, through development of different conceptual solutions, to designing a favoured solution and working out the details of the physical artefact (Salter and Gann 2001; Yazdani 1999). It is a recursive practice, a continuous cycle of trial and error focusing on the creation of a physical product and drawing upon the fundamental laws of nature (Constant 2000). In a more precise manner, Bell (2007) defines D&E capabilities as those that transform knowledge from a generally applicable form into increasingly specific and concretised forms. Engineering is the application of scientific knowledge to solving problems in the real world. While science (physics, chemistry, biology, etc.) allows us to gain an understanding of the world and the universe, engineering enables this understanding to come to life through problem-solving, designing and building things. Engineers can be distinguished from other professions by their ability to solve complex problems and implement solutions in cost-effective and practical ways.[1]

The development of the field of engineering has made a significant difference in the scope and the speed with which new knowledge is translated into technical change. Technological capabilities are needed to carry out various kinds of D&E activity, ranging from initial studies to lifelong upgrading (Bell 2007). These activities include a series of successive tasks, namely: studies, concept elaboration, basic design, fabrication, procurement : these are two different steps commissioning start-up and, finally, upgrading. The first step is always a process of 'discovery' as put forward by Haussmann et al. (2005). D&E in an important stage in the innovation process (Bell and Dantas 2009). It is also key to embodying sustainability concerns such as pollution reduction, longer life-cycle and more robust products, eco-efficient energy consumption and so forth. In newly industrialising countries, *adaptive and design capability* are more important than R&D (Intarakumnerd and Virasa 2004).

---

[1] Source: What is engineering http://whatisengineering.com/ (visited May 2016).

D&E feeds from the R&D sphere and contributes to it through feedback and accumulated experience and experimentation. It also feeds from other spheres, such as technician skills and craft capabilities, and from below the basic operator skills and capabilities (Arnold et al. 2000). This is where most of the DUI (doing, using, interacting) occurs and where the technology use and operations and maintenance provide the opportunity to foresee incremental changes. This is at the firm level. Externally, recent studies suggest that the technology required by the business sector does not come from fundamental or even applied research generated by R&D laboratories, but is generated by D&E activities spawned by interaction with customers, suppliers and competitors. This helps to explain why clusters, competition and linkages with other firms are so important to the technology development process. In addition, the ICT revolution has drastically modified the D&E function (2000). Applications for computer-aided design (CAD) amongst others brought significant advantages in handling general data in D&E by the 1970s. It is now clear that we are moving to a different world with recent technological advancements such as 3D printing. Nonetheless, designers still rely on tacit knowledge and face-to-face exchanges to solve problems and innovate (Bucciarelli 1994; Henderson 1999; D'Adderio 2001; Nightingale 1998; Salter and Gann 2001).

The Situation of D&E in Africa

There is a growing awareness of the importance of design and engineering for African development along with the need to re-industrialise African economies. Calestous Juma's Hinton Lecture to the Royal Academy of Engineering in the UK (Juma 2006) emphasised its role in 'redesigning African economies', focusing heavily on engineering capabilities in connection with infrastructure development, but recognising its much wider significance across other sectors of the economy (cited by Bell 2007:72). Product design and process improvement are important in the emerging innovation systems (EIS) (Djeflat 2011) as a whole in view of the different paths innovation trajectories are likely to take. Industrial policy requires increased productivity based on intensive research into local raw materials, which are better adapted and usually more eco-efficient and more sustainable as inputs to manufacturing, and the acquisition of engineering design and fabrication skills, as well as adaptation of modern technologies and machinery (Emovan 1999).

The ability of a developing country to produce engineering goods is especially important, partly because this requires skills in metal processing and fabrication that are fundamental to manufacturing as a whole. Moreover, the engineering sector functions as the training ground for a wide spectrum of managerial and entrepreneurial skills. It also plays a fundamental role in the assimilation of foreign imported technology. The non-R&D dimensions of technology development may be especially important for the vast majority of enterprises in developing countries that are not engaged in R&D, are far from the technological frontier, and do not require cutting-edge R&D to improve their competitive standing. Achinivu (1999), using the oil sector in Nigeria, distinguishes between rehabilitation engineering, which allows for the possibility of reverse engineering, and classical design engineering. Reverse engineering and reverse design are opportunities to introduce sustainability concerns.

The reality is that D&E suffers from many shortcomings in the African continent. Several studies have analysed D&E in Africa, namely the African technology gap: United Nations Conference on Trade and Development (UNCTAD) (2003), the African Technological Outlook (2011), International Development Research Centre (IDRC) studies on STI in Africa, and others. They all conclude that there is little D&E in Africa and that capital goods and design engineering are almost all foreign due to passive imports of relatively simple-to-use technology with low levels of technical efficiency and sometimes high environmental risks. Industrial engineering as a distinct function has been rather absent in the face of excessive use of turnkey products. Design capabilities are inadequate and often simple testing is called D&E. The lack of local research and design capability is one factor keeping African producers at the bottom of the global value chain (GVC) and outside complex product segments.

These weaknesses have several root causes. The first one is the legacy of import substitution and the effects of structural adjustment programmes (SAPs). Following independence, state-led and elite-managed development strategies targeted industrialisation as a central part of the development agenda in many African countries. The import substitution industrialisation (ISI) model that most African countries adopted in the 1960s and 1970s mobilised investment for domestic industries (nurturing the infant industries). Burgeoning initiatives to develop D&E in industry in some countries included unpacking the technology bundle and disembodying the engineering component. D&E was bought from a different source, with the possibility of outsourcing certain tasks locally. In parallel, several schools and universities introduced engineering training in their syllabuses. The second era started in the early 1980s, when SAPs set batteries of measures such as liberalisation, corrective signals and incentives for the manufacturing sector. This liberalisation process led to industry restructuring and pushed firms to further reduce costs, downsize personnel and cut down on maintenance expenses, an importance source for the development of D&E capabilities. This led to the brutal end of the development of domestic engineering in industry. Since the 1990s, de-industrialisation in several African countries has led to the de-engineering of domestic industry (Djeflat 2014). The collapse of the demand for domestic design and engineering (e.g., for petroleum engineering in Algeria) has resulted in substantial losses of high-level human capital through brain drain, political conflicts, civil war and so on.

Secondly, Africa suffers from the effect of the Dutch disease (for commodity producers), which made it easier to resort to foreign sources for D&E, and the neglect of local competencies both in the industrial sphere and in the training sphere. This contributed to the *de-engineering* phase of African countries and resulted in the loss of interest in the engineering function and the decline in effort made initially by local industry. This is also reflected in the research sphere in engineering and technology in several sub-Saharan African countries. With the exception of Ghana, where the proportion of researchers in engineering reached 19.4 % of the total number of researchers, it does not exceed 8 % in the other countries : Malawi (6 %), Mozambique (4.8 %), Senegal (4.4 %), Tanzania (7.4 %) and Uganda (1.9 %) (NEPAD 2010). It is reflected through the weak demand for D&E consultancy. Out of 138 consultancy bureaus in Algeria, only four are explicitly geared towards engineering consultancy (Ministry of Industry 2011).

The third problem is the foreign-dominated D&E sector in Africa. The failure or lack of regulation in relation to foreign engineering firms has been damaging to local capacity. Local content laws often do not exist, and when they do exist, they are often not appropriately enforced to ensure knowledge transfer from foreign companies to local engineers (Wright 2013). Learning-centred arrangements with international engineering companies supplying design, engineering and project management services for industry and infrastructure projects in Africa are rare.

Fourthly is the major deficit in engineers. As pointed out in earlier studies, the first and most critical skills shortages are in engineering (Lall 1992). Apart from building and construction and civil works, where the rates of locally supplied services appear to be significant, the remaining sectors rely heavily on engineering services supplied by foreign firms. For example, with only 880 men/year (300 engineers and 580 technicians), the local supply of engineering does not exceed 20 % of local needs in Tunisia. The country suffered a deficit of 2,920 men/year, that is, about 4,867 specialists in engineering.

Several obstacles have hindered the development of engineering. Lack of organisation of the sector, limited financial tools designed to cater for the specific needs of the activity, heavy taxation, lack of guarantees and lack of incentives are the most important problems reported. To overcome the weaknesses of local engineering, Tunisian firms resorted to foreign engineering services through two channels. In the first one, local firms hired the services of foreign engineering firms directly, namely in the mechanical and electrical industries and in the fabrication of transport equipment.

The Situation of D&E in Algeria: Empirical Findings

A brief historical analysis shows that the engineering function benefited from an early awareness at the level of policymaking. From the beginning of the industrial strategy, which was part of the first development plan (1967–1969), the steel sector was managed by a group of recent graduates of the top French training institutions, including the Polytechnic of

Paris, the Ecole des Mines and Telecom Paris, where most of the French elite are trained.[2] Two sectors managed by these brilliant engineers, the energy (electricity) sector and the steel sector, were particularly active in the development of D&E capabilities. In the steel sector, a decision was made very early on to open a design office and put local engineers in direct and permanent contact with foreign partners in mixed professional teams. Foreign engineers were compelled to carry out their D&E in these offices. Local engineers had to work with them on all stages through to the realisation of the projects and be involved in the design process. The teams, led by polytechnicians,[3] were comprised of competent, well-trained and dedicated members. Three specialised companies were created to lead the development of effective D&E capabilities; one of these teams, for example, managed to design a complete gas cylinder unit.

All this drive for D&E came to a halt in the late 1970s when the new labour legislation, called the General Statute of Workers (SGT),[4] aligned the salaries of engineers with those of administrative personnel, which reduced the motivation and commitment of the former. Later, in 1980, the government decided to restructure the industrial sector to be dominated by state companies, allegedly to encourage greater efficiency.[5] By restructuring industry, the link between D&E and production was broken, with no possibility of interactive learning. Moreover, the teams of workers who had managed to accumulate D&E know-how throughout the 1970s were dispersed.

Importance of Engineering Personnel The engineering function varies in terms of size from one sector to the other. Its importance is measured in terms of size of personnel, that is, the proportion of engineers in the professional group. The results show that the proportion of engineers is small (5–20 %) compared to the proportion of technicians, who are the

---

[2] I am indebted for this section to the kind contribution of Mr Omar Lassel, former Head of Engineering at the SNS Company, the major state-owned steel company in the country.

[3] Mohamed Liassine, who was Director General of the steel complex, later became Minister of Industry.

[4] Established by law n° 78–12 of 5 August 1978.

[5] The restructuring of Algerian enterprises was promulgated by the Presidential decree of 4 October 1980.

dominant group (70 %) in some companies in the professional group. In addition, not all engineers are involved in the D&E function. The proportion of engineers involved effectively remains the same, while in some cases, for example electricity, D&E is performed entirely by technicians.

Involvement of Workers in D&E The majority of firms in the sample (60 %) do not involve workers in the D&E function as a result of a lack of capacity to adequately manage workers and the excessive centralisation of decision-making (e.g., in the agricultural machinery sector). This is an indication that the view that D&E is the domain of highly qualified engineers, and eventually technicians, but not of workers still prevails. The DUI process is completely ruled out.

Relationship of D&E and Training Institutions Companies in the sample appear to be fairly open to the training world: 53 % recruit newly graduated engineering students. These are from petrochemicals, pharmaceuticals, energy and building materials sectors. The rest (47 %) who do not recruit their engineers from the training system (agro-food, energy, liquefied natural gas (LNG), mechanical industry, chemical industry and plastics) offer different explanations. These include the existence of their own training facilities (energy sector), internal obstacles such as weak recruitment function (the LNG case), lack of experience and inadequate profile (agricultural equipment) and the quality of engineering graduates, which is considered below standards (in the case of plastics and printing).

Sources of D&E Used by Local Firms To satisfy their D&E needs, local firms use different sources. Nearly half of them (46 %) use their own D&E services which they have developed over the years. These include both public and private companies across all sectors. Bearing in mind the de-industrialisation and de-engineering phenomenon, the score seems fairly high. The second-most important source are the research centres (27 %) used by the agro-food and chemical industries. Algeria has a relatively active research community in both agronomy and biotechnology and hosts the African Agency for Biotechnology (AAB). Local universities come in third (9 %), showing the negligible role they play as a source of D&E services. Their technological trajectory has been different from the trajectory of industry, as we have shown in previous work (Djeflat 1992). Consultancy bureaus also occupy a relatively negligible position (9 %). It is surprising that foreign companies are rarely used (4.5 %), given that many technologies in various development projects are relatively new and sophisticated and require the help of technology suppliers. Finally, own retired personnel (engineers and technicians) are in a weak position (4.5 %), essentially used only by the agricultural equipment sector.

Integration of the D&E Function Within the Organisation The D&E function appears to be well integrated within the organisation in 60 % of cases. Thus, the potential for interactive learning appears relatively high for a number of companies from both the public and the private sector and in various industrial sectors (agricultural equipment, energy, oil refining, petrochemicals, pharmaceuticals, building materials and printing/plastics). In the rest of the sample, D&E is not well accepted. Several reasons are put forward for not accepting the D&E function within the organisation, ranging from the lack of motivation of personnel to the dominant position of the informal sector.

Three reasons given are of particular interest. The first is the preference for foreign sources of D&E: this preference comes also from the consumers and users. For example, farmers tend to prefer imported agricultural machinery, such as tractors and combine harvesters from European and US companies, over that produced locally. The second is the lack of confidence in the concepts and ideas of local personnel within the company. Often, the engineers and technicians who come up with brilliant ideas leading to important improvements in the production process receive no reward. For example, in a public lamp company, one of the technicians managed to improve the productivity rate of the filament production process from 60 % to 120 %, through re-engineering the design of the process. In the face of total ignorance and lack of recognition, he stopped proposing the new incremental changes he had in mind. The third reason given is the significant role played by the informal sector in discouraging the use of local products and services. Competitive products are imported informally and provide tough competition for home-grown products and services. This is the case in the mechanical sector, where spare parts are imported through informal channels.

The Decision-Making Process (Governance) In big state companies, the decision-making process is centralised at head office level, giving little freedom to the production units of the group. This is the case in the LNG sector. The reasons can be attributed to the complexity of the process, where the production units are not considered qualified to interfere with the process. This view, largely held by major industrial public companies, has often annihilated any form of initiative to bring in technological change at the shop floor level, in total ignorance of the doing, using, interacting process taking place at this level.

Conclusions and Recommendations

Based on this analysis, some conclusions can be drawn and recommendations made to promote D&E as a tool for innovation and accelerated growth and development in Africa.

The first conclusion is at policymaking level. D&E cannot be promoted if the level of policymaking awareness of its importance remains low. It rests on three important components: firstly, reinforcement of the importance of the industry option at the level of decision-making in the face of a growing tendency to encourage services and ready-made products and technologies; secondly, the need to encourage productive enterprises in relation to importing ones to reverse the trend of de-industrialisation; and thirdly, the need to encourage, through proper laws and regulations, the development of the D&E function at the enterprise level.

The second conclusion relates to the issue of training and capacity building. Various forms of training are involved: traditional training at the university level (adding more sessions through revision of the curriculum and enhanced internships) and in high technical schools, as well as at the industry level, both in-house regular training and continuous training to update the knowledge and capabilities of both management and employees in the field of D&E. The ICT revolution has made life-long learning crucial. Several suggestions can be made to improve the recruitment of engineers from the training system and to provide a profile better adapted to the requirements of industry. It relates also to updating the curricula in universities and training centres and regular review of training programmes, training that is better adapted to the specific domains of activity, more specialised training for engineers and technicians, deeper engineering training and project management, continuous training, and more internships. The reinforcement of links with universities and high schools is vitally important. Developing partnerships with foreign firms to use more locally trained engineers and technicians and to train them in D&E needs to be systematically explored in major industrial projects.

The third conclusion is that awareness of the relationship between D&E and the research and development sphere is severely limited. It is important to raise this awareness and to institute policies and strategies to enhance the linkages between research and D&E both at policymaking level and at enterprise level.

The fourth conclusion concerns the creation of more D&E consultancy bureaus in various fields. These are relatively scarce in African countries (only seven bureaus for all the industry needs currently in Algeria) and often companies, particularly the small ones that are unable to import these services, feel the deficit. They are both process-based and product-based.

The fifth conclusion is centred on the role of consumers and users in enhancing D&E through actively encouraging locally designed and engineered products. This role could be even more proactive through open source or open innovation, a proper policy of involving consumers and users in the design of the products.

The sixth conclusion is centred on the need for a strategy to provide access to technology and know-how through imitation. D&E requires in this particular case the development of capabilities to unbundle the technological package through reverse engineering and possibly reverse design, and to incorporate both local design and local inputs. The potential of reverse engineering as a tool for innovation requires specific skills and capacity building. Exploring reverse engineering in a more systematic way, which is within reach of African capabilities in view of the important learning and competence building which has taken place, is crucial. For instance, engineers in South Africa, facing persistent levels of unemployment in the country, are rediscovering the potential of using labour-intensive road construction techniques (Bell 2007).

Finally, existing D&E models may not be appropriate for analysing the evolution of network forms that occur in late industrialising countries, in particular the importance of networks in the development of D&E capabilities, as shown in the example of Petrobras in Brazil (Bell and Dantas 2009). The proposed multi-stage approach to build D&E capabilities (Salter and Gann 2001) mentionned earlier could be applied to African economies both to the industrial and the mineral sector (possibly to the agricultural sector as well).

Further research is needed on why African industry D&E did not evolve to the adaptive capacity and generative stage. Another question is how to involve communities in the entire design process, from problem identification to idea generation, concept evaluation, detailed design, fabrication, and testing and evaluation. Finally, what prospects for South-South collaboration to develop joint D&E capacity in particular in industries where countries have common interests—for example, offshore oil, particular kinds of mining, particular kinds of infrastructure projects and so forth.

References

Achinivu, O. I. (1999) cited by Abubakar Abdullahi. *An impact assessment of science and technology policy on national development of Nigeria*, Phd Thesis – 2008.

Arnold, E., Bell, M., Bessant, J., & Brimble, P. (2000, December). *Enhancing policy and institutional support for industrial technological development in Thailand: The overall policy framework and the development of the industrial innovation system*. Bangkok: NSTDA.

NEPAD 2010 The African Innovation Outlook, African Science, Technology and Innovation Indicators Initiative (ASTII) South Africa, 135 pages.

Bell, M. (2007). *Technological learning and the development of production and innovative capacities in the industry and infrastructure sectors of the least developed countries: What role for ODA?* UNCTAD, background paper n°10.

Bell, M., & Dantas, E. (2009). Latecomer firms and the emergence and development of knowledge networks: The case of Petrobras in Brazil. *Research Policy, 38*, 829–844.

Bucciarelli, L. (1994). *Designing engineers.* Cambridge, MA: The MIT Press.

Constant, E. (2000). Recursive practices and the evolution of technical knowledge. In J. Ziman (Ed.), *Technological innovation as an evolutionary process.* Cambridge: Cambridge University Press.

D'Adderio, L. (2001). Crafting the visual prototype: How firms integrate knowledge and capabilities across organizational boundaries. *Research Policy, 30*, 409–424.

Djeflat, A. (1992). *Technologie et Système Educatif en Algérie.* Alger/Paris: Unesco/CREAD/Medina.

Djeflat, A. (2011). Emerging innovation systems (EIS) and take off: Evidence from the North African countries. *African Journal of Science, Technology, Innovation and Development, 3*(2), 16–45.

Djeflat, A. (2014). *Design & engineering and innovation for African development: Element for a research project.* Paper given at the Globelics 2014 conference – Addis Ababa – Ethiopia.

Emovon, E. U. (1999). National research policy and sustainable development. In P. O. Adeniyi (Ed.), *Research capacity building for sustainable development* (pp. 31–36). Lagos: Unilag Consult.

Hausmann, R., Hwang, J., & Rodrik, D. (2005). *What you export matters: CIC Working paper no. 123.* Cambridge, MA: Centre for International Development, Harvard University.

Henderson, K. (1999). *Online and on paper visual representation, visual culture, and computer graphics in design engineering.* Cambridge: MIT Press.

IDRC The African Technological Outlook. (2011). *IDRC report.* Ottawa, Canada.

Intarakumnerd, P. and Virasa, T. (2004). Government policies and measures in supporting technological capability development of latecomer firms: a tentative taxonomy, *Journal of Technology Innovation, 12*(2), 1–19.

Juma, C. (2006). *Redesigning African economies: The role of engineering in international development.* London: Hinton Lecture, The Royal Academy of Engineering.

Lall, S. (1992). Technological Capabilities and Industrialization, *World Development, 20*(2), 165–186.

Ministry of Industry (2011) «Catalogues des bureaux d'études et du Consulting» Ministère de l'industrie de la PME et de la Promotion des Investissements,

Direction Générale de la vieille stratégique, des études économiques et des statistiques, Document de travail n°26, DGVSEES, Algiers, 138 pages.

Nightingale, P. (1998). A cognitive model of innovation. *Research Policy, 27*(7), 689–709.

Salter, A., & Gann, D. (2001). *Sources for ideas for innovation in engineering design*. Brighton: Science and Technology Policy Research SPRU.

UNCTAD (2003). *Africa's technology gap, Case Studies on Kenya, Ghana, Uganda and Tanzania*, UNCTAD/ITE/IPC/Misc.13, United Nations Publications, July, 123 pages.

Wright, H. (2013). *The engineering capacity needs in sub-Saharan Africa*. London: The Royal Academy of Engineering.

Yazdani, B. (1999). Four models of design definition: Sequential, design centered, concurrent and dynamic. *Journal of Engineering Design, 10*(1), 25–37, Taylor & Francis.

9

Absorptive Capacity of Human Capital and International R&D Spillover on Labour Productivity in Egypt

Eman Elish and Hany Elshamy

Introduction

The theoretical and empirical economic literature provides evidence that knowledge transfer between countries or regions has contributed to the productivity growth of other geographic areas (see Coe and Helpman 1995; Coe et al. 2009; Kao et al. 1999; Litchtenberg and Brouno 1998).

In addition, empirical evidence has been also presented with respect to the direction, the magnitude and the effectiveness of different channels through which such spillover effect is transmitted.

However, few studies have examined the effect of international R&D spillover transmission from industrial countries to developing countries. Those that have been conducted in this respect focused on the macro

E. Elish (✉)
Department of Economics, Faculty of Business Administration, Economics and Political Science, The British University, Cairo, Egypt

H. Elshamy
Associate Professor of Economics and Acting Head of Economics Department, Faculty of Commerce, Tanta University, Cairo, Egypt

© The Author(s) 2017   **153**
A. Ahmed (ed.), *Managing Knowledge and Innovation for Business Sustainability in Africa*, DOI 10.1007/978-3-319-41090-6_9

level and the overall effect on total factor productivity. Very few empirical studies have been conducted on how international R&D spillover affects labour productivity in developing countries.

The main objective of this chapter is to survey the literature on international R&D spillover transmitted from industrial countries to developing countries and its effect on labour productivity, then to build a model whose basic assumption suggests that, technology and innovation can be transmitted to the Egyptian manufacturing industries through various channels. However, the effect of international R&D spillover can be insignificant in enhancing labour productivity if there is a low absorptive capacity of human capital.

Hence, the chapter will examine the relationship between the labour productivity of the Egyptian manufacturing industries, relative to international R&D capital stock, and human capital.

The chapter is organised as follows: the second section discusses the literature pertaining to international R&D spillover and how it affects productivity in developing countries. The third section outlines the methodology and model application, using time series analysis to examine the effect of international R&D spillover and school enrolment on labour productivity in the Egyptian manufacturing industries. The fourth section analyses estimation results and interpretations. The final section concludes with the main findings and recommendations of the research.

Literature Review

International R&D was originally discussed in several studies, the most significant being Coe and Helpman (1995) (as cited from Coe et al. 2009). They contributed new estimates of R&D spillovers that differed from those of earlier research studies, which only examined spillover across sectors or industries for a single country.

Their estimates of R&D spillovers used a pool of macroeconomic data for 21 OECD countries plus Israel over the period 1971–1990. They estimated the relation of a country's total factor productivity as a function of the domestic research and development capital stock and foreign R&D capital stock as a proxy for the stock of knowledge embodied in a country's trade position. All the measures of foreign and domestic research and development capital were constructed from the business sectors' research and development activities.

The model used the estimated elasticity of total factor productivity in relation to domestic and foreign R&D capital stock. In another study, Coe et al. (1997) estimated elasticity of the total production function in relation to the change in domestic and foreign R&D capital stocks, imports of machinery and equipment, and secondary school enrolment ratio. Another contribution of the Coe and Helpman model (1995) is using this function as empirical evidence that research and development spending in industrial countries can be transmitted to developing countries and increase these countries' total productivity.

Many studies advocated this model but using advance statistical techniques. Coe et al. (2009) adopted the modern panel cointegration method that was not available in the early 1990s. In addition they did an expansion of the panel to the same model.

Another study by Kao et al. (1999) used the same model and adopted methods of OLS, FM and DOLS estimators in panel data. The study concluded that the estimated coefficients in the Coe and Helpman model (1995) are subject to estimation bias, but they have correct signs. However, the results support the argument for international R&D spillover.

Litchtenberg and Brouno (1998) examined two important characteristics of the Coe and Helpman model (1995). Firstly they argued that the foreign R&D weighting scheme suffers from 'aggregation bias' and suggested a less biased weighting scheme. They also corrected an indexation bias and found that the more a country enjoys trade openness, the more probability of gains from R&D spillover.

Muller and Michaela (1998) argued that the choice of an appropriate model for behaviour of panel data can affect the results of the Coe and Helpman model (1995), in other words, the choice between fixed coefficient methods previously used in the model and the use of a random coefficient model in this study. Applying the model using fixed regression gave unreliable results when compared to random coefficient analysis results.

The channel through which international R&D is transmitted was debated in several studies on the macro level (across borders of countries) and on the micro level (across firms or industries in the same country).

Cincera and Bruno (2001) distinguished between rent spillover of technology transfer that occurs from trading transactions of factor imports and machinery that embodies innovative technology on the one hand, and international knowledge spillover across countries via foreign direct investment, international research collaboration, scientific publications or brain drain on the other hand. Both are difficult to measure due to high collinearity between them. Wolf and Ishraq (1993) depicted a channel of R&D spillover embodied in new investments that enter a sector in the economy.

The absorptive capacity of a recipient country for international R&D spillover was taken into consideration when analysing the magnitude of impact on productivity. Several determinants of absorptive capacity were suggested in various studies.

The first is the quality of human capital as an important catalyst for absorption (Sunkwark and Young 2006). They built their assumption on the idea that domestic human capital is an important factor in understanding the foreign high technology embodied in imported goods and absorbing it for domestic use. McNeil (2007) specified the quality of the labour force and capital accumulation as two vital determinants of absorptive capacity of spillover.

The second is the technology gap between countries, where studies questioned the impact of international R&D on total factor productivity with a wide technology gap in developing countries (Blomstrom and Kokko, as cited from Bouoiyour 2005).

Zhu and Bang (2007) showed that innovation in information technology has played a significant role in facilitating the transmission of international R&D spillovers among OECD countries and Israel and consequently improving productivity growth.

Finally, Coe et al. (2009) added a group of institutional determinants which impact the absorptive capacity of international research and development spillover in recipient countries. These include the ease of doing business, the quality of the tertiary education system, the strength of patent protection laws in the country and their effectiveness in copyright protection, and the origin of the country's legal system. All these determinants were found to be highly correlated to the improvement of total factor productivity through enhancing the absorptive capacity of spillover.

Other contributions were made to the literature of international R&D spillover by examining its impact on other economic variables. Costa and Stefano (2004) focused on the effect of technology innovation spillover on economic growth. They made use of the dynamic growth model, which facilitates the evaluation of regional convergence and innovation on long-run labour productivity, without the technology index that is usually used in the technology gap model for developing countries.

Borras, Serrano and Simarro (2011) examined the effect of intersectoral direct and indirect knowledge spillover on a sector's labour productivity on a disaggregated level. Their interpretation of knowledge included innovation, research and development, and tacit knowledge.

Gera, Wulong and Frank (1999) presented an empirical model that estimates the effect of information technology investments and R&D spillover from the information technology sector on labour productivity between Canadian and US industries. They relied on the Coe and Helpman (1995) model for estimating foreign research and development capital and domestic research and development capital. They agreed on the transmission channels introduced in this model. However, they regressed the annual average labour productivity rate of an industry on the information technology and non-information technology investments for five sub-periods from 1971 to 1993. They regressed the mean values of the research and development variables over the same results.

Their result showed a significant effect of international R&D spillover from information technology sectors on labour productivity for both sectors, with low significance from non-information technology sectors.

Empirical studies of international R&D in relation to total factor productivity in few Middle East countries like Morocco and Egypt were conducted but with a narrow scope. McNeil (2007) examined the effect of international R&D spillover on total factor productivity through its diffusion in the intermediate products imported from OECD countries to the Egyptian and Moroccan manufacturing sectors. He used the same model which Coe and Helpman model (1995) have used. In addition, his study showed the significance of cross-border research and development spillover on total factor productivity, where Human capital, is a core determinant of the magnitude of spillover in the model. Bouoiyour (2005) conducted a study on the Moroccan manufacturing industries, indicating that the channel of R&D spillover is through foreign direct investment, which has a significant positive effect on domestic labour productivity. He introduced the technology gap as a measure of absorptive capacity. It is calculated as the ratio between total factor productivity of foreign firms to the total factor productivity of domestic firms. This technology gap is a condition set in the model to have a higher positive magnitude effect of international R&D on domestic labour productivity.

The final conclusion of this literature survey, from which this chapter builds its basic assumptions, is that international R&D can be transmitted from industrial countries to developing countries through different mechanisms. It can significantly affect total factor productivity given the presence of high absorptive capacity. The main catalyst of this capacity is the quality of human capital, a narrow technology gap and innovation in information technology.

Methodology

In this section, we first present the empirical model used to estimate the effect of R&D spillover and human capital on labour productivity growth in the Egyptian manufacturing sector. We then discuss the methodology used to construct the international R&D spillover and capital stock.

Empirical Model

The empirical model depends on Cobb-Douglas production function. This model was developed by Corves (1997) and Gera et al. (1999):

$$Y_t = L_t^{\alpha_1} H_t^{\alpha_2} K_t^{\alpha_3} RD_t^{\alpha 4} e^{0t} \tag{9.1}$$

where α_1, α_2, α_3, and α_4 are the output elasticities of labour input, human capital, capital stock and international R&D capital respectively. α_4 represents the rate of exogenous technical change. All of the other variables are explained in Table 9.1.

From Eq. 9.1, we can derive the following equation that expresses the labour productivity growth rate of the manufacturing sector in Egypt.

Table 9.1 Sources and descriptions of data

Variable	Description	Expected sign	Source of data
Y	Labour productivity in manufacturing sector in Egypt. Y = GDP in manufacturing sector divided by employment	Dependent variable	Ministry of planning in Egypt, annual series
L	Employment level in manufacturing sector in Egypt	–	Ministry of planning in Egypt, annual series
H	Years of primary schooling	+	World Bank
K	Capital stock. It is calculated from the investment data by using the PIM technique explained in this section	+	Ministry of planning in Egypt, annual series
RD	International R&D, which is calculated from the R&D expenditure data by using the PIM technique explained in this section	+	STAN dataset, OECD

$$\left(\frac{\dot{y}}{y}\right) = \beta_0 + \beta_1\left(\frac{\dot{L}}{L}\right) + \beta_2\left(\frac{\dot{H}}{H}\right) + \beta_3\left(\frac{\dot{K}}{K}\right) + \beta_4\left(\frac{\dot{RD}}{RD}\right) + \epsilon \qquad (9.2)$$

Where $\left(\frac{\dot{y}}{y}\right)$ is the labour productivity growth; $\left(\frac{\dot{H}}{H}\right)$ is growth rate of the human capital; $\left(\frac{\dot{K}}{K}\right)$ is the growth rate of the capital stock; and $\left(\frac{\dot{RD}}{RD}\right)$ is the growth rate of the international R&D.

Measurement of R&D Spillovers

We calculated the international R&D as follows:

First, we calculated R&D expenditures for the G7 countries (USA, UK, Germany, France, Italy, Japan and Canada) by using the STAN dataset.

Second, we calculated the values of R&D at constant prices.

Third, we transferred these data from flows to stock by using the Perpetual Inventory Method (PIM)[1] by applying Eq. 9.3 for the benchmark year and Eq. 9.4 for the rest of the years (Elshamy 2009).

$$RD = \frac{RD \text{ flow in } 1982 / 83}{\text{Average annual growth rate} + \text{Depreciation rate}} \tag{9.3}$$

$$RD_i = RD_{i-1(1-\text{Depreciation rate})+RD \text{ flow in year } i} \tag{9.4}$$

Measurement of Capital Stock in Egypt

We calculated the international R&D as follows:

First, we collected the investment data for the manufacturing sector in Egypt during the period 1982/83–2010/11.

Second, we calculated the values of investments at constant prices.

Third, we transferred these data from flows to stock by using the Perpetual Inventory Method (PIM) by applying Eq. 9.5 for the benchmark year and Eq. 9.6 for the rest of the years.

$$K = \frac{\text{Investment flow in } 1982 / 83}{\text{Average annual growth rate} + \text{Depreciation rate}} \tag{9.5}$$

$$K_i = K_{i-1(1-\text{Depreciation rate})+\text{Investment flow in year } i} \tag{9.6}$$

Empirical Results

This section discusses the estimated results of Eq. 9.2. Regression was performed on a time series data consisting of 29 years (1982/83–2010/11) for the manufacturing sector in Egypt. First we conducted the cointegration analysis. Table 9.2 shows the results of the Augmented Dickey

---

[1] For more details about this method, see Elshamy (2009). Details of these findings can be interpreted as follows: in the Egyptian manufacturing sector, international R&D has a positive influence.

Table 9.2 Cointegration analysis

Dependent variable (growth of labour productivity)	Coefficients	Significant
Independent variables		
Constant	0.007	*
Growth of labour input	−0.411	***
Growth of human capital	0.012	**
Growth of capital input	0.019	*
International R&D spillover	0.056	***
CDRW	1.75	
ADF tests	Favoured lag length = 2	Favoured lag length = 2
ADF(0)	0.004	0.003
ADF(1)	0.052	0.022
ADF(2)	0.041	0.006
ADF(3)	0.031	0.004

*** = significant at 1 %
** = significant at 5 %
* = significant at 10 %
ADF figures show the Mackinnon approx P-value

Fuller (ADF) test on the first difference based upon the Mackinnon P values at various lag lengths. The preferred lag length based upon the Akaike Information Criterion (AIC) indicate that cointegration is generally accepted.

Table 9.2 shows the estimation results using cointegration analysis. We find that labour productivity has a positive and significant relationship with the growth rate of human capital, capital stock and international R&D. However, the relationship between labour productivity and the growth rate of employment is negative and significant. All of these results are correct according to the economic theory.

Details of these findings can be interpreted as follows: in the Egyptian manufacturing sector, international R&D has a positive influence on labour productivity, with a 1 % rise in international R&D increasing labour productivity by 5.6 %. Moreover, in the Egyptian manufacturing sector, human capital has a positive influence on labour productivity, with a 1 % rise in human capital increasing labour productivity by 1.2 %.

Table 9.3 shows the error correction mechanism (ECM). It indicates the same results as cointegration. Most importantly of course, the lagged

Table 9.3 Error correction mechanism (ECM)

Dependent variable (LFDI)	Coefficients	Significant
Independent variables		
Constant	0.006	*
Growth of labour input	−0.366	**
Growth of human capital	0.009	**
Growth of capital input	0.	*
International R&D spillover	0.048	**
Lagged error	−0.116	***
No. of observations	29	
F- statistics	8.33	***
Adjusted R²	0.76	
DW	2.15	
AR(1)	1.42	
ARCH(1)	1.82	
Normality	2.12	

*** = significant at 1 %
** = significant at 5 %
* = significant at 10 %

error is negative and significant. This confirms the acceptance of the long-run relationship, which is further validated given that there are no problems with any of the diagnostic tests presented (the AR(1) test for first-order residual autocorrelation, the ARCH(1) test for autoregressive conditional heteroscedasticity and the Jarque-Beta test for normality).

Conclusions

This chapter empirically analyses the relationship between labour productivity, human capital and international R&D spillover during the period 1982–2011, by estimating a single model equation which employs long-run cointegration analysis and short-run analysis (ECM). The analysis uses annual data from 1982 to 2011.

Conventional results for international R&D and human capital are found. It is inferred from the model that significant role played by international R&D and human capital has strongly shaped labour productivity. These results are consistent with all literature surveyed in this research chapter, which supports the basic assumption that international research and development spillover is transmitted from industrial countries to developing countries like Egypt. In addition, this spillover affects labour productivity given the quality of human capital formation in Egypt.

The more developed the educational level of human capital in the industrial sector, the more significant its role will be in absorbing international research and development spillover and benefiting labour productivity.

References

Borras, B., Serrano Domingo, G., & Simarro Parreno, R. (2011). *Direct and indirect intersectoral knowledge and labour productivity in the Spanish economy.* University of Valencia. Retrieved from http://www.webmeets.com/SAEe/2011/prog/getpdf.asp?p:d

Bouoiyour, J. (2005). Labour productivity, technological gap and spillovers. Evidence from Moroccan manufacturing industries. *African Finance Journal, 7*(2), 1–17.

Cincera, M., & Bruno, P. (2001). International R&D spillovers: A survey. *Cahier Economiques de Bruxells, 69*(1), 169–180.

Coe, D., & Helpman, E. (1995). International R&D spillovers. *European Economic Review, 39*(5), 859–887.

Coe, D., Helpman, E., & Hoffmaister, A. W. (1997). North–South R&D spillovers. *The Economic Journal, 107*(440), 134–149.

Coe, D., Helpman, E., & Hoffmaister, A. W. (2009). International R&D spillovers and institutions. *European Economic Review, 53*(7), 723–741.

Costa, M., & Stefano, I. (2004). Technology spillover and regional convergence process: A statistical analysis of the Italian case. *Statistical Methods and Application, 13*(3), 375–398.

Covers, F. (1997). The impact of human capital on labour productivity in manufacturing sectors of the European union. *Applied Economic, 29*, 975–987. RePEc:dgr:umaror:1996001.

Elshamy, H. (2009). *Productivity growth in the manufacturing sector in Egypt.* Conference of the Scottish economic society, held from 22/4/2009 to 24/4/2009, Perth-Scotland.

Gera, S.,Wulong, G., & Frank, L. (1999). Information technology and labour productivity growth: An empirical analysis for Canada and the USA. *The Canadian Journal of Economics, Working Paper Series* (Canada. Industry Canada), *32*(20), 384–407.

Kao, C., Minttsien, C., & Bangtin, C. (1999). International R&D spillovers: An application of estimation inference in panel cointegration. *Center for Policy Research Working Paper(4)*, RePEc:max:cprwps:4.

Litchtenberg, F., & Brouno, P. (1998). International R&D spillovers : A comment. *European Economic Review, 42*(8), 1483–1491.

McNeil, L. (2007). *The international diffusion of technological knowledge: Industry level evidence from Egypt and Morocco*. Howard University. Retrieved from http://www.unidep.org/Release3/.../IDEP-AFEA-07-12.pd...

Muller, W., & Michaela, N. (1998). A panel data analysis: Research and development spillover. *Economics Letter, 64*(1), 39–41.

Sunkwark, N., & Young, S. (2006). International R&D spillovers revisited: Human capital as an absorptive capacity for foreign technology. *International Economic Journal, 20*(2), 179–196.

Wolf, E., & Ishraq, N. (1993). Spillover effects, linkage structure, and research and development. *Structural Change and Economic Dynamics, 4*(2), 315–331.

Zhu, L., & Bang, J. (2007). International R&D spillovers: Trade, FDI and information technology as spillover channels. *Review of International Economics, 15*(5), 955–976.

Part V

Investment

10

Foreign Direct Investment in Zimbabwe and Botswana: The Elephant in the Room

Mavis Gutu, Constantia Anastasiadou,
Maktoba Omar, and Collins Osei

Introduction

Sub-Saharan Africa (SSA) has 54 countries, some experiencing good inflows of foreign direct investment (FDI) and economic expansion, whereas others are shrinking as FDI inflows are weak. Africa's inability to attract significant levels of FDI requires close attention, because FDI is crucial in capital formation and for stimulating sustainable economic development in the region. However, FDI is unevenly distributed among nations and regions (UNCTAD 2015; IMF 2013; Asiedu 2013; Anyanwu

M. Gutu (✉) • C. Anastasiadou • C. Osei
Edinburgh Napier Business School, Craiglockhart Campus,
Edinburgh Napier University, Edinburgh, EH 14 1DJ, UK

M. Omar
Coventry University, William Morris, Priory Street City, Coventry,
CV1 5FB, UK

Coventry University Business School, UK

© The Author(s) 2017   **167**
A. Ahmed (ed.), *Managing Knowledge and Innovation for Business
Sustainability in Africa*, DOI 10.1007/978-3-319-41090-6_10

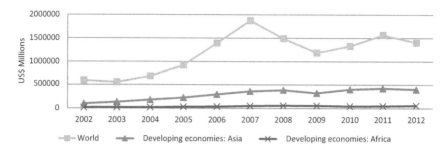

Fig. 10.1 FDI trends in US$ million: World, Asia and Africa, 2002–2012 (*Source*: Adapted from UNCTAD: UNCTADstat)

2011). This chapter examines FDI determinants for the SSA region with particular emphasis on the comparison between Zimbabwe and Botswana.

Africa as a whole has recently gained more prominence as an attractive location for FDI, and the SSA region's FDI inflows are increasing. However, FDI into the African region remains relatively stagnant, as evidenced in Fig. 10.1.

Foreign Direct Investment Defined

FDI is considered a firm internationalisation strategy. The firm establishes a physical presence in the host country by acquiring and transferring resources such as capital, technology, labour, land, plant and equipment, giving investors partial or full ownership, and is long lasting (Cavusgil et al. 2013; IMF 2004).

Foreign Direct Investment: Empirical Determinants

Determinants of FDI generally fall into four categories, as shown in Table 10.1.

These motives will be integrated into the discussion of the variables in relation to Zimbabwe and Botswana.

Table 10.1 FDI categories and objectives

FDI category	Objective
Resource-seeking	MNEs aim to invest in host country in order to benefit from lower-cost resources, such as natural or physical resources, cheap labour, technological and managerial
Market-seeking	MNEs enter foreign countries with the main objective to increase market share and sales growth
Efficiency-seeking	MNEs attempt to rationalise resources and market-seeking by centralising production in host country while servicing multiple markets. The aim is to reduce transaction costs through economies of scale
Strategic-asset-seeking	The long-term internationalisation strategy of a firm's objective through acquisition of host country assets or by forming strategic alliances

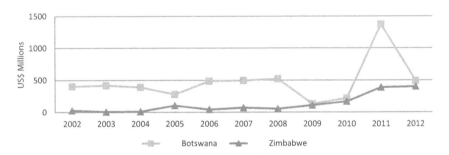

Fig. 10.2 FDI inflows in US$ million: Zimbabwe and Botswana comparison, 2002–2012 (*Source*: Adapted from UNCTAD: UNCTADstat)

The State of FDI in Zimbabwe and Botswana

Zimbabwe and Botswana, with populations of 14.2 and 2.2 million respectively, have received varying amounts of FDI, as shown in Fig. 10.2.

FDI in Zimbabwe is substantially lower than in Botswana (Fig. 10.2). Historically, FDI in Botswana is low (Selelo and Sikwila 2012) but higher than in Zimbabwe. The following section analyses the factors that explain some of these differences in FDI attraction.

Factors Influencing FDI Location Choice

Political Factors

Political Stability

Political risk arises where a host government can change the rules of how businesses operate without notice. The assessment of the political environment by multinational enterprises (MNEs) varies according to location, as the degree of political instability as a determinant could be more profound in some countries than in others (Alcantare and Mitsuhashi 2012). Political risk in the twenty-first century is widespread, with host governments' political institutions (political parties, trade unions and the legal system) being the major sources, as they create, enforce and apply laws that mediate conflict and governmental policies on the economy and social systems. Political instability negatively impacts on FDI inflow as it may interrupt business activities and alter investors' perceptions on location choice, and violence could harm the operations of the firm (Jakobsen 2010; Reiter and Steensma 2010).

Though political risk is a threat to FDI inflows, opportunities such as higher returns on investment offered in politically unstable environments could support a firm's achievement of its internationalisation strategy (Jime'nez et al. 2014; Rios-Morales et al. 2009). During the period 1998–1999, Angola attracted the highest FDI inflows among SSA countries, even though it was considered politically unstable. The returns in petroleum were huge compared to the risk, thus attracting FDI (Asiedu 2002).

Comparing the political environments of Zimbabwe and Botswana for the period 2002–2012, Zimbabwe's reflected instabilities (Fig. 10.3), with the negative scores largely associated with pre- and post-election periods. Furthermore, controversial political events (Land Acquisition Act 1992; Indigenisation Act 2007) destabilised the business environment, impacting negatively on FDI inflows (Copley et al. 2014; Marawanyika and Latham 2014). However, the introduction of new policies by the

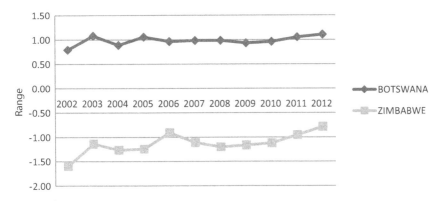

Fig. 10.3 Political stability and absence of violence/terrorism: Zimbabwe and Botswana comparison, 2002–2012 (*Source*: Adapted from World Bank – Worldwide Governance Indicators)

inclusive coalition government (2008–2012) resulted in an improvement in FDI inflows.

By comparison, Botswana, perceived as successful and as a model African country characterised by political stability (Fig. 10.3), with credible, regular, peaceful elections—though the same ruling party has been in power since 1965—attracts constant flows of FDI (Hendricks and Musavengana 2010). Furthermore, there is observance of property rights, correlating with FDI attraction, as ownership advantages (Dunning 2000) are important, as they grant MNEs the right to exercise control of host country subsidiaries (Gwenhamo 2011; Busse and Hefeker 2006; Globerman and Shapiro 2002).

Figure 10.3 compares political stability and absence of violence or terrorism in Zimbabwe and Botswana.

Additionally, FDI is attracted to a host country with the propensity to uphold the rule of law and respect voice accountability. Zimbabwe's tolerance of voice is limited (Fig. 10.4) and internal conflict impacts negatively on FDI. In contrast, Botswana's index is stable and continuously shows signs of improvement, hence it is a favourable location for FDI inflows.

Figure 10.4 illustrates the dimension of these variables.

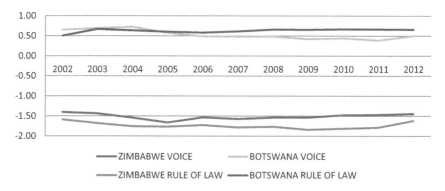

Fig. 10.4 Voice accountability and rule of law: Zimbabwe and Botswana comparison, 2002–2012 (*Source*: Adapted from World Bank – Worldwide Governance Indicators)

Corruption

Corruption is defined as the demanding of bribes from firms in return for the right to operate in a sector, country or location, or the misuse of public power for private benefit (Hill 2014; Rugman and Collinson 2012). It is prevalent in the public sector, and it undermines the decision-making process and retards participants' capabilities (Mudambi et al. 2013; Osei and Gbadamosi 2011). Institutional structures make it difficult to measure corruption; however, as it increases the cost of doing business, it negatively impacts on FDI inflows (Omar and Osei 2015; Al-Sadig 2009; Egger and Winner 2005).

The association of natural resources with corruption results in noticeable adverse effects on economic development and governance, thus making the location unattractive to FDI (Asiedu 2013; Mudambi et al. 2013; Sparks 2011; Reiter and Steensma 2010). Companies that perceive corruption as an unfair practice do not invest in environments that appear to promote corruption. Clinton (2014) viewed corruption and a host country's lack of capacity (human capital, technology, level of openness) to absorb FDI as contributory impediments to inward FDI.

Zimbabwe has more negative corruption indicators than does Botswana (Fig. 10.5), with 2002 being the worst year owing to the land invasions. Zimbabwe does experience some FDI inflows—though the amount is

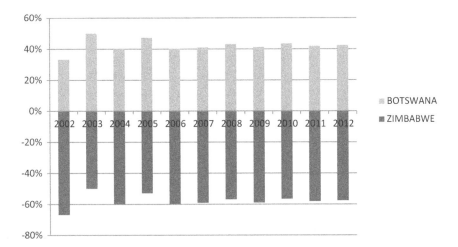

Fig. 10.5 Control of corruption: Zimbabwe and Botswana comparison, 2002–2012 (*Source*: Adapted from World Bank – Worldwide Governance Indicators)

insignificant—because corruption can have a positive impact on FDI, as some MNEs will enter locations shunned by others based on underhanded negotiations by the host government (Egger and Winner 2005).

The Botswana government's active efforts to control corruption have produced positive indicators, with the highest score recorded in 2003. Transparency International ranked it as the least corrupt country in Africa (Njau 2013; Transparency International 2012; van Wyk 2010; Economist Intelligence Unit 2008). Botswana's positive ranking in terms of corruption confirms its attractiveness to FDI.

Taxation Policy

Favourable taxation policy and low tax rates (Suh and Boggs 2011) are incentives for investors and therefore attract larger amounts of FDI inflows (Gondor and Nistor 2012). Countries with small market size normally enact favourable taxation policies to attract FDI, with the Netherlands (Halvorsen 2012) and Botswana falling into this category.

Zimbabwe's tax system is complex, and some aspects are rigid. A change in taxation policy and the introduction of incentives could lure MNEs (Trading Economics 2014; Bloch 2013).

By comparison, Botswana has low taxes with investment incentives (The Heritage Foundation 2014), creating a positive attitude towards investments.

Country Brand and Image

The negative image the world has of Africa may be due to a lack of information about the continent, which consequently affects the ability of individual countries to attract FDI (Osei and Gbadamosi 2011; Cleeve 2008). This is why managing national economic development presents a marketing or business challenge. It requires countries to be managed as brands in order to reap the benefits of full participation on international markets (Magobo and Wakeham 2014; Marundu et al. 2012). Thus the current Zimbabwe brand image, represented in its name, flag and political ideology to portray its functionality, has not yielded the intended benefits. This is due to the period of hyperinflation, the land invasions and, more recently, the indigenisation law, which was perceived as having grabbed assets from firms (Kwinika 2015; Dzirutwe 2014; Maswanganyi and Karombo 2013; Ndlovu 2013; Coomer and Gstraunthaler 2011; Plaut 2011).

On the other hand, Botswana has an exemplary African country brand created through conscious efforts. In 2008, the president of Botswana, Festus Mogae, launched 'Branding Botswana', appointing a company solely to promote and position Brand Botswana on the global map, thus sustaining competitive advantage (Setshogo 2008). In order for Brand Zimbabwe to correct the negative image currently associated with it, substantial effort and participation from country stakeholders and massive promotion internally and externally are crucial.

Economic Factors

Macroeconomic factors (inflation, exchange rates, GDP, unemployment rate, disposable income, consumer confidence and labour costs) and host government policies affect where companies invest. Thus weak institutions often lead to poor macroeconomic policy implementation and negatively affect consumer confidence (Ahmed and van Hulten 2014; Inekwe, 2013; Cleeve 2008; IFC and FIAS 1997). Hence, host countries experience growth from FDI when they have liberalised trade policies, an educated workforce and where the macroeconomic environment is stable (Adams 2011).

Inflation

High inflation rates deter international investors as they have a negative impact on business profitability and could signal poor economic conditions. Inflation rate is also an indicator of monetary and macroeconomic stability that determines a country's economic growth prospects, an important consideration for market-seeking FDI (Suh and Boggs 2011).

The hyperinflation era in Zimbabwe, triggered by the land redistribution programme, reached a peak in 2007, resulting in the Zimbabwean dollar losing value. The government relied on money printing to finance activities, resulting in further weakening of the economy and leading to its total collapse (Coomer and Gstraunthaler 2011). However, the Zimbabwe dollar was abandoned in 2008 and a multi-currency regime was introduced in 2009, leading to stabilisation of the inflation rate. The resultant stability of inflation confirms the effect of inflation on location attractiveness, as in 2009 FDI inflows marginally increased.

Botswana's inflation rate (Fig. 10.6) is relatively stable and fluctuated within normal limits from 2002 to 2012. Botswana's highest rate of inflation was 12.7 % (2008), which, combined with the global financial crisis,

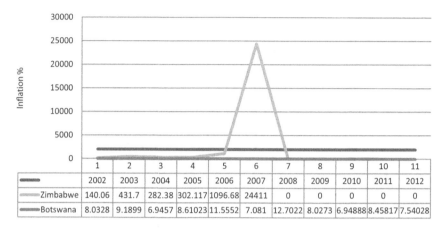

	1	2	3	4	5	6	7	8	9	10	11
▬▬	2002	2003	2004	2005	2006	2007	2008	2009	2010	2011	2012
Zimbabwe	140.06	431.7	282.38	302.117	1096.68	24411	0	0	0	0	0
Botswana	8.0328	9.1899	6.9457	8.61023	11.5552	7.081	12.7022	8.0273	6.94888	8.45817	7.54028

Fig. 10.6 Inflation: Zimbabwe and Botswana comparison, 2002–2012 (*Source*: UNCTAD, UNCTADstat (data is not available from 2008 to 2012 for Zimbabwe))

impacted negatively on FDI inflows. However, the overall stability in Botswana's inflation could make it a more attractive location for FDI (Suh and Boggs 2011).

Exchange Rates

Flexibility in exchange rate policy, with an absence of unfavourable exchange controls, has a positive impact on investors' location decisions. In an imperfect market firms tend to invest in a host country experiencing a devaluation of currency, as borrowing in the host country becomes cheaper (Owusu-Antwi et al. 2013; Basu and Srinivasan 2002). The depreciation of the currency increases location attractiveness to FDI as exports increase (Schmidt and Udo 2009). The volatility of the exchange rate can attract or discourage FDI (Owusu-Antwi et al. 2013).

In Zimbabwe, the use of the multi-currency regime introduced in 2009 has stabilised the economy. The exchange rates follow international markets and hence there is no domestic exchange risk.

Botswana's official currency is the pula. Exchange controls were abolished in 1999, increasing the country's attractiveness to FDI. The pula is pegged against major currencies and is convertible with them.

Gross Domestic Product (GDP) Per Capita

The GDP per capita is considered a determinant for FDI as it is a good indicator of the purchasing power of a country (Vinesh et al. 2014; Bayraktar 2013).

Zimbabwe's GDP tends to fluctuate. In 2002, it was higher than Botswana's, but the deteriorating economic and political environment resulted in a subsequent fall as companies closed down. Low GDP indicates uncertain purchasing power, thus market-seeking FDI could consider the location unattractive. Zimbabwe's income base is distorted owing to high levels of unemployment, with many people working in the informal sector where GDP cannot formally be accounted for. GDP could be important when analysing the purchasing power of a country and useful when firms are considering market-seeking FDI (Vinesh et al. 2014), thus making Zimbabwe unattractive to market-seeking FDI.

Botswana's GDP shows an upward trend, with a high level of economic activity positively impacting on FDI inflows. About 57 % of its population are formally employed as compared to Zimbabwe's 5 %. The purchasing power of the country is improving with the rise of middle-income earners. Botswana's highest contributor to GDP (99.78 %) in 2012 was exports of its commodities from the mining sector.

Figure 10.7 shows a comparison of GDP per capita purchasing power parity (PPP) between Zimbabwe and Botswana for the period 2002–2012.

Unemployment

While recognising the importance of FDI in job creation through technological spillovers (Adams 2011), FDI has also been linked to the destabilisation of domestic employment, degradation of working conditions and exclusion of host country nationals from high-paying positions (Mucuk and Demirsel 2013). The ratio of jobs created as compared to the amount of FDI is small, which could be attributed to the capital-intensive production and labour-saving techniques used by MNEs in host countries.

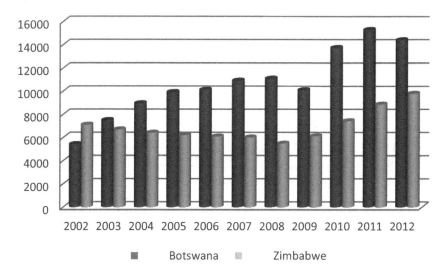

Fig. 10.7 Zimbabwe and Botswana GDP per capita PPP, 2002–2012 (*Source*: Adapted from UNCTAD, UNCTADstat)

Ideally, the number of jobs created by FDI inflows should exceed those lost in the host country through FDI-related activities such as job lay-offs resulting from mergers and acquisitions and closure of local firms (Gohou and Soumare 2011) for FDI to be beneficial to a host country.

While Zimbabwe's unemployment rate is increasing, Botswana's is declining (Fig. 10.8). In Zimbabwe, resource-seeking FDI in the mining sector initially reduced unemployment as mining workers were recruited. However, due to the depletion of alluvial diamonds and the limited capacity of current MNEs in deeper minerals extraction expertise and technology, workers were laid off, worsening the unemployment situation. Thus, resource-seeking FDI has a negative impact on employment (Gohou and Soumare 2011).

Botswana's unemployment rate is 7.5 % (Fig. 10.8). Government is the single largest employer with 47 %, others being mining (3.5 %), agriculture (2 %), and self-employed and informal (35 %) (Botswana Country Profile 2014). The government actively funds programmes that create jobs and reduce unemployment and continues to stimulate economic growth (Bakwena 2012). Although FDI is concentrated in Botswana's mining sector, with 3.5 % of the labour force, it does not seem to play

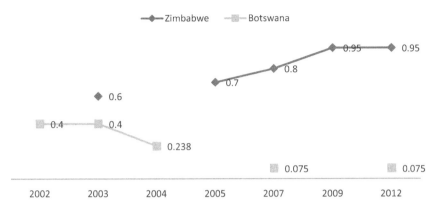

Fig. 10.8 Unemployment rate: Zimbabwe and Botswana comparison, 2002–2012 (*Source*: Adapted from Indexmundi 2014)

a major role in employment creation (World Bank 2011; Alter 1994). Thus, Clinton (2014) mentioned that poverty reduction is the responsibility of the government.

Labour Costs

Labour costs could be linked to the quality of labour, with labour-intensive industries attracting low labour costs as compared to capital-intensive industries (Chan et al. 2013). A firm's major objective is profitability. Thus a location where profit realisation is linked to low production costs such as low wages influences FDI, particularly in resource-seeking FDI (Halvorsen 2012; Kurtish-Kastrati 2013). In contrast, Demirhan and Musca (2008) found no clear link between wages and FDI. However, when labour costs are insignificant, the skills of the labour force can have an impact on FDI location.

Though Zimbabwe has an educated workforce, the labour market is skewed because of the high rate of unemployment. The economy is unable to absorb most of its highly trained, educated and skilled people, leading to skilled people taking up low-paid employment. Resource-seeking FDI directed towards the manufacturing sector could absorb the unemployed at lower cost (Halvorsen 2012; Kurtish-Kastrati 2013).

Botswana has a sophisticated and educated workforce. It has higher costs of labour, and its public sector offers the highest wages in the SSA region. However, the high labour costs (skilled and unskilled) do not correlate with productivity, and total factor productivity such as transport and Internet connectivity costs place a barrier on the diversification of FDI from the mining sector, because MNEs associate quality and productivity with profitability when considering locations (Chan et al. 2013).

Disposable Income

The income distribution of a host country can negatively or positively impact on FDI location choice (Huifang 2006). Studies suggest that FDI increases production and raises income levels.

Zimbabwe is classified as a low-income economy, with a gross national income per capita (GNI) of US$1,035 or less (The World Bank 2013). The implementation of radical policies saw middle-income earners disappear as foreign companies offering attractive wages closed down. Additionally, the low-income earners' disposable income was reduced further, decreasing the consumption rate of goods and services.

Botswana is ranked as a middle-income economy, with a GNI of US$4,126 to US$12,745 per capita and GDP per capita of US$14,696 in 2012 (The World Bank 2013). The economy is growing and FDI inflows into the mining sector have contributed to the development of the economy and increased disposable income. The potential higher demand for products due to higher employment, increased wages and economic growth as a result of the multiplier effect attracts FDI (Ezeoha and Cattaneo 2012).

Socio-Cultural

A social and cultural atmosphere that is sufficiently flexible to embrace foreign influence can encourage FDI (Suh and Boggs 2011). Though MNEs tend to invest in countries that are culturally close to their own home culture (Omar and Osei 2015), FDI inflows can create social divisions owing to the gaps created by wage differentials (Chintrakarn et al. 2011; Georgieva et al. 2012).

Demographics

Countries with strong demographics could use FDI in labour-intensive manufacturing industries leading to job creation and capital accumulation, thus resulting in increased efficiency and technological capabilities. Demographics could influence FDI inflows as cheap labour could be made available by shifting rural labour into manufacturing, potentially influencing FDI inflows ((Neogi 2013; Research and Markets 2005).

Zimbabwe has a population of 14.2 million, and Botswana 2.2 million. Their population annual growth rates stand at 4.38 % and 1.48 % respectively (World Bank 2012). Zimbabwe's market size is bigger, making its demographics attractive to FDI. However, instability in the economic and political environment prevents the country from benefiting from FDI.

Both countries have the same ability to attract Western FDI based on cultural affinity, since they are both former British colonies. However, they differ in their capacity to attract FDI because Botswana's economic and political atmosphere is more conducive to inflows.

Human Capital

The host country's human capital is of importance in the determination of FDI, due to a direct correlation between workforce skills set and FDI attraction (Choong 2012). Therefore, the success of human development hinges on the involvement, commitment and motivation of the host government in pursuing policies that enhance the skills level of the population and build human resource capabilities (Clinton 2014; Reiter and Steensma 2010). Technology-intensive FDI is directed to countries with a highly educated workforce, consequently further developing human capital, while a host country with a less skilled workforce initially attracts less technology-intensive FDI and the pace of development is slower.

Thus, the educational level of human capital and managerial skills are determining factors for firms to invest in a particular sector in a host country (Bayraktar 2013; Nkechi and Okezie 2013).

Zimbabwe had the highest educated and skilled workforce in Africa prior to the reforms that commenced in 2000, with a literacy rate of 95 %. The land reform programme led to a rise in external debt, a drop in GDP and increased political instability. Furthermore, this prompted the political and economic emigration of skilled Zimbabweans to neighbouring countries, as well as abroad, leaving Zimbabwe with a reduced skilled workforce and a severely depleted pool of available talent, affecting resource capacity (Nkechi and Okezie 2013). Therefore, Zimbabwe's human capital base could be creating a barrier to FDI inflows because of the reduced pool of talent.

Botswana's population was historically mostly rural, with its human capital mostly unskilled. In 1987, the government implemented the World Bank global education promotion programme, offering free primary and junior high school, subsequently elevating its literacy rate to 85 % (Tabulawa 2011). Thus its labour market now is generally educated. In effect, the importance of host country government involvement in the development of human capital to facilitate FDI attraction cannot be overemphasised (Reiter and Steensma 2010; Clinton 2014). However, Botswana has limited human capital with the right skills, and shortages in semi-skilled and skilled manual workers are still experienced as more people opt for white collar jobs in the public sector. Botswana's human capital's limited skills set could be impacting on attracting higher levels of, and more diversified, FDI (Basu and Guariglia 2007).

Infrastructure

Infrastructure is categorised as soft (transparent institutions and wider reforms) and hard (highways, rail and airports) (Glass 2009). Generally, good infrastructure is linked to the promotion of productivity and reduction of production costs, while poor infrastructure is considered a major constraint in low-income countries (Vinesh et al. 2014; Behman 2012). However, underdeveloped infrastructure could attract FDI in construction and telecommunications (Marr 1997). But where infrastructure is under government control, there appear to be inefficiencies in service delivery (Suh and Boggs 2011; Glass 2009; Kessides 2004).

Hard Infrastructure

Most of Zimbabwe's hard infrastructure is in desperate need of rehabilitation. Roads, railway, hospitals, schools, water and sewage, and power have deteriorated as the government has little capacity or financial resources to restore them. The state of hard infrastructure could be an incentive for MNEs to invest in this sector (Marr 1997). However, the continuous interruptions of power and water supplies affect normal business operations and result in MNEs incurring additional costs in doing business, making the country unattractive to FDI.

In comparison, Botswana has developed its location advantages (Dunning 2000) in a number of ways. The government has played a significant part in improving its infrastructure (road networks, dams and coal mining), with further plans to invest in railway and information and communication technology. With the increase in middle-class income earners and growth in GDP per capita, the demand on infrastructure for water supplies and utilities is expected to grow, thus creating an opportunity for FDI (Behman 2012).

Soft Infrastructure

Zimbabwe's soft infrastructure is complex, inconsistent and lacks clarity as government policies, the banking system and other organisations lag behind world standards. There is ambiguity and conflicting legislation, making the legal framework uncoordinated. According to Ezeoha and Cattaneo (2012), all aspects of soft infrastructure are important when evaluating location attractiveness.

Botswana has effective state institutions in place, making the legal and regulatory framework environment transparent. Processes and procedures are enforced, making FDI applications and approvals efficient, thus encouraging FDI inflows.

Natural Resources

A host country's comparative advantage in the natural resource sector attracts resource-seeking FDI. Most FDI to Africa, particularly the SSA region, and Zimbabwe and Botswana is targeted towards natural resources, especially the extractive industry (Ezeoha and Cattaneo 2012).

Zimbabwe and Botswana are both rich in natural resources. In Zimbabwe most of the vertical FDI in the extractive industry originates from China. There has been no noticeable improvement in economic growth, unemployment or poverty reduction from realised mineral revenues. Thus, natural resources have no significant impact on economic development, but increase corruption tendencies (Mudambi et al. 2013; Sparks 2011; Jenkins and Edwards, 2006).

Botswana is the second-largest diamond producer in the world by volume and the largest producer in terms of output value (UNCTAD 2003), contributing 40 % to GDP. Consequently, mining sector FDI has transformed its economy. The availability of natural resources in some cases makes a location attractive (Asiedu 2006), as seen in Botswana.

Legal and Regulatory Framework

The state of the legal regulatory framework influences MNEs in location choice. Protective and restrictive trade policies might prohibit international competition, as they protect the domestic market while suppressing firms' options for managing operations (Ahmed and van Hulten 2014; Dewit et al. 2009). Therefore good governance, in the form of legal and regulatory frameworks, constitutes one of the determinants of FDI (Buss and Hefeker 2006; Globerman and Shapiro, 2003; 2002).

Employment Law

Locations with more labour union involvement deter FDI, as firms are reluctant to move production facilities to those locations (Floyd 2003).

Zimbabwe's trade union movements are closely monitored by the government, which interferes in most aspects of the law and economy, and is detrimental to FDI inflows. In Botswana, the size of the population and its small market led to noticeable shortages in skilled human resource. However, the country made favourable changes to its policies, making it easier to employ foreign workers, in order to close the gap in human capital and make the labour market flexible (Suh and Boggs 2011).

Company Law and Business Regulation

Locations that display weaknesses in institutional structures may beshunned. Evidence has shown that some countries within the SSA regionfall into this category (Marr 1997). In order to mitigate this drawback, most foreign investors use joint ventures and merger as mode of entry. A weak legal and regulatory framework in the host country also facilitates easier exit for MNEs (Georgieva et al. 2012).

The laws and business regulation frameworks in Zimbabwe can be changed arbitrarily (Land Acquisition 1992; Indigenisation and Empowerment Act 2007), without weighing the impact on society and the economy, and negatively impacting on FDI (Jenkins and Edwards, 2006).

In comparison, in Botswana the regulatory framework is adhered to, as the government respects company laws and business regulations, which are viewed as a necessity for doing business. The stability in the legal and regulatory framework prompted De Beers Diamond Trading Company to relocate from London to Botswana in 2013 (Kariuki et al. 2014; van Wyk 2010), a favourable FDI indicator.

Openness to Trade and Bilateral Agreements

Openness to trade is described as the ease and cost by which goods and services, factors of production (capital, labour and skills) and technology can flow in and out of a country freely (Anderson 2005). Countries that have active membership with various trading partners often attract FDI, as there are benefits that accrue from being a member that are beneficial to investors. Minimal government interference in the economy leads to FDI inflows (Brafu-Insaidoo and Biekpe 2014; Globerman and Shapiro, 2003).

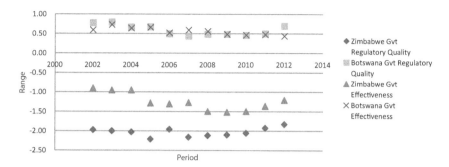

Fig. 10.9 Regulatory quality and government effectiveness: Zimbabwe and Botswana comparison, 2002–2012 (*Source*: Adapted from World Bank – Worldwide Governance Indicators)

Zimbabwe is a member of various trading organisations, and has bilateral trade agreements with neighbouring countries, such as the Trade Agreement Group. All the arrangements provide frameworks for further liberalisation of trade. Botswana's openness to trade facilitated the placement of its commodities on the global market. The country's 2014 economic freedom score was 72, and it was ranked the 27th freest economy out of 178 countries in 2014, taking second place in the sub-Saharan African region of 54 countries (Van Wyk and Lal, 2010).

Figure 10.9 shows a comparison of the two countries.

Conclusions

This chapter has addressed foreign direct investment in SSA, with particular emphasis on the comparison between Zimbabwe and Botswana. It is clear that FDI inflows differ significantly between Zimbabwe and Botswana. FDI is an important topic that has received a great deal of attention from researchers. However, this particular research is unique, as the study concentrates on an area that has not been explored before. This chapter brings into sharp focus the crucial determinants of FDI in these neighbouring countries with contrasting fortunes in FDI attraction. Essentially, the fortunes of these countries hinge largely on how their location variables have been managed. In addition, the significance of FDI determinants may vary from country to country.

Specifically, the results from the research showed key determinants that affect location attractiveness for Zimbabwe and Botswana. Political stability, economic, socio-cultural, technology and legal factors are key considerations when MNEs consider investing in a host country. However, the evidence from this study shows that these key determinants are not universally applicable as FDI determinants, as economies differ geographically, in addition to the factors listed above. Caution should be applied when analysing and applying these determinants. The FDI location attractiveness in relation to Zimbabwe and Botswana is generally in line with the theories of foreign direct investment, albeit with different experiences and results, depending on implementation.

With a bigger market than Botswana, and a larger human capital base, Zimbabwe could create favourable conditions for MNEs to provide FDI. Dependence on advantages from risky FDI considerations alone is not enough to pull Zimbabwe into a favourable FDI position, as all the other determinants are more critical and provide a wider and bigger attraction rating for FDI.

In accordance with FDI theories and key determinants findings, this chapter concludes that Botswana has systematically and consistently improved its political and economic environment for the period under study (2002–2012), in an effort to be an attractive country for FDI. The political environment is stable, corruption is not tolerated, taxation is low, GDP is high, legal and regulatory frameworks are favourable, and so is the highly educated human capital—all key determinants for attracting FDI. The recognition of and adherence to the principles that govern FDI inflows have been observed for the benefit of the economy, resulting in higher inflows of FDI as compared to neighbouring Zimbabwe. During the same period, Zimbabwe was experiencing political instability due to the implementation of unfavourable policies (land seizures, controversial elections and indigenisation) and high taxation rates were announced. All this culminated in a falling GDP, high unemployment and poverty, a depleted workforce and rampant corruption. Though Zimbabwe has the capability to recognise the key factors for attracting FDI, it has not been consistent in its policy application, causing confusion in both the political and economic environment, creating an unfavourable environment that does not attract meaningful FDI to redress the political and economic woes.

Political stability is one of the key determinants making Botswana an attractive place to do business. Zimbabwe and Botswana are similar politically in that their ruling parties have been in government since independence. However, Botswana has a stable political environment that respects democracy, shuns corruption, allows voice and upholds the rule of law. Zimbabwe seems to be the opposite in all these factors.

It is interesting that two neighbouring countries with similar colonial backgrounds can have paradoxically different results in their economies, as the result of a conscious but different application of and attitude towards similar policies that have a direct bearing on attracting FDI. The results, over the period in consideration, clearly show that one country prefers to reap the benefits from positive and consistent implementation of beneficial policies, while the other appears to wilfully ignore international norms and theories, and haphazardly carries out policies that are both detrimental and counter-productive to FDI attraction, leading to dire economic consequences.

References

Adams, S. (2011). Foreign direct investment, domestic investment, and economic growth in sub-Saharan Africa. *Journal of Policy Modeling, 31*(6), 939–949.

Ahmed, A. D., & Van Hulten, A. (2014). Financial globalization in Botswana and Nigeria: A critique of the thresholds paradigm. *The Review of Black Political Economy, 41*(2), 177–203.

Alcantara, L. L., & Mitsuhashi, H. (2012). Make-or-break decisions in choosing foreign direct investment locations. *Journal of International Management, 18*, 335–351.

Ali Al-Sadig, A. (2009). The effects of corruption on FDI inflows. *Canton Journal, 29*(2), 267–294.

Alter, R. (1994). Foreign investment: Engine for employment? *OECD Observer, 190*, 4.

Anderson, E. (2005). Openness and inequality in developing countries: A review of theory and recent evidence, Overseas Development Institute, London, UK. *World Development, 33*(7), 1045–1063.

Anyanwu, J. C. (2011). Why does foreign direct investment go where it goes?: New evidence from African countries. *Annals of Economic and Finance, 13*(2), 425–462.

Asiedu, E. (2002). On the determinants of foreign direct investment to developing countries: Is Africa different? *World Development, 30*(1), 107–119.

Asiedu, E. (2006). Foreign direct investment in Africa: The role of natural resources, market size, government policy, institutions and political instability. *The World Economy, 29*(1), 63–77.

Asiedu, E. (2013). *Foreign direct investment, natural resources and institutions.* International Growth Centre, Working paper (Online). http://www.theigc. org/wp-content/uploads/2014/09/Asiedu-2013-Working-Paper.pdf

Bakwena, M. (2012). The recent economic reforms in Botswana: A critical assessment. *Botswana Journal of African Studies, 26*(1), 39–49.

Basu, A., & Guariglia, A. (2007). Foreign direct investment, inequality and growth. *Journal of Macroeconomics, 29*(4), 824–839.

Basu, A., & Srinivsan, K. (2002). *Foreign direct investment in Africa—Some case studies* (IMF working paper WP/02/61). Washington, DC: International Monetary Fund.

Bayraktar, N. (2013). Foreign direct investment and investment climate. *International Conference on Applied Economics, 5*, 83–92.

Behname, M. (2012). Foreign direct investment and urban infrastructure: An evidence from southern Asia. *Journal in Advances in Management & Applied Economics, 2*(4), 253–259.

Bloch, E. (2013). More tax changes critical for Zimbabwe, Zimbabwe independent (online). *The Independent.* Available at: http://www.theindependent. co.zw/2013/11/15/tax-changes-critical-zimbabwe/

Botswana Country Profile (2014). *The programme of action for sustainable development in Botswana with specific reference to the cross-cutting issues, introduction,* Action for Southern Africa (ACTSA): London.

Brafu-Insaidoo, W. G., & Biekpe, N. (2014). Determinants of foreign capital flows: The experience of selected sub-Saharan African countries. *Journal of Applied Economics, 17*(1), 63–88.

Busse, M., & Hefeker, C. (2006). Political risk, institutions and foreign direct investment. *European Journal of Political Economy, 23*, 397–415.

Cavusgil, S. T., Knight, G., & Riesenberger, J. R. (2013). *A framework for international business, international edition.* New York: Pearson.

Chan, M. W. L., Hou, K., Li, X., & Mountain, D. C. (2013). Foreign direct investment and its determinants: A regional panel causality analysis. *The Quarterly Review of Economics and Finance, 54*(4), 579–589.

Chintrakarn, P., Herzer, D., & Nunnenkamp, P. (2011). Fdi and income inequality: Evidence from a panel of U.S. *States, Economic Inquiry, 50*(3), 788–801.

Choong, C. K. (2012). Does domestic financial development enhances the linkages between foreign direct investment and economic growth? *Empirical Economics, 42*(3), 819–834.

Cleeve, E. (2008). How effective are fiscal incentives to attract FDI to sub-Saharan Africa? *The Journal of Developing Areas, 42*(1), 135–153.

Clinton, B. (2014). *Inclusive capitalism conference.* Mansion House, Guildhall, London.

Coomer, J., & Gstraunthaler, T. (2011). The hyperinflation in Zimbabwe. *The Quarterly Journal of Austrian Economics, 141*(31), 311–346.

Copley, A., Maret-Rakotondrazaka, F., & Sy, A. (2014). *The U.S.—Africa leaders' summit: A focus on foreign direct investment.* Brookings Institution, USA.

Demirhan, E., & Masca, M. (2008). Determinants of foreign direction investment flows in developing countries: A cross-sectional analysis. *Prague Economic Papers, 4*, 356–369.

Dewit, G., Gorg, H., & Montagna, C. (2009). Should I stay or should I go? Foreign direct investment, employment protection and domestic anchorage. *Review of World Economics, 145*, 93–110.

Dunning, J. H. (2000). The eclectic paradigm as an envelope for economic and business theories of MNE activity. *International Business Review, 9*(2), 163–190.

Dzirutwe, M. (2014, May 22). New Zim land invasions raise concerns for foreign firms (online). *Mail & Guardian Africa.*

Egger, P., & Winner, H. (2005). Evidence of corruption as an incentive for FDI. *European Journal of Political Economy, 21*(4), 932–952.

Ezeoha, A. E., & Cattaneo, N. (2012). FDI flows to Sub-Saharan Africa: The impact of finance, institutions, and natural resource endowment. *Comparative Economic Studies, 54*(3), 597–632.

Floyd, D. (2003). How can a flexible labour market influence the amount of foreign direct investment attracted by a host nation. The case of UK. *European Business Review, 15*(5), 334.

Georgievaa, D., Jandikb, T., & Lee, W. Y. (2012). The impact of laws, regulations, and culture on cross-border joint ventures. *Journal of International Financial Markets, Institutions & Money, 22*, 774–795.

Glass, A. J. (2009). *Infrastructure and foreign direct investment.* Princeton: Princeton University Press.

Globerman, S., & Shapiro, D. (2002). Global foreign direct investment flows: The role of governance infrastructure. *World Development, 30*(11), 1899–1919, 20.

Globerman, S., & Shapiro, D. (2003). Governance infrastructure and US foreign direct investment. *Journal of International Business Studies, 34*(1), 19.

Gohou, G., & Soumare, I. (2011). Does foreign direct investment reduce poverty in Africa and are there regional differences? *World Development, 40*(1), 75–95.

Gondor, M., & Nistor, P. (2012). Fiscal policy and foreign direct investment: Evidence from some emerging EU economies (8th International strategic management conference). *Procedia – Social and Behavioural Sciences, 58*, 1256–1266.

Gwenhamo, F. (2011). Foreign direct investment in Zimbabwe: The role of institutional and macroeconomic factors. *South African Journal of Economics, 79*(3), 211–223.

Halvorsen, T. (2012). Size, location and agglomeration of inward foreign direct investment (FDI) in the United States. *Regional Studies Association, 46*(5), 669–682.

Hendricks, C. and Musavengana, T (2010). *The Security Sector of Southern Africa* Institute of Security Studies Africa (online). Available at: http://www.issafrica.org/uploads/Mono174.pdf

Hill, C. W. L. (2014). *International business: Competing in the global marketplace* (10th Global ed.). Berkshire: McGraw-Hill Education.

Huifang, L. (2006). The theory basis on location choice in FDI of the multinational enterprise. *Canadian Social Science, 2*(6), 72–75.

IMF. (2013). *World economic and financial surveys, regional economic outlook, Sub-Saharan African*. International Monetary Fund, Publication Services, USA (online) available at: https://www.imf.org/external/pubs/ft/reo/2016/afr/eng/pdf/sreo0416.pdf

Indexmundi. (2014). *Unemployment rate index* (online). http://www.indexmundi.com/g/g.aspx?v=74&c=zi&l=en

Inekwe, J. N. (2013). FDI, employment and economic growth in Nigeria. *African Development Review, 25*(4), 421–431.

International Finance Corporation and Foreign Investment Advisory Service. (1997). *Foreign direct investment*. Washington, DC: Library of the Congress Cataloguing.

International Monetary Fund (IMF). (2004). *IMF committee on balance of payments and OECD workshop on International investment statistics direct investment technical expert group (DITEG)*. Definition of foreign direct investment (FDI terms, issue paper (DITEG) 20 (online)).

Jakobsen, J. (2010). Old problems remain, new opens crop up: Political risk in the 21st century. *Business Horizons, 53*(5), 481–490.

Jenkins, R., & Edwards, C. (2006). The economic impacts of China and India on sub-Saharan Africa: Trends and prospects. *Journal of Asian Economics, 17*(2), 207–225.

Jime'nez, A., Luis-Rico, I., & Benito-Osorio, D. (2014). The influence of political risk on the scope of internationalization of regulated companies: Insights from a Spanish sample. *Journal of World Business, 49*(3), 301–311.

Kariuki, P., Abraha, F., & Obuseng, S. (2014). *Botswana 2014, African Economic Outlook, OfDB, OECD, UNDP* (online). Available at: http://www.africaneconomicoutlook.org/fileadmin/uploads/aeo/2014/PDF/CN_Long_EN/Botswana_EN.pdf

Kessides, I. N. (2004). Reforming infrastructure privatization, regulation, and competition. *A World Bank Policy Research Report*. A co-publication of the World Bank and Oxford University Press.

Kurtishi-Kastrati. (2013). Impact of FDI economic growth: An overview of the main theories of FDI and empirical research. *European Scientific Journal, 9*(7): ISSN 1857-7881.

Kwinika, S. (2015, July 6). Zimbabwe 51% local ownership law applies only to fine products like minerals; minister (online). *Mail & Guardian Africa.*

Magobo, V. V., & Wakeman, M. (2014). Re-branding Zimbabwe: A transformative and challenging process. *Mediterranean Journal of Social Sciences, 5*(27), 298–310.

Marawanyika, G., & Latham, B. (2014). *Zimbabwe wants 2015 FDI to double as ownership law clarified* (online) http://www.bloomberg.com/news/articles/2014-06-30/zimbabwe-wants-2015-fdi-to-rise-to-2-billion-on-empowerment-law.

Marr, A. (1997). *Foreign direct investment flows to low-income countries: A review of the evidence overseas development institute* (Briefing paper 3), (online) Available at: http://www.oecd.org/env/1819582.pdf.

Marundu, E. E., Amanze, D. N., & Mtagulawa, T. (2012). Nation branding: An analysis of Botswana nation brand. *International Journal of Business Administration, 3*(2), 17–27.

Maswanganyi, N., & Karombo, T (2013, April 25). Zimbabwe asset grab like South Africa's BEE (online). *African Business.*

Mucuk, M., & Demirsel, M. T. (2013). The effect of foreign direct investment on unemployment: Evidence from panel data for seven developing countries. *Journal of Business, Economics and Finance, 2*(3), 2146–7943.

Mudambi, R., Navarra, P., & Delios, A. (2013). Government regulation, corruption and FDI. *Asia Pacific Journal Management, 30*(2), 487–511.

Ndlovu, R. (2013, January 18). 'Fear' drives indigenisation in Zimbabwe (online). *Mail & Guardian Africa.*

Neogi, S. (2013). FDI is now looking beyond China, to India. *Financial Express.* New Delhi.

Njau, B. (2013, August 13). Botswana shines brightly (online). FDI intelligence, London, *The Financial Times Limited.*

Nkechi, O. A., & Okezie, O. K. (2013). Investigating the interaction between foreign direct investment and human capital on growth: Evidence from Nigeria. *Asian Economic and Financial Review, 3*(9), 1134–1151.

Omar, M., & Osei, C. (2015). An investigative analysis of the factors influencing degree of involvement in a foreign market. *Transnational Marketing Journal, 3*(1), 45–60.

Osei, C., & Gbadamosi, A. (2011). Rebranding Africa. *Marketing Intelligence and Planning, 29*(3), 284–304.

Owusu-Antwi, G., Antwi, J., & Polu, P. K. (2013). Foreign direct investment: A journey to economic growth in Ghana – empirical evidence. *International Business & Economic Research Journal, 12*(5), 573–584.

Plaut, M. (2011, December 1). Are Zimbabwe's new farmers winning, 10 years on? (online). *BBC News, World Service Africa.*

Reiter, S. L., & Steensma, H. K. (2010). Human development and foreign direct investment in developing countries: The influence of FDI policy and corruption. *World Development Journal, 38*(12), 1678–1691.

Research and Markets. (2005, April 21). With over 51 million people in India owning mobile phones – there are significant opportunities for content providers. *PR Newswire*, New York.

Rios-Morales, R., Tom, D. G., & Azuaje, S. F. (2009). Innovative methods in assessing political risk for business internationalization. *Research in International Business and Finance, 23*(2), 144–156.

Rugman, A. M., & Collinson, S. (2012). *International business* (6th ed.). Harlow: Pearson Education Limited.

Schmidt, C. W., & Udo, B. (2009). Real exchange-rate uncertainty and US foreign direct investment: An empirical analysis. *Review of World Economics, 145*(3), 513–530.

Selelo, S. E., & Sikwila, M. N. (2012). Determinants of fixed foreign direct investment in Botswana. *Journal of Economics and Behavioural Studies, 4*(7), 414–422.

Sethogo, T. (2008, January 30). *Branding Botswana on course – Makgato-Malesu* (online) Wednesday. Available at: http://www.mmegi.bw/index. php?sid=4&aid=17&dir=2008/January/Wednesday30

Sparks, D. L. (2011). India and China's growing economic involvement in sub-Saharan Africa. *Journal of African Studies and Development, 3*(4), 65–75.

Suh, T., & Boggs, D. J. (2011). Communications infrastructure and traditional determinants of inward foreign investment: A comparison of developed and emerging markets. *International Business Journal, 21*(2), 205–223.

Tabulawa, R. (2011). The rise and attenuation of the basic education programme (BEP) in Botswana: A global local dialectic approach. *International Journal of Educational Development, 31*(5), 427–436.

The Economist Intelligence Unit Limited (2008) Botswana Economy: The southern star, Available at: ABI/INFORM Complete ProQuest (Accessed 29th June 2014).

The Heritage Foundation. (2014). *2014 Index of economic freedom, Botswana.* Available at: http://www.heritage.org/index/country/botswana. Accessed 30 July 2014.

The World Bank. (2011). *World Development Indicators Statistics for small states a supplement to the World Development Indicators 2011.* Available online: http://cetglad.org/OPEN%20REPOSITORY/World_Development_Indicators_2011.pdf

The World Bank (2012). Countries and Economies, (online) Available at: http://data.worldbank.org/country/

The World Bank. (2013). *Population growth rate, World developmental indicators* (online) Available at: http://data.worldbank.org/indicator/SP.POP.GROW.

Trading Economics. (2014). *Zimbabwe corporate tax rate.* (online) Available at: http://www.tradingeconomics.com/zimbabwe/corporate-tax-rate

Transparency International. (2012). *Corruption perceptions index* (online). Available at: http://www.transparency.org/cpi2012/results

United Nations Conference on Trade and Development. (2003). *World investment report, 2003 FDI policies for development.* New York/Geneva.

United Nations Conference for Trade and Development (2015). Investment Trends Monitor No. 20. FDI Can Be An Important Source Of External Development Financing For Ldcs, Lldcs And Sids. New York/Geneva.

Van Wyk, J. (2010). Double diamonds, real diamonds: Botswana's national competitiveness. *Academy of Marketing Studies Journal, 14*(2), 55–76.

Van Wyk, J., & Lal, A. K. (2010). FDI location drivers and risks in MENA. *Journal of International Business Research, 9*(2).

Vinesh, S. R., Boopendra, S., & Hemraze, D. (2014). Determinants of foreign direct investment in SADC: An empirical analysis. *The Business and Management Review, 4*(4), 46–158.

Part VI

Banking and Finance

11

The Kenyan Banking Industry: Challenges and Sustainability

Samuel Muiruri Muriithi and Lynette Louw

Introduction

The banking industry plays an important role in an economy and is often regarded as the engine that drives economic development and the lifeline of the economy and society in both developed and developing nations (Adeyemi 2007; Kumbirai and Webb 2010). As such the banking industry is able to influence a country's economic development and long-term sustainability by offering different services (UNEP FI 2007). The main services provided by the banking industry include facilitating money transfers between countries and ensuring that savers and borrowers are brought together in well-organised structures, as well as borrowing and lending, agency services, trade facilitation and money control

S.M. Muriithi (✉)
School of Business and Economics, Daystar University, Nairobi, Kenya

L. Louw
Department of Management, Rhodes University, Grahamstown, South Africa

© The Author(s) 2017   **197**
A. Ahmed (ed.), *Managing Knowledge and Innovation for Business
Sustainability in Africa*, DOI 10.1007/978-3-319-41090-6_11

(Nagar et al. 2011; Kashyap et al. 2002). These services by the banking industry are instrumental in enhancing world development and financial stability.

In Africa, the banking industry is playing an increasingly important role in sustainable development. Across the African continent, numerous banks are championing sustainability and re-engineering their operations in order to integrate the environment, technology, social responsibility and governance (UNEP FI 2005). The growing trend toward sustainability is evident in countries like Botswana, Kenya, Nigeria, Senegal and South Africa. These countries have introduced strategies and mechanisms meant to make their banking industries sustainable in the long run.

Despite the importance of the banking industry for economic and social development and its focus on sustainability, the banking industry worldwide has experienced several financial challenges which have threatened to cripple the industry, thereby negatively affecting the economic performance of most countries. Notable banking crises occurred in the 1940s–1950s, 1980s–1990s and from 2007–2009. However, the 2007–2009 financial crisis is considered the worst, as it almost brought major world economies to a standstill, with most nations still recording negative economic growth, a trend that may continue for several years (Grant Thornton 2013). The period has been described as the most turbulent in relation to the world economy (Deloitte 2012).

It has been asserted that the past and present challenges facing the banking industry worldwide can be associated with lack of strong leadership and management (Donnelly 1994). The banking industries of African countries, among them Kenya, have also been victims of poor leadership and management, especially between the 1970s and the 2000s, a situation that has threatened the industry's sustainability (Waweru and Kalani 2009).

The purpose of this chapter is to examine the Kenyan banking industry in relation to performance and sustainability. First, the chapter examines the overall importance of the banking industry and the challenges it faces. Second, it focuses on the Kenyan banking industry, including its history and the reasons for its poor performance and recovery. Third, the chapter addresses the contemporary Kenyan banking industry. Finally, the future of the Kenyan banking industry in terms of performance and sustainability is explored.

The Importance of the Banking Industry

Given the positive role played by the banking industry in a given economy, it is essential to identify the specific activities performed by the banks in order to steer development and sustainability. These activities, which include borrowing and lending, agency services, facilitating trade, and money supply control, will subsequently be discussed.

Borrowing and Lending The banking industry provides a number of economic services to its customers. The leading service is borrowing and lending to customers. Through its role of borrowing and lending, the banking industry facilitates money supply by taking deposits from customers and then lending the money to those who need it (Kumbirai and Webb 2010:35). These services not only increase the production capacity of the community or nation but also accelerate the pace of economic growth and sustainability (Russo and Ugolini 2008).

Agency Services The banking industry provides a range of investment services to its customers. Upon opening various accounts, such as current and savings accounts, the banks offer services like settling of indebtedness between customers by facilitating credit transfers, standing orders, clearing cheques, access to loans and overdraft facilities, payment of dividends and debt transfers (Hoyle and Whitehead 1982:42; Kumbirai and Webb 2010). By doing so, banks have become the lifeline of businesses and the gatekeepers to capital provision. Similarly, banks provide loans and credit to millions of businesses and individuals throughout the world (UNEP FI 2007).

Facilitating Trade In addition, the banking industry plays an important role in facilitating trade within and between countries and providing logistical support. This role has eased business operations and ensured the survival of businesses which would otherwise find it difficult or impossible to operate. The specific activities that the banks facilitate include: foreign exchange transactions, executorships and trust services, export trade payments, tax advice, investment management and stock blocking (Hoyle and Whitehead 1982:42). In an effort to offer overseas trading

services, some banks have set up branches in foreign countries specialising in trade financing and advising. The branches, for instance, are
able to provide a comprehensive network of services for businesses and
persons interested in foreign transactions. The banks or their branches
have also acted as sources of information on overseas trading opportunities and challenges. The results of such activities are savings in time and
money, as well as smooth business transactions among businesses located
in different parts of the world (Economic Commission for Africa 2011;
Kumbirai and Webb 2010).

Money Supply and Control The banks, through the coordination
efforts of the central banks, are able to facilitate money supply and regulation in an economy. This enables commercial banks to control the money
available in the economy by gathering small savings from customers and
combining them into larger deposits which are then channelled into the
right enterprises (Kumbirai and Webb 2010). By controlling money supply, the banks are able to regulate the level of sustainable development in
an economy.

The Challenges of the Banking Industry

Although the banking industry has played, and continues to play, a critical role in facilitating world economic development, the industry still
continues to face a number of challenges. The main challenges are non-
performing loans, global financial difficulties, poor leadership and sustainability pressure.

Banks' Non-performing Loans The challenge of banks' non-performing
loans continues to plague the banking industry worldwide. The problem
is mostly associated with the crisis resulting from 'rapid accumulation of
nonperforming loans in the banking industry and a deterioration of asset
quality in the face of increased credit risks' (Fofack 2005:5). In Africa, for
instance, the proportion of non-performing loans reached over 30 % of
total loans. This was the highest level ever for the developing world. In
fact, during the Asian financial crisis of 1997, which was said to be the

worst, the rate did not exceed 25 % of total loans (Fofack 2005:5). The problem of non-performing loans is not unique to Africa. According to Kroszner (2002), non-performing loans are closely linked to banking crises and overall sustainability. In Japan, for example, the banking industry continued to suffer the effect of non-performing loans experienced in the 1990s, leading to the loss of billions in yen as a result of the collapse in asset prices (Sultana 2000). The Japanese government had to intervene to rectify the situation in an effort to regain market confidence and ensure a stable financial environment (Waweru and Kalani 2009:13). As such, non-performing loans impact negatively on the banking industry and present challenges to realising its sustainability.

Global Financial Crisis   Between 1970 and 2000, the world witnessed several financial crises that greatly hindered smooth operations of the banking industry worldwide. Given the critical role played by the banking industry in economic development, financial crises have an adverse effect on the economic stability of countries. Many banks collapsed during the global crisis of 2007–2009, leading to worsening economic situations in many countries. In spite of the deteriorating global financial situation, some countries' banking industries were able to withstand the pressure and continued to prosper against all odds. For instance, the Canadian banks remained relatively stable, while the neighbouring US banks continued to experience major financial shocks (Elliot 2008). The global financial crisis posed a serious threat to banks' sustainability and overall performance (UNEP FI 2005).

Poor Leadership   The role of effective leadership is instrumental in the attainment of successful performance by banks. Besides the positive role played by the banking industry, the industry has been in the spotlight due to its undesirable leadership practices. According to Donnelly (1994:12), 'management and leadership issues are critical' to bank success. It is interesting to note, however, that leadership has received very little attention within the banking industry. In fact, the biggest challenge facing the banking industry could easily be summarised as 'poor leadership' (Waweru and Kalani 2009). It is further notable that those involved in banking management 'lack the skills to provide leadership in a deregulated environment' (Donnelly 1994:12). With poor leadership, no sustainability mechanisms will work.

Sustainability Pressure Like elsewhere in the world, the need for sustainable banking practices has put pressure on African banks to comply. The major drivers of sustainability within the banking industry have been the development of regulatory frameworks aimed at making financial institutions responsible for their environmental and social impacts, expansion of international standards and governance code, and increasing pressures from stakeholders (UNEP IF 2005). However, even with these efforts, various challenges still hinder the attainment of the desired level of sustainability. Such challenges include corruption, currency fluctuations, political interference, inadequate infrastructures and poor technical know-how (UNEP IF 2005). These challenges threaten African banks' competitiveness and survival, a situation that also affects the Kenyan banking industry.

The History of the Kenyan Banking Industry

Between the years 1963 and 1982, the Kenyan economy was very prosperous compared to those of its neighbouring countries. The prosperity of the industry was attributed to good monetary and fiscal policies instituted by the government. This made the financial industry very industrious, resulting in sound economic growth (Central Bank of Kenya,1994).

In the 1980s and 1990s, several countries, both developed and developing, experienced severe banking crises which affected their financial, social and economic performance. To overcome the challenges, the International Monetary Fund (IMF) demanded that countries overhaul their banking systems (IMF 1998). Kenya was no exception, and as such had its share of banking crises.

The crises in Kenya started in 1982 after the government relaxed financial control measures, making way for an increase in the number of financial institutions. Unfortunately, this action by the government opened up what had been a professional and disciplined career to non-professional business people whose interest was in profit and self-gratification

(Ambutsi 2005). As a result, professional management was replaced by poor governance, mismanagement and political interference, which led to the collapse of a number of banks (Ambutsi 2005). To rectify the situation, the Central Bank of Kenya introduced strict measures in the industry between 1994 and 2002. These measures included the establishment of a reserve and deposit protection fund, insurance schemes and an increase in minimal capital requirements for bank starters (Central Bank of Kenya 1994). However, despite these strict measures, 32 banks were liquidated or put under receivership, with 14 of them collapsing in 1993 (Central Bank of Kenya 2004). The situation deteriorated further, and by 1998 37 banks had collapsed despite the Central Bank of Kenya's efforts to salvage them (Kithinji and Waweru 2007; Ngugi 2001). In 1998, the losses arising from non-performing loans stood at Ksh. 80 billion, or 30 % of advances, an increase from Ksh. 58.4 billion in 1997 (Central Bank of Kenya, 1999). By world standards, the Kenyan non-performing loans were too high (30 %) in 1999, putting the banks at even greater risk in recovering them. By the year 2000, the Kenyan banking industry had plunged into a crisis mostly associated with under-capitalisation, high levels of non-performing loans, political interference, corruption and poor governance (Honohan and Laeven 2005). This meant that the sustainability of the banking industry was severely affected.

Causes of Past Poor Banking Performance in Kenya

The banks' overall poor performance has been blamed on non-performing loans, weak internal control measures, political interference, corruption and lack of leadership.

Non-performing Loans In the past, the major challenge within the Kenyan banking industry was non-performing loans, which accounted for 42 % of banks' loan portfolios. According to the Kenyan Central Bank, non-performing loans were loans not serviced as per the contract with the borrower, thus subjecting the financial institution to potential losses (Central Bank of Kenya 2001). In an effort to address this challenge, the Central Bank of Kenya demanded to be a partner in controlling the bad debts at a manageable level (Economic Report on Africa 2002:143). However, the actions taken by the Central Bank of Kenya to assist banks in reducing non-performing loans was just one way to react to the worsening performance of the banks. Unfortunately, more banks in Kenya did not perform well and eventually closed down. Between the years 2000 and 2001, five banks were put under statutory management, while one building society was placed under investigation. Three of the banks were able to reopen, one was liquidated, while one remained under statutory management (Economic Report on Africa 2002:143). For two years the non-performing loans stood at Ksh. 73.6 billion (2001) and Ksh. 76.1 billion (2002) respectively. A summary of the Kenyan banking industry non-performing loans during the period of the worst financial crisis is represented in Table 11.1.

Table 11.1 shows an increase in non-performing loans from Ksh. 31.8 billion in 1995 to Ksh. 74.6 billion in 2003, or 134.6 %. During the same period, the year 1999 had the worst non-performing loan rate of Ksh. 97.2 billion. Similarly, the loans issued during the same period ranged from Ksh. 180.2 billion in 1995 to Ksh. 270.1 billion in 2003. Likewise, 1997 was the worst performing year, with total loans of Ksh. 284.2 billion. This indicates that compared to loans given during the same period, non-performing loans far exceeded what was issued, a very gloomy picture for the banking industry. It is also notable that the period 2001–2003 showed a

Table 11.1 Kenyan banking industry non-performing loans 1995–2003

Year	Non-performing loans (in Ksh. billion)	Total loans (in Ksh. billion)	Percentage (%)
1995	31.8	180.2	17.6
1996	37.9	213.7	17.7
1997	69.0	248.2	27.8
1998	83.5	268.6	31.1
1999	97.2	284.2	34.2
2000	90.2	272.9	33.1
2001	73.6	245.0	30.0
2002	76.1	255.0	29.8
2003	74.6	270.1	27.6

(*Source*: Waweru and Kalani 2009:14).

decrease in non-performing loans compared to the three previous years. The decrease was not as a result of good policies but was attributed to the collapse of some financial institutions, including Trust Bank and Euro Bank (Waweru and Kalani 2009:15). Similarly, some banks wrote off part of their loans in order to ensure healthy balance sheets (Central Bank of Kenya 2003). According to Waweru and Kalani (2009:15), non-performing loans were attributed to poor decision-making by individual investors, although this could be caused simply by bad luck or poor economic eventualities. Comparing non-performing loans to those of developed countries like Japan and Spain, Waweru and Kalani (2009) maintain that bank managers may have been aware of the repercussions of their actions but still acted wrongly because of competition pressure and the desire for high profits. In Kenya, almost 50 % of bank failures were associated with non-performing loans resulting from insider lending during the 1980s and early 1990s (Sokpor 2006). By world standards, the Kenyan non-performing loans were too high (30 %) in 1999, putting the banks at even higher risk of recovering them. The non-performing loans for similar developing countries stood at 7.7 % for Taiwan (2002), 16.81 % for the Philippines (2001), 24 % for Zimbabwe (2000), 11 % for Nigeria (2000) and 3 % for South Africa (2000) (Batino 2001; Central Bank of Kenya 2001). The Kenyan government's inability to manage its banking crisis was alarming compared to similar economies. It is also notable that a large proportion of non-performing loans were associated with government-owned and controlled banks as well as some well-capitalised banks (Beck et al. 2009:7). Again, the banks' failures were blamed on poor management, lack of strong internal control measures and poor governance, all affecting bank stability. However, the government's efforts to reduce non-performing loans eventually worked. Since then, the percentages of non-performing loans dropped from 37.2 % in 2000 to 8.4 % in 2008 and eventually to 4.7 % in 2012, which shows improved performance and progress (Central Bank of Kenya 2012).

Weak Internal Controls As in the past, the poor performance of the Kenyan banking industry has been blamed on weak internal controls, bad governance and poor management practices (Sokpor 2006:5). According to the Economic Report on Africa (2002:143), poor banking performance was caused by mismanagement. The report states that although several measures continued to be implemented which seemed to yield positive results through visible improved financial effectiveness, bank operations remained a significant risk. The risks were 'compounded by economic stagnation. Thus regulatory authorities needed to maintain regulatory vigilance' (Economic Report on Africa 2002:143). It appeared that the right internal measures were not put in place and the banks suffered the consequences.

Political Interference External forces also played a major role in the Kenyan banking industry's problems. For instance, political leaders used their positions in government to borrow from banks without repaying the loans, a problem that led to increased non-performing loans (Sokpor 2006). According to Brownbridge (1998:16):

> Most of the larger local bank failure in Kenya, such as the Continental Bank, Trade Bank and Pan Africa Bank involved extensive insider lending, often politicians. The threat posed by insider lending to the soundness of the banks was exacerbated because many of the insider loans were invested in speculative projects such as real estate development, breaching large-loan exposure limits, and were extended to projects which could not generate short-term returns (such as hotels and shopping centres), with the result that the maturities of the bank's assets and liabilities were imprudently mismatched.

It is notable that the political pressure arising from bank ownership and external influence led to major bank failures (Brownbridge 1998).

Corruption Widespread corruption has continued to wreck the Kenyan economy for the last five decades. This has led to low investor confidence and insufficient foreign direct investment and other forms of foreign aid. Despite several government measures to fight corruption, the efforts have not had a significant impact. For instance, in 2006, two major scandals in government led to the resignations of three ministers. Considering this insufficient, both the World Bank and the IMF delayed their loans to the country (CIA World Factbook, 2007). The problem of corruption remains a major hindrance to the country's economic standing while at the same time affecting the confidence of investors and consumers.

Poor Leadership Numerous studies have indicated that lack of leadership continues to be a major challenge for most banks. Donnelly (1994:12) further pointed out that those involved in banking management lack the skills required for effective banking. The crises in the banking industry worldwide during the 1980s and 1990s corresponded to poor leadership of the banking industry in most countries (Donnelly 1994; Brannigan and de Lisser 1993; Meechan 1992). Given that failures of private banks in Kenya have mostly been associated with poor management and governance, and thus poor leadership (Sokpor 2006; Kinyua 2006), the importance of effective leadership in ensuring that banks attain their goals cannot be neglected, as it is central to effectiveness and good performance.

After struggling with dismal performance as a result of non-performing loans, weak internal controls, political interference, corruption and poor leadership, the Kenyan banking industry made a remarkable turnaround and reversed its undesirable performance. The next section discusses the banking industry recovery trend which has put the industry on a positive sustainable track (UNEP IF 2005).

The Kenyan Banking Industry Recovery

The problem of bank failures that impacted the banking industry in the 1980s and 1990s most strongly affected the local banks rather than foreign-owned banks. It is also evident that non-performing loans, weak internal controls and political interference, all arising from poor management and leadership, were challenges facing the indigenous banking industry in Kenya (Waweru and Kalani 2009). However, it is also notable that the Kenyan banking industry started to show signs of recovery by the beginning of the 2000s.

In fact, since 2003, many Kenyan banks have reported positive growth and a turnaround in their operations, although a few banks still performed poorly until 2009. One example of a successful bank was the Cooperative Bank of Kenya, whose good performance was associated with good management and good leadership practice (Wahome 2004).

Its success was also attributed to 'aggressive cost management, focus on non-funded income, debt recovery and prudent liquidity management' (Waweru and Kalani 2009:31). The implementation of financial sustainability measures such as reducing non-performance loan portfolios, introducing basic corporate governance mechanisms and incorporating principles of sustainability in the banking system are all associated with the positive trend (UNEP IF 2005).

To ensure sustainability and sound financial performance of the Kenyan banking industry, the Kenyan government introduced additional measures to the industry. According to the *Kenya Gazette Supplement No. 90* (2008), a Financial Act 2008 which took effect in January 2009 required that all banks and mortgage institutions increase their minimum core capital to Ksh. 1 billion (US$12 million) by December 2012, up from Ksh. 250 million (US$4 million) in 2008. The aim of the Financial Act was also to make small banks become more stable by ensuring that they had adequate capital. The goal of the Financial Act 2008 was to consolidate and transform small banks into more stable organisations. By introducing financial measures, the government hoped to avert future financial crises by making sure that the banks are able to 'withstand financial turbulences and therefore increase banking industry stability' (Gudmundsson et al. 2013:3). For some banks, financial restrictions remain a challenge due to their inability to raise the required capital. Such banks may be required either to merge with other financial institutions or to sell out. The banks were also expected to deal with deposits mobilisation and reduction in trade volumes (Gudmundsson et al. 2013). The effort of the government was expected and continued to show positive fruits. With continued recovery of the banking industry, the positive performance is expected to increase.

The Contemporary Kenyan Banking Industry

The 2007–2009 financial crisis had major implications for the world financial sector, especially the banking industry. However, while the rest of the world experienced negative to minimal growth, the sub-Saharan African countries reported average growth of 4.7 % in 2008 and 6.2

% in 2009 (United Nations 2009). Some countries did very well during this period, including Congo, Tanzania, Uganda, Ghana, Nigeria, Cameroon and Côte d'Ivoire, while others like Kenya, Ethiopia, Sudan and South Africa deteriorated in performance, falling by 5.4 %, 3.0 %, 1.7 % and 1.3 % respectively. Due to efforts by individual countries' central banks to revive the banking industry through the injection of monetary supports to the economy, the years 2009 and 2010 experienced slight economic growth (IMF 2009). Consequently, while the rest of the world continued to experience negative effects from the financial impact of 2007–2009, the sub-Saharan Africa region reported an average of 5–7 % growth, which was far above the rest of the world's economic performance (European Investment Bank 2013).

The period 2007–2009 was not favourable for Kenya. While the rest of Africa experienced substantial growth, Kenya experienced its worst political crisis arising from post-election violence (resulting from election disputes between the government and the main opposition party). The result was an economic growth slump from 7.1 % in 2007 to about 1.7 % in 2008 (Central Bank of Kenya 2008:23). In 2009, economic growth was 2 % due to the worsening financial crisis, as cited by the Kenya Institute for Public Policy Research and Analysis (KIPPRA) (2009). Likewise, the country's balance of payment declined from a surplus of Ksh. 63,250 million in 2007 to a deficit of Ksh. 33,161 million in 2008. At the same time, the capital and financial sector recorded a surplus of only Ksh. 81,055 million in 2008 compared to Ksh. 150,090 million recorded in 2007, a decline associated with deteriorating world economic performance, minimal inflows of foreign direct investment (FDI) and reduced short-term capital inflows (KIPPRA 2009). By 2013, however, Kenya had fully recovered from the 2007–2008 post-election violence and although its recovery from the global financial crisis was slow, the country remained a leader in the Eastern Africa region in terms of economic development (Njuguna 2013).

Surprisingly, despite the Kenyan economy performing poorly between 2007 and 2008 as a result of the post-election violence, the country's banking industry remained upbeat and recorded relatively positive performance. In the last 10 years, the Kenyan banking industry is said to have fared quite well overall compared to other world markets. Unlike in previous years, the contemporary Kenyan banking industry is considered the most mature and the largest financial service leader in sub-Saharan Africa. Accordingly, the Kenyan financial industry is currently one of the fastest growing in the continent (Njuguna 2013). The banking industry is governed by the Companies Act, the Banking Act, the Central Bank of Kenya Act and various prudential guidelines and instructions issued by Central Banks of Kenya as contained in the Laws of Kenya: Banking Act, 2010, Chapter 488 incorporating all the Acts from 1985 to 2009 (Central Bank of Kenya 2010).

By 2011, banking industry growth was even more encouraging, with an impressive increase of 20.4 % in total assets, which amounted to Ksh. 2.02 trillion, up from Ksh. 1.68 trillion realised in 2010. There was also a reduction in gross non-performing loans of 8 %, from Ksh. 57.6 billion in 2010 to Ksh. 53 billion in 2011 (Central Bank of Kenya 2011). In terms of branch network expansion, Kenya's banking industry registered growth of 20 %, going from 740 branches in 2007 to 887 branches in 2008. The country's capital, Nairobi, had the highest branch network growth, accounting for 41 % of all branches or 60 out of the total 147 branches (Central Bank of Kenya 2008). This means that in Nairobi, the number of bank branches grew from 293 in 2007 to 353 in 2008 (Central Bank of Kenya 2008:5–6). By 2012, the number of bank branches countrywide reached 1,272, an increase of 75 from the 1,197 branches reported in June 2011 (Central Bank of Kenya 2012).

By the end of September 2012, the Kenyan banking industry had improved its performance both in assets and customer deposits. Industry assets stood at Ksh. 2.3 trillion, up from Ksh. 2.02 trillion in 2011, an increase of 15.3 %. Similarly, customer deposits grew to Ksh.1.49 trillion in 2012 from Ksh. 1.71 trillion in 2011, an increase of 14.8 %. During the same period, profit before tax rose from Ksh. 89.5 billion in 2011 to Ksh. 107.9 billion in December 2012, a growth of 20.6 % (Central Bank of Kenya 2012). By June 2013 the banking industry had enhanced its performance and increased its assets to Ksh. 2.5 trillion, loans and advances rose to Ksh. 1.5 trillion, while bank deposits stood at Ksh. 1.9 trillion. Likewise, profit before tax was Ksh. 61.5 billion, customer deposits stood at 18.9 million, while loan accounts amounted to Ksh. 3.8 million (Central Bank of Kenya, June 2013). Similarly, the Credit Information Sharing (CIS) mechanism has advanced in terms of usage since its establishment in June 2010. By June 2013, the number of credit reports requested by institutions increased by 12 % to stand at 2,907,375, up from 2,596,600 reported in March the same year. Likewise, agency banking has seen tremendous growth since its introduction in 2010, as more and more customers are able to access the service (Central Bank of Kenya, June, 2013). The Deposit Taking Microfinance Institutions (DTM) also grew and by June 2013, DTM had gross loans amounting to Ksh. 22.5 billion while deposits stood at Ksh. 19.7 billion.

As of 31 December 2014, the Kenyan banking industry comprised 44 banking institutions, namely 43 commercial institutions and one mortgage finance company. Of the 44 banking institutions, 30 were locally owned while 14 were foreign-owned. There were also eight representative offices of foreign banks. A further breakdown of the banks shows that of the locally owned banks, three were co-owned in partnership with the government while the other 27 banks were privately owned commercial banks. The 27 privately owned financial institutions included one privately owned mortgage company. There were also 87 private forex bureaus, eight Deposit-Taking Microfinance Financial Banks (DFBs), two Credit Reference Bureaus (CRBs) and 13 Money Remittance Providers (MRPs) (Central Bank of Kenya 2014:1), as shown in Fig. 11.1.

In terms of ownership and asset control, local public commercial banks (those with government shareholding) account for 7 % of total banking assets, local private commercial banks account for 62.8 %, while foreign commercial banks account for 30.2 % of total assets, as shown in Table 11.2 (Central Bank of Kenya, Supervision Annual Report 2014:5). It is believed that the banking industry will continue to be a major player in steering economic development in Kenya, thereby emphasising its critical importance to the country (Njuguna 2013).

As Table 11.2 shows, local public commercial banks control only a small percentage of the ownership and assets of the banking industry, while local private commercial banks control the majority of total assets. It is notable that foreign commercial banks control a substantial percentage of total assets despite the fact that there are very few of them.

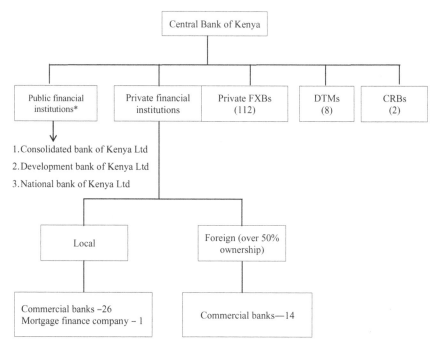

Fig. 11.1 Structure of the banking industry (*GOK shareholding includes shares held by the state corporation) (*Source:* Central Bank of Kenya 2014:xiv)

Table 11.2 Ownership and asset base of commercial banks (Ksh. million)

Ownership	No.	%	Total net assets	%
Local public commercial banks	3	7	154,896	5
Local private commercial banks	27	62.8	2,061,517	64
Foreign commercial banks	13	30.2	982,983	31
Total[a]	43	100	3,199,396	100

[a]Charterhouse Bank excluded due to being under statutory management (Central Bank of Kenya 2014: 5)

However, overall the Kenyan banking industry and the economy have greatly improved as a result of restructuring in the industry and improved governance. Given the present banking industry's positive performance, the industry is projected to continue its improved performance.

Is the Current Positive Performance Sustainable for the Banking Industry?

The Kenyan banking industry still remains the largest and most developed in the Eastern Africa region. According to banking industry 2013 update (Central Bank of Kenya 2013), the Kenyan banking industry is expected to maintain its momentum and robust growth against the backdrop of a favourable stable macro- and microeconomic environment. Other factors associated with the positive growth include aggressive domestic and regional expansion by banks and other financial institutions, as well as increased economic activity arising from the devolved system of government as a result of the new constitutional dispensation focusing on county development (Central Bank of Kenya 2013). Despite this, the banking and financial industry still faces some challenges which may hinder its expected prosperity and strategic leadership in East Africa. The challenges arise from the threat of rampant corruption which may undermine the gains made. However, the industry is still faced with the threat of rampant corruption which may undermine the gains made. Specifically, the barriers include the bank consolidation, inaccessible banking services, fragmentation, poor leadership, rampant corruption and overall sustainability.

Bank Consolidation The *Kenya Gazette Supplement No. 90* (2008) requiring all banks and mortgage institutions to increase their minimum core capitalisation and consolidation aims to increase bank efficiency and stability in the future. However, the effectiveness of the new policy is dependent on the types of ownership arising from such mergers, associated competition and client response. Similarly, the banks' performance will depend on how government-owned banks are managed, quality of services and the level of financial infrastructure (Beck et al. 2009).

Banking Services The Kenyan banking industry is credited for its size and diversification. In relation to private credit to gross domestic product

(GDP) (a standard measure of financial development), the Kenyan banking industry stood at 23.7 % compared to a median of 12.3 % for Sub-Sahara African countries (Thorsten et al. 2010:2). It is also notable that the country has well developed financial systems including banks, insurance, stock and bond markets. However, according to Beck et al. (2009:2), Kenya has failed 'to provide adequate access to banking services to the bulk of the population' and concentrates on large private and public enterprises in urban areas while neglecting rural communities. Similarly, financial services are very expensive as evidenced by high interest rates, making them inaccessible to the majority of the population. In 2006, 23 % of the Kenyan population was still living on less than US$1/day, while approximately 10 % of the population controlled more than 42 % of the country's income (Fitzgibbon 2012). It will be essential to harmonise the economic standards of citizens and financial access across the country to ensure a stable and efficient banking industry.

Fragmentation In recent years the banking industry has taken major steps to ensure stability and efficiency through various efforts like writing off non-performing loans, reducing government influence and managing interest rates. However, the industry still continues to face a fragmentation challenge. There are many small banks operating in Kenya to serve specific niches but having very little impact on the industry in terms of competition and social influence (Beck et al. 2009). Although the government through its consolidation effort is expected to solve the problem of the fragmentation of small banks, the challenge still remains as the effort might divert the banks from their intended missions and objectives.

Leadership A major challenge facing the banking industry worldwide is lack of effective leadership. Most banking management lacks the leadership skills required to cope with the changing environment (Donnelly 1994:12). In fact, studies by Ambutsi (2005), *Kenya Magazines* (2011), Waweru and Kalani (2009) and Kaplan (2012) advocate strong leadership in the industry. The lack of effective leadership has negatively affected the Kenyan banking industry for years, as illustrated by non-performance of the locally incorporated commercial banks rather than the foreign-owned banks. It is important to ensure that effective leadership is maintained in the sector to guarantee stability and continued growth.

Rampant Corruption Kenya is ranked among the most corrupt countries in the world (Transparency International 2014). The government, through it anti-corruption body, needs to introduce and strictly enforce laws that impose heavy penalties on offenders. Failure in this area will undermine all achievements attained so far and in the future (Ambuts 2005; Brownbridge 1998; Kinyua 2006).

Overall Sustainability The financial crisis has put the financial sector worldwide under scrutiny both in terms of monetary performance and social impact. From international and local regulators to the public (clients, investors, employees), there is a growing concern and expectation that banks must not just make money but must play a positive role in national and international development agendas to promote green and low carbon economies (PWC 2012:1). This new challenge means that whether in Kenya or elsewhere, banks must adopt a multidimensional and comprehensive approach to issues relating to the environment and climate change and to social responsibility, while at the same time operating ethical and profitable businesses (PWC 2012:1).

The Future of the Kenyan Banking Industry

Despite its positive contributions, the Kenyan banking industry has undergone several decades of financial difficulty which, in turn, have generated financial and social imbalance in the economy (Sokpor 2006; Kinyua 2006). A major obstacle to the development and stability of the banking industry during the 1980s and 1990s was the presence of high non-performing loans, resulting from heavy borrowing without good mechanisms of repayment or enforcement. As discussed previously, the industry was also open to non-bankers who established more banks, leading to an increase in non-professionalism in the industry, as investors whose interest was profit and self-gratification invested in the industry. These actions resulted in a banking industry dominated by non-performing loans, weak internal controls, political interference, corruption and poor leadership (Ambutsi 2005; Brownbridge 1998; Sokpor 2006; Kinyua 2006).

However, since the year 2000, major changes in the financial sector have led to positive performance of the Kenyan banking industry (Gudmundsson et al. 2013; Wahome 2004; Waweru and Kalani 2009). The industry is expected to continue its upward trend in the future in line with the government's 2030 Vision of ensuring that the financial sector attains stability and efficiency in service delivery and is accessible to the majority of the population. However, the achievement of these goals is still threatened by uncertainty about the proposed bank consolidation, market reactions, poor infrastructure to reach the majority of the population in rural areas, the presence of many small fragmented banks serving different niches, and finally rampant corruption (Beck et al. 2009; Brownbridge 1998; Fitzgibbon 2012; Waweru and Kalani 2009).

In an effort to address these challenges, the Financial Act 2008 recommended that the small banks should consolidate to form large banks, thus reducing costs and enhancing their operational efficiency. Again, this is a challenge that can only be met with strong effective leadership, a clear vision and the ability to propel the banking industry to the desired end. According to Kaplan (2012), the banking industry must invest in leadership because the demand for strong leadership is high. This means that the Kenyan banking industry must refocus its attention on leadership if it is to be assured of effectiveness and a positive role in enabling the country to achieve its development agenda. To further facilitate its role in enhancing the future development of the banking industry, the Central Bank of Kenya has pledged to continue with three main tasks considered critical for the future survival of the banking industry (Njuguna 2013). Firstly, the Central Bank of Kenya promises to strengthen the financial stability of the country through strict and robust supervision and regulatory mechanisms. Secondly, the Central Bank of Kenya aims to enhance financial integrity within the banking industry as a way to curb corruption in the form of money laundering and financing of terrorism-related activities in line with international best practices. Finally, the supervisory and regulatory body plans to promote financial activities aimed at strengthening banking's financial standing and development as outlined in the country's Vision 2030.

Besides the internal measures instituted by the Central Bank of Kenya and the banks themselves to safeguard their future survival, a more urgent concern relating to sustainability poses a major threat to the banking industry worldwide (including in Kenya). This is the need for banks to develop strategies for an integrated and comprehensive approach to environmental, social and profit motives and other sustainability dynamics. The banking industry is expected to be a major player in ensuring a green and lower carbon economy. How involved the banks become will determine their sustainability due to renewed demands by key stakeholders both at international and local levels (UNEP FI 2005, PWC 2012). According to International Finance Corporation (n.d.), banks can benefit immensely from reassessing their approach to business practice to focus on sustainability-oriented risk management and develop products geared toward such ends. Thus, sustainability is increasingly identified as central to bank growth and cannot be neglected, a challenge that Kenyan banks must embrace.

Conclusion

The Kenyan banking industry has a crucial role to play in strengthening the country's financial position as a hub for the Eastern Africa region. In the last 10 years, the banking industry has experienced very significant growth and its prospects for future growth are very encouraging. However, the banking industry in Kenya has undergone both positive and negative growth. For over three decades the industry was plagued with weak internal control, poor management, political interference, poor governance and corruption. However, following the positive growth seen in the last ten years, the industry needs to maintain its upward trend by ensuring that sustainability strategies are put in place. The most appropriate moves toward sustainability are both internal and external. While maintaining the momentum of growth through the consolidation of small and fragmented banks into large institutions and the expansion of banking services to the majority of the population are important, future success and growth will mostly be determined by the banks' involvement in sustainability practices. This means that long-term business success will only be achieved by banks that contribute to healthy economic, social and environmental activities aimed at a stable society, an increasing trend that Kenyan banks must embrace.

References

Adeyemi, K.S. (2007, June). Banking sector consolidation in Nigeria issues and challenges. *Union Digest, 9*, 3–4.

Ambutsi, P. B. (2005). *A survey of corporate governance practices in selected commercial banks in Kenya.* Unpublished MBA thesis. Nairobi: Daystar University, Faculty of Post Graduate Studies.

Batino, C. S. (2001, June 25). *Government vows tighter money-laundering laws. Philippine Inquirer.*

Beck, T., Demirgüç-Kunt, A., & Levine, R. (2009). *Financial institutions and markets across countries and over time: Data and analysis* (World Bank Policy Research Working Paper 4943). Washington, DC: World Bank.

Brannigan, M. & de Lisser, E. (1993, July 8). The end of banking as we know it … changing climate: Two big rival banks in southeast take on new age competitors. *Wall Street Journal*, A1, 1–4.

Brownbridge, M. (1998). Financial distress in local banks in Kenya, Nigeria, Uganda and Zambia: Causes and implications for regulatory policy. *Development Policy Review, 16*(2), 173–188.

Central Bank of Kenya. (1994). *Annual report.* Nairobi: Central Bank of Kenya.

Central Bank of Kenya. (1999). Reforming Kenya's financial. *Monthly Economic Review.* Nairobi: Central Bank of Kenya (CBK).

Central Bank of Kenya. (2001). *Bank supervision annual report.* Nairobi: Central Bank of Kenya.

Central Bank of Kenya. (2003). *Monthly economic review.* Nairobi: Central Bank of Kenya.

Central Bank of Kenya. (2004). *Kenya monthly economic review.* Nairobi: Central Bank of Kenya.

Central Bank of Kenya. (2008). *Bank supervision annual report.* Nairobi: Central Bank of Kenya. Retrieved on February 24, 2010 from: http://www.central-bank.go.ke

Central Bank of Kenya. (2010). *Kenya monthly economic review.* Nairobi: Central Bank of Kenya. Retrieved on March 20, 2010, from http://www.ouhk.edu. hk/ PAU/AlumniLink/Alumni Talk/040828/speech_ marvincheung.pdf

Central Bank of Kenya. (2011). *Financial sector development.* Nairobi: Central Bank Of Kenya Annual Report.

Central Bank of Kenya. (2012). *Bank supervision annual report 2012.* Nairobi: Central bank of Kenya. Retrieved on August 13, 2010, from http://www. centralbank.go.ke/images/docs/Bank%20Supervision%20Reports/ Annual%20Reports/bsd2012-r.pdf

Central Bank of Kenya. (2013). *Economic update.* Nairobi: Central Bank of Kenya Retrieved on April 24, 2010, from http://www.centralbank.go.ke

Central Bank of Kenya. (2014). *Bank supervision annual report 2014.* Nairobi: Central bank of Kenya.

CIA World Factbook (2007). Kenya economy 2007. Retrieved on October 30, 2016, from http://www.allcountries.org/wfb/2007/kenya/kenya_economy. html

Deloitte. (2012). *Global powers of consumer products industry 2012.* London, UK: Deloitte Global Service Limited.

Donnelly, J. H. (1994). Reframing the mind of the banker: The changing skill set and skills mix for effective leadership. *International Journal of Bank Marketing,* 12(8):12-16 . Retrieved on February 8, 2010, from http://www. emeraldinsight.com/Insight/viewPDF.jsp?contentType=Article&filename=h tml/Output/Published/EmeraldFullTextArticle/Pdf/0320120802.pdf

Economic Commission for Africa. (2011). *Economic report of Africa 2011: Governing development in Africa – The role of the state in economic transformation.* Addis Ababa: Africa Union.

Economic Report on Africa. (2002). Kenya—Weak governance hobbles economy. *Economic Report on Africa: Tracking Performance and Progress.* Retrieved on February 24, 2010, from: http://www.uneca.org/era2002/chap5.pdf

Elliot, R. (2008). In crisis, Canadian banks survive and thrive. *Forbes.com.* Retrieved on February 26, 2010, from: http://www.forbes.com/2008/12/11/ Canada-banking-crisis-oped-cx_re_121elliott.html

European Investment Bank. (2013). *Banking in sub-Sahara Africa: Challenges and opportunities.* Luxembourg: European Investment Bank.

Fitzgibbon, C. (2012). Economics of resilience study: Kenya country report. Retrieved on April 30, 2014, from https://www.gov.uk/government/uploads/ system/uploads/attachment_data/file/228500/TEERR_Kenya_ Background_Report.pdf

Fofack, H. (2005). Nonperforming loans in sub-Sahara Africa: Causal analysis and macroeconomic implication. *World Bank Policy Research Working Paper 3769.* WPS3769:2–36.

Grant Thornton. (2013). *2013 banking outlook: Surviving and thriving in the new normal world of banking regulations.* Chicago: Grant Thornton LLP.

Gudmundsson, R., Ngoka-Kisinguh, K., & Odongo, M. T. (2013). *The role of capital requirements on bank competition and stability: The case of the Kenyan banking industry.* Nairobi: Kenya Bankers Association.

Honohan, P., & Laeven, L. (Eds.). (2005). *Systemic financial crises: Containment and resolution.* Cambridge: Cambridge University Press.

Hoyle, K., & Whitehead, G. (1982). *Money and banking.* London: William Heinemann Ltd.

International Finance Corporation. (n.d). *Banking on sustainability financing environmental and social opportunities in emerging markets.* Retrieved on March 14, 2016, from http://www.ifc.org/wps/wcm/connect/9486d980488 658f8b7b2f76a6515bb18/Banking_on_Sustainablity_Launch.pdf?MOD= AJPERES&CACHEID=9486d980488658f8b7b2f76a6515bb18

International Monetary Fund (IMF). (1998). *Code of practices on fiscal transparency: Declaration on principles.* Washington, DC: International Monetary Fund.

International Monetary Fund (IMF). (2009). *Regional economic outlook: Sub-Sahara Africa.* Washington, DC: *International monetary fund (IMF).* Retrieved on June 15, 2012, from http://www.inf.org/external/pubs/ft/reo/2009/afr/eng/sreo0409.pdf

Kaplan, A. J. (2012). *Banking on leaders.* Retrieved on August 12, 2014, from http://www.kasearch.com/Articles/ICBA%20Banking%20on%20 Leaders%20Article%202012.pdf

Kashyap, A. K., Rajan, R., & Stein, J. C. (2002). Banks as liquidity providers: An explanation for the coexistence of lending and deposit-taking. *Journal of Finance, American Finance Association, 57*(1), 33–73.

Kenya Institute For Public Policy Research and Analysis (KIPPRA). (2009). *Kenya economic report 2009.* Nairobi: KIPPRA.

Kenyan Magazines Online. (2011). James Mwangi – *Equity bank CEO – Managing Generation Y – Leading a young workforce.* Retrieved on June 20, 2011, from http://www.kenyanmagazines.com/james-mwangi-equity-bank-ceo-managing-generation-leading-young-workforce-management-march-2011/

Kinyua, J. (2006). *Exploration of factors influencing fraudulent activities in banks in Kenya.* Unpublished master's thesis, Nairobi: Daystar University, Faculty of post graduate studies.

Kithinji, A., & Waweru, N. M. (2007). Merger restructuring and financial performance of commercial banks in Kenya. *Economic, Management and Financial Markets Journal, 2*(4), 9–39.

Kroszner, P. (2002). Nonperforming loans, monetary policy and deflation: The industrial country experience. *Economic and social research institute.* Tokyo: Cabinet office, Government of Japan.

Kumbirai, M., & Webb, R. (2010). A financial ratio analysis of commercial bank performance in South Africa. *African Review of Economics and Finance, 2*(1), 30–53.

Meechan, J. (1992). America's bumbling bankers: Ripe for another fiasco. *Business Week, 2*(March), 86–87.

Nagar, N., Masih, E., & Badugu, D. (2011). Retail banking: The new buzzword of today's world of banking. *Journal of Banking Financial Services and Insurance Research, 1*(8), 1–10.

Ngugi, R. (2001). An empirical analysis of interest rate spread in Kenya. *AERC Research Paper 106, African Economic Research Consortium.* Nairobi: African Economic Research Consortium (AERC).

Njuguna, N. (2013). *The importance of the banking sector in the Kenyan economy.* Nairobi: Speech at the Bank of India, Kenya Branch, Diamond Jubilee Celebrations.

PricewaterhouseCooper. (2012). *Go green. Stay competitive: Sustainability for banks.* Retrieved on March 13, 2016, from www.pwcsustainability.lu

Russo, M., & Ugolini, P. (2008). *Emerging markets forum.* Washington, DC: Centennial Group.

Sokpor, C. K. D. (2006). *The role of central bank of Kenya in controlling bank failures: An investigative study.* Unpublished MBA thesis, Nairobi: Daystar University, Faculty of post graduate studies.

Sultana, W. (2000). Banking crisis in Japan: Prediction of nonperforming loans. Retrieved on March 1, 2009, from: http://www.inq7.net/bus/2001jul/16/bus_5-1.htm

Thorsten, B., Asli, D. & Ouarda, M. (2010). *Islamic vs. conventional banking: business model, efficiency and stability* (Policy Research Working Paper Series 5446). Washington, DC: The World Bank.

Transparency International. (2014). *Transparency international corruption perceptions index 2014.* Berlin: Transparency International.

United Nations. (2009). *World economic situations and prospects (2009)*. New York: United Nations.

United Nations Environment Programme Finance Initiative (UNEP FI). (2005). *Sustainability banking in Africa*. Paris: UNEP.

United Nations Environment Programme Finance Initiative (UNEP FI). (2007). *Banking on value: A new approach to credit risk in Africa*. South Africa: University of South Africa Center for Corporate Citizenship (UNISA CCC).

Wahome, M., (2004, March 20). Cooperative bank's profit up seventy percent. *Saturday Nation*. Nairobi: Daily Nation Publishers.

Waweru, N. M., & Kalani, M. V. (2009). Commercial banking crises in Kenya: Causes and remedies. *African Journal of Accounting, Economics, Finance and Banking Research.*, 4(4), 12–32.

12

Assessment and Way Forward of the Douala Stock Exchange in Cameroon

Alain Ndedi

Introduction

This chapter discusses the assessment and the way forward of the Douala Stock Exchange (DSX) in Cameroon based on the results of empirical research. In the first part, the historical background of the market is discussed, with the focus on shareholding. The second part presents the methodology used to conduct the research, and the last part gives the results.

Historical Background of the Douala Stock Exchange

Having launched in 2001 and with trading beginning on 30 June 2006, the Douala Stock Exchange is a financial market, a public limited

A. Ndedi (✉)
School of Business and Public Policy, Saint Monica University, Cameroon, UK

© The Author(s) 2017
A. Ahmed (ed.), *Managing Knowledge and Innovation for Business Sustainability in Africa*, DOI 10.1007/978-3-319-41090-6_12

company with a Board of Directors and capital of 1.8 billion francs CFA, distributed as follows: 63.7 % by banks and financial institutions, 23 % by spin-offs from the state, and 13.3 % by insurance companies. The Douala Stock Exchange is the sole agent authorised to carry out stock exchange transactions and functions within the territory of the Republic of Cameroon (Douala Stock Exchange Website 2015).

According to Douala Stock Exchange (2015), the principal functions of the market include to create, organise and manage the stock market; to monitor and supervise the smooth running of negotiations on the stock market; and to administer the negotiation of negotiable public stocks and securities (OTZ). The final function of the DSX is to establish the rules which regulate access to the market; admission of listed stocks; the organisation of transactions; the suspension of negotiations of one or several stocks; the recording and advertising of negotiations; the delivery of share certificates and settling of accounts; the custody of shares; and the invoicing and collection of commissions. Unfortunately, nearly 14 years after its creation, the DSX is struggling to fulfil its noble objectives.

Theoretical Framework: The Stock Exchange Purpose and Operation

According to Ndedi (2009), the major reason for the development of stock exchanges in recent years has been government privatisation programmes. In order to sell stock in state-owned enterprises to the public, there must exist a secondary market for the public to later trade the shares among themselves. That is the role of an exchange, as a secondary market. Here, the securities that are bought and sold on an exchange are bought and sold by shareholders, not by the issuing company. A company sells its shares in a primary offering directly to shareholders through the use of underwriters and other intermediaries. The sale by the company is a direct transaction between the company and the shareholder and is not done on an exchange. This is true even for companies that already have shares listed on the exchange and then decide to sell more shares. Even companies with shares already listed on an exchange do not sell new, additional shares on the exchange.

Those shares are also sold in direct transactions off the exchange (Ndedi 2009).

Because an exchange is a secondary market, it is not absolutely necessary to have an exchange in order for companies to sell their shares. Companies can sell shares in the primary market and let the investors figure out on their own how they will later trade and sell those shares. Obviously this is not a happy prospect for investors, and that is why exchanges are formed early in the capital market development process. If there is no exchange, investors will be reluctant to buy shares in privatisations or other offerings, because the investors will not have a ready and available forum in which to sell their shares at a later time. However, an over-the-counter (OTC) market can operate as a forum for trading shares in the secondary market. The OTC market can exist with or without an exchange. There are very few countries that have OTC markets without exchanges. Some countries, such as Zimbabwe and Nigeria, have exchanges and no OTC market. In most developed countries, exchanges and OTC markets both operate concurrently.

Some questions generally arise regarding the stock exchange. The first of these is 'Who owns a stock exchange and who makes its rules?' Most statutes require that exchanges be non-profit entities, as it is considered most appropriate from a public policy standpoint that an exchange serves the public investors and keeps costs of trading as low as possible. In most countries, the model followed is that an exchange is formed as a not-for-profit company by licensed broker-dealers. Although an exchange is usually a not-for-profit corporation, this does not mean that it has no revenues. All not-for-profit organisations are permitted under law to charge for their services and to pay salaries to employees. The exchange therefore charges a small fee for every transaction. The fee is generally a small amount, no more than is necessary to provide for exchange expenses and expansion plans. Although a stock exchange begins its existence through a government-issued license, it is treated as a self-regulatory organisation (SRO). That means that the exchange selects its own Board of Governors and officers and determines its own rules of membership and trading subject to review and approval by the securities commission. Exchanges have the authority to discipline, suspend or expel members or floor traders for violation of exchange rules (Ndedi 2009, 2012).

Methodology

Unlike quantitative research which uses a random sample generalisable to a larger population, qualitative research uses a purposive sampling method. Purposive sampling involves the selection of informants based on an important characteristic under study, such as what they know about the subject under study, or where they live in order to ease the task of the researcher (Nayab in Bowen 2009). Triangulation (confirmation of the same information by different methods or sources) is used to indicate that two (qualitative and quantitative) methods are used in the study in order to check the results of the various methods of data gathering used during the study. The purpose of triangulation in qualitative research is to increase the credibility and validity of the results.

According to Nayab (in Bowen 2009), validity shows the soundness of the research methodology and the results generated, based on the extent to which the research remains in congruity with universal laws, objectivity, truth and facts. The validity of statistics-driven quantitative research depends on the soundness of the instrument adopted. Validity in qualitative research, however, depends on the ability and effort of the researcher, as the researcher is the instrument.

For the current research, data were derived from both primary and secondary sources. Secondary data consisted of articles and reports on the development of the Douala Stock Exchange in Cameroon; these included government policy documents, consultancy reports, community-based financial market reports and other financial reports, and the historical background on financial market development in Africa.

To really understand the issues pertaining to the Douala Stock Exchange, empirical research was conducted with a sample of 75 business managers, academics and other financial analysts acquainted with the activities of the institution. These informants, purposively chosen, both in Cameroon and abroad, constitute the sample under a cross-sectional study. The data gathering consisted of a questionnaire of seven items aiming at interrogating these informants on their reluctance, and that of the public in general, to trade at the DSX. The research also used the Likert Scale Questionnaire for questions 4 and 6.

Results and Discussion

This section discusses the data gathered during field research along with the results obtained and recommendations that need to be implemented to achieve desirable goals at this important capital market. Based on the empirical research, the following information was gathered.

1) The first question was: 'Launching the capital market, what Cameroon as a country wanted to achieve?' The goals and the motivations when launching a capital market are multiple. It is very tempting to rush into the maze of securities laws, stock exchange rules and licensing regulations without asking the basic question, which is 'why are we doing this?'

This basic question should be the starting point of analysis. In the case of the Douala Stock Exchange, based on the information gathered, almost all informants said that the Cameroonian government launched the DSX after the launching of the Libreville Capital Market. Therefore, the launching of the DSX was not genuine as it was not based on local and/or regional needs of a stock exchange.

In general, the principal objectives for the DSX were supposed to be one of the following: privatisation programmes that could not be undertaken without a capital market infrastructure; the desire to create investment opportunities for Cameroonians; or, finally, the desire to stimulate the growth of small and medium-sized businesses in Cameroon.

2) The second question discussed with respondents was: 'Should government regulation precede or adapt to the trading market?'

Some countries have adopted full-scale securities laws, licensing requirements, registration provisions and so on, before a single company was listed on the local stock exchange. This was true of the DSX. In this case, there is a danger that market forces will be hindered by rules that are not responsive to local conditions. Market forces include such factors as the supply of capital, the supply of investment opportunities, the competition from foreign capital markets, the impact of government fiscal policies, and the number and activities of broker-dealers and investment advisers.

The point raised through this research question is that capital markets should not refrain from regulation. But the recommendation made for this point is that regulation should consider trading practices that have been developed informally, that conform to the efficient practices that have developed, and that cover areas where potential problems could arise.

3) The third question asked was: 'Should regulations be developed for an over-the-counter (OTC) market?'

An OTC is a secondary trading market that is not on an exchange. The OTC is usually operated by broker-dealers among themselves. The broker-dealers are market makers because they put out quotations as to the price at which they will buy or sell specific OTC securities. Almost all the respondents (90 %) were keen on such a move.

4) The fourth question was: 'What does transparency really mean and require at the DSX?'

The informants, all 100 % of them, said that the Douala Stock Exchange is not transparent. Figure 12.1 presents the results of the respondents in the Likert scale from 1 to 5, with 5 agreeing that the DSX is transparent, while 1 means the financial market is not transparent. According to the respondents, to be an effective doctrine at the DSX, transparency must be defined by notions of materiality, and there must also be an acknowledgement of company interests regarding the timing of disclosure and confidentiality of some matters.

Without doubt, transparency is an indispensable element of an efficient securities market. Although transparency is clearly accepted as a common good, when applied to government actions, transparency does not extend to matters for which public disclosure is contrary to national interests.

What is the goal of the transparency requirement at the DSX? From the perspective of government regulators, transparency is required so that the reviewing and supervising agencies can determine whether government-established investor protection goals are met. For potential investors, transparency is required so that they can determine the potential risks and rewards of the investment—something that most respondents mentioned. Generally, government and investor interests in transparency

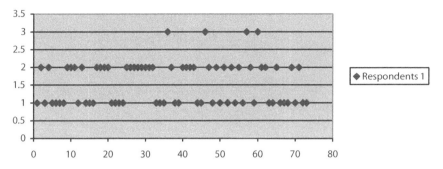

Fig. 12.1 Scattered plots from respondents' responses

overlap, and transparency standards serve both interests. However, there might be differences in emphasis.

What are the standards for transparency at any financial market? One might think that transparency is equated with full disclosure. Full disclosure of material facts and events is a standard that gets one closer to the goal of transparency. A fact is material when it is important. In the securities world, two types of material information exist side by side. One is called hard information, the other soft information.

5) The fifth question discussed with the sample of managers was: What is your assessment of the corporate governance at the Douala Stock Exchange.'

In the case of the DSX, and in the light of the recent history of economic crimes in Cameroon, almost all respondents (87 %) raised the issue of lack of corporate governance.

The role of corporate governance in any institution is increasingly important. Good corporate governance might not assure the success of a company, but bad corporate governance will often destroy or severely limit a company. Moreover, good corporate governance engenders public confidence that management is devoting itself as best it can to the best interests of the company. Public confidence translates into a willingness to invest capital. For many investors, certainly for unit trusts and other institutional investors, good corporate governance is one of the primary factors leading to an investment decision. Good corporate governance includes transparency with regard to board decisions and periodic full disclosure to shareholders of corporate results and plans. Without an effective enforcement procedure, good corporate governance standards alone are insufficient.

6) The sixth question raised with respondents is: 'The Douala Stock Exchange manipulation.'

It was appropriate to discuss with our respondents the public confidence in the DSX, and in particular in the buying and selling of securities. Many respondents (76 %) raised the issue of lack of public confidence due to market manipulation, which is the single greatest problem with regard to the DSX. The scattered plots (Fig. 12.2) represent respondents' views on the market manipulation with the Likert scales, with 5 being totally agree, and 1 totally disagree.

Market manipulation probably began the day the first stock market opened, and it has continued to this day. In every country in the world the temptation exists to make money through deceptive and unfair measures.

The recommendation made to deal with this issue is how to prevent the misuse of information. The DSX and securities commission rules should provide for some minimum period of time before which a company or insiders can begin to trade on the basis of publicly released information. Too few people trust the system enough to put their money into it. Many people continue to believe that it is safer to put their money under their bed, or in a bank account, than to give it to a stockbroker to invest in a company listed in the DSX. Unfortunately, this belief sometimes has historical roots in local corrupt practices such as misleading privatisation offerings that have not been effectively prevented or sanctioned. There is probably no greater challenge to government officials than to overcome public distrust. This chapter indicates several issues that should be addressed by government officials who want to create a positive atmosphere for an active public market.

Government ministries have spent much time, money and energy preparing the infrastructure for securities trading, but companies often have not responded with the enthusiasm that was hoped for. In discussing this issue with some small and medium enterprise (SME) managers in Cameroon, the single most important theme that is heard is the lack of public confidence in the fairness of the DSX. Years of corruption in government and financial sectors have taken their toll.

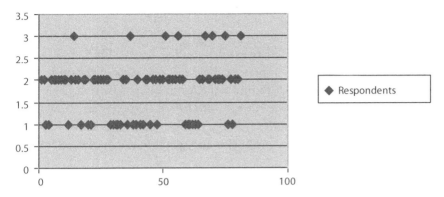

Fig. 12.2 Scattered plots of respondents

Can the DSX be trusted? Despite every effort to develop a securities commission staffed with knowledgeable and dedicated staff, it is nevertheless a government agency and therefore is subject to potential mistrust. Furthermore, the DSX has been created through government action and is managed by a government appointee.

Public confidence is an intangible yet essential element in the infrastructure necessary for a viable DSX. What are the factors that affect public confidence? There are several that appear to be the most important, according to our research.

The first is *market integrity*. No one is willing to buy or trade securities without confidence that they are being treated fairly. Fair treatment means that all investors and potential investors at the DSX are dealing with the same information, and that the information is accurate. This can be achieved through two fundamental requirements: timely disclosure of material information by companies, and prohibition against use of confidential information by insiders. The public must be aware of this development.

The second issue to look at is *broker and investment adviser neutrality*. Customers have an implicit faith in their brokers and advisers, a faith based upon the licensing process and the appearance of good faith and objectivity. If such advisers do not treat their customers with absolute fairness, the DSX will be seriously hurt. For neutrality, strong licensing standards and swift and effective disciplinary sanctions are needed.

The third element required for public confidence is *transferability and liquidity*. The ability to attract investors at the DSX is linked directly to potential investors' perceived risks of liquidity. At the DSX, it is risky enough to buy a stock not knowing how the company will fare in the future. It is even more risky to buy a stock not being sure that it will be readily transferable when the time comes to sell. Experiences show that in many markets, the amount of public investor activity is so low that at any given time there are too few buyers and sellers in the market to ensure immediate liquidity.

The fourth point for public confidence is an *effective enforcement process with the Douala Stock Exchange*. Investors know that occasionally there will be companies or persons who try to make money in the market through illegal means. That is an inevitable but unfortunate part of the securities market. Temptation often proves too great a force for some people.

Investors will not lose faith in the DSX because of a few bad apples, but they will quickly lose faith if there is a lack of effective enforcement.

Effective enforcement means:

1) Criminal prosecution, whenever appropriate;
2) Administrative sanctions by the securities commission;
3) The availability of private remedies for investors who have suffered losses as a result of the misconduct.

Each of these enforcement mechanisms requires input from the Cameroonian government. There must be adequate funds provided for the investigation and prosecution of criminal conduct, there must be a sufficient budget for the securities commission to afford its own investigators and lawyers, and there must be civil procedure statutes that allow effective private causes of actions. If the public sees that these are in place and that wrongdoers are promptly apprehended and punished, there will be a sense that enforcement will have a deterrent effect and thereby create a fairer marketplace. If the public perceives otherwise, there will be no interest in taking part in the trading market, as all will perceive that such trading will be equivalent to playing poker with persons who 'deal from the bottom of the deck'. There are other factors that also impact upon public confidence, including for example the quality of the companies being offered, and the quality of corporate governance procedures.

7) The seventh question discussed was around an effective way to educate and develop an interest of the public on the advantages of investing at the Douala Stock Exchange?

The DSX cannot thrive without active participation by local companies. Institutional traders, such as pension plans, bank trust funds and insurance companies, have neither the commitment nor the capacity to fund the capital needs of an entire market. The movement of investments from private savings accounts to publicly traded companies is a vital element in capital market growth. One may wonder how it is possible to have an active DSX in a country that has a low per capita income like Cameroon.

The problem of educating and attracting potential investors is a global phenomenon. Even in highly developed markets in Europe, for example, less than 20 % of the population participates through investments in the market. Therefore, we should not set our sights too high.

In summary, the findings have shown that unfortunately, despite financial liberalisation and the emergence of new markets and institutions in Cameroon, in the absence of adequate oversight and an adaptive regulatory structure the DSX can only malfunction. According to Chami, Fullenkamp and Sunil Sharma (2009), the development of the financial market occurs when market players are able to reach mutually acceptable compromises regarding the terms of financial transactions. Agents strike grand compromises, such as those between maturity and collateral, and between seniority and control, as well as myriad smaller ones. A financial market will generally fail to develop because the instrument traded does not meet the requirements of some of the players; such is the case with the DSX.

Summary

A number of issues have been discussed in this chapter. In summary, the role of government in establishing, supervising and facilitating the growth of the DSX is complex. It involves much more than simply establishing rules and creating supervising authorities. The content of those rules must be developed based upon both 'what is the on the ground' and the goals to be achieved. Rules cannot be static, because the market is changing all the time.

Flexibility must be written into the rules, and discretion must be accorded to agencies that support the DSX to act without going back to Parliament. Government regulators will not know what the market looks like or how it is changing without continual examination. Finally, no market will succeed without public confidence. All the factors that affect public confidence must be kept at the top of policymakers' lists, and each factor must be continually examined to assure that its requirements are being achieved. These are challenging tasks. The responsibility placed upon government regulators is high, but the opportunities are great. An efficient, viable DSX will result in significant economic gains, which will in turn have major benefits for the welfare of all of Cameroon and the Central African Economic and Monetary Community (CEMAC) sub-region. The Cameroonian regulators therefore stand at the head of a process that offers enormous promise and opportunity, and their response to these challenges will very much determine the growth and prosperity of Cameroon.

The chapter has developed an appropriate strategy for sequencing the development of the DSX. It has argued that instruments that require simpler and more easily verifiable compromises must be launched in the first place at the DSX. The chapter also shows that the path of development will depend on economic, legal, political, institutional and cultural factors—the framework that prompts policymakers to ask the right questions in diagnosing the deficiencies and hurdles. The chapter finally provides guidance for designing suitable policies for the development and functioning of the Douala Stock Exchange that will contribute to the emergence of Cameroon by 2035. The chapter concludes that when they function properly, financial markets allow the transfer of resources from savers to investors, and contribute to making the economy more robust to shocks by enabling risks to be allocated appropriately—something that is needed in Cameroon with the DSX.

References

Bowen, G. A. (2009). Supporting a grounded theory with an audit trail: An illustration. International Journal of Social Research Methodology, 12(4), 305–316. doi: 0.1080/13645570802156196

Ndedi, A. A. (2009). *Financial markets regulations.* Pretoria: University of Pretoria Printing. Pretoria.

Ndedi, A. A. (2012). *Financial markets regulations: Theory and practice.* Lambert Academic.

Chami, R, Fullenkamp, C., & Sharma, S. (2009). *A framework for financial market development* (IMF working paper; WP /09/156).

Index

© The Author(s) 2017   **237**
A. Ahmed (ed.), *Managing Knowledge and Innovation for Business
Sustainability in Africa*, DOI 10.1007/978-3-319-41090-6